Markets for Schooling

In recent years many countries have experimented with extending the role of market forces in their state schooling systems. These changes have often produced fierce debates about their rationale and consequences, not least because of their origins in a specific political and economic philosophy. The basis of this philosophy is economic liberalism: a belief in the efficiency of the market as a rationing and allocative mechanism. This book examines the appropriateness of this belief for schooling markets.

Nick Adnett and Peter Davies develop an economic analysis of schooling markets, emphasising both the strengths and weaknesses of orthodox analysis. They explain the economic and social contexts that have generated widespread desire to reform state schooling and develop a systematic analysis of the key policy components examining both theory and international evidence. The authors employ a framework based upon economic analysis that is informed by research by educationalists and other social scientists. They assess:

- The changes made to the funding of state schooling and the move towards open enrolment.
- The response of parents and teachers to these reforms and the impact on the licensing, training and pay of teachers.
- The rationale for, and the consequences of, the greater devolution of management control to school and the growth of performance monitoring, including the publication of school performance tables.
- How schools have responded to these policies and the overall impact on the level, mix and distribution of schooling outcomes.
- The effect of market incentives on the degree of stratification of pupils by ability, class and ethnic origin.
- The tensions between teacher professionalism and the new 'managerial culture' and examine the consequences of targeting incentive pay.

Markets for Schooling is designed to be accessible and of interest to all researchers, administrators and policy-makers concerned with education.

Nick Adnett is Professor of Economics at Staffordshire University. **Peter Davies** is Reader and Head of the Centre for Economics and Business Education at Staffordshire University.

Routledge Research in Education

Markets for Schooling
An economic analysis

Nick Adnett and Peter Davies

Routledge
Taylor & Francis Group

LONDON AND NEW YORK

First published 2002
by Routledge
2 Park Square, Milton Park, Abingdon, Oxfordshire OX14 4RN

Simultaneously published in the USA and Canada
by Routledge
711 Third Avenue, New York, NY 10017

Routledge is an imprint of the Taylor and Francis Group, an informa business

First issued in paperback 2015

© 2002 Nick Adnett and Peter Davies

Typeset in Goudy by Taylor & Francis Books

British Library Cataloguing in Publication Data
A catalogue record for this book is available from the British Library

Library of Congress Cataloging in Publication Data
Adnett, Nick.
Markets for schooling : an economic analysis / Nick Adnett
and Peter Davies.
p. cm.– (Routledge research in education; 5)
Includes bibliographical references and index.
1. Education–Economic aspects–Cross-cultural studies. 2. Public
schools–Cross-cultural studies. 3. School choice–Cross-cultural studies.
4. Educational change–Cross-cultural studies. I. Davies, Peter, 1954–
II. Title. III. Series.
LC65 .A36 2002
338.4'737–dc21
                                                    2001045710

ISBN 978-0-415-25333-8 (hbk)
ISBN 978-1-138-01018-5 (pbk)

To Karen and Liz and Ellen, Neil and Alison

Contents

Illustrations

Tables

Figure

Preface

This work investigates the theory and practice of market-based reforms of state schooling systems. These reforms are more the product of a particular political and economic philosophy than an attempt to imitate successful educational systems in other countries. In other words, the motivation for the reforms we are analysing in this work was ideological rather than evidential. At the heart of this ideology was economic liberalism: a belief in the efficiency of the market as a rationing and allocative mechanism. Accordingly, our investigation is based upon an economic analysis of these market-based reforms. The primary objective of this work is to make that economic analysis accessible to all researchers, administrators and policy makers. Our starting presumption is that in modern capitalist economies, the presence of market forces in education is inevitable. The fundamental policy debate concerns the desired extent and nature of those forces.

The rationale for this work rests upon three propositions. First, that economic analysis can provide unique insights into educational decision-making. Second, that both its proponents and detractors have too often equated economic analysis with unequivocal support for the extension of market forces in education. Third, that when carefully deployed, economic analysis can provide complementary insights into schooling decision-making to those achieved by other disciplines. We attempt to build our economic analysis of schooling markets using the techniques of both orthodox and heterodox analysis. Since our intention is to promote an inclusive readership, we do not utilise formal algebraic analysis or discuss in detail the modelling and econometric issues underlying empirical work in this area. We make no claim to provide a comprehensive coverage of the economic analysis of education. While we hope that our distinct objectives and innovative approach will be of interest to our fellow economists, they are not our only intended audience. Our analysis should be seen as intending to complement the existing studies of market reforms, which in Europe largely employ a sociological approach. In seeking to lower harmful inter-disciplinary barriers, wherever possible we point out both the strengths and the weaknesses of orthodox economic analysis.

A further characteristic of our approach is our attempt to examine the precise interactions between different elements of the market-based reforms. In particular, we show how any analysis of school choice reforms needs to incorporate a consideration of the associated reforms to school governance and performance monitoring. We further broaden conventional analysis by including assessments of the changes introduced to teacher training and employment contracts, particularly remuneration.

Since the developments we seek to analyse are not limited to a single country, our study is of necessity international. However, we do concentrate largely upon experience in developed economies. In the first part of the study we develop a theoretical framework for analysing educational decision-making. This framework is continuously 'tested' against evidence concerning actual schooling market behaviour. As the work progresses we focus upon specific market-based policy reforms and how they have affected the behaviour of particular groups of decision-makers. In analysing policy details we increasingly rely upon evidence drawn from England and Wales, while pointing out any contrasts with developments elsewhere. Our study is of necessity limited in certain other ways. We concentrate upon actual rather than potential market-based policies, analysing the various quasi-markets created in parts of North America, Australasia and Europe. Our focus is upon compulsory state schooling and we largely neglect pre-primary and post-16 compulsory schooling. We therefore do not consider many important policy issues related specifically to further and higher education or lifelong learning.

This book is the product of a research programme undertaken by the Centre for Economics and Business Education, Staffordshire University Business School. This research commenced in 1997 with funding from Staffordshire University. The empirical part of this programme consisted largely of extensive interviews and questionnaire-based surveys in two local schooling markets. We are exceedingly grateful for the co-operation of the relevant LEAs, heads, teachers, pupils and parents in these two locations. Our work in this area has also benefited from the comments of our colleagues in the Centre: Gwen Coates, Helen Howie, Jean Mangan, Geoff Pugh and Shqiponja Telhaj. We have also gained a lot from the responses we have received to our presentations at the following conferences: British Educational Research Association, Education and Employment Economics Workshop, European Conference on Educational Research and the Quasi-market Conference. Some of the analysis and arguments that follow have already been 'market-tested' in various journals. We wish to thank referees and editors of the following journals for their comments which have helped to further refine our arguments: *British Journal of Educational Studies*, *Cambridge Journal of Economics*, *Economics of Education Review*, *Journal of Education and Work*, *Journal of Education Policy*, *Oxford Review of Education*, *Research in Post-Compulsory Education*, *Review of Policy Issues* and *The Curriculum Journal*. In addition we need to give special thanks to colleagues who have been of particular assistance in the development of our research in this area: Spiros Bougheas, Mike Barrow, Ros Levačić and Jason Tarsh. We also wish to acknowledge the assistance of the library staff at Staffordshire University, especially Gill Round and the encouragement of our editor at Routledge, Robert Langham. For the errors, omissions and inconsistencies which follow we take sole responsibility.

Nick Adnett & Peter Davies
July 2001

1 The economic theory of schooling markets
An introduction

1.1 Introduction

In this chapter we introduce the economic analysis relevant to an understanding of schooling markets. Too often in recent debates advocates of particular viewpoints have preferred to present caricatures of economic analysis rather than carefully defining key terms and systematically developing that analysis. As Finkelstein and Grubb (2000) point out, the debate about schooling quasi-markets has settled into a ritual. Supporters of markets cite the advantages of choice and flexibility and the resulting efficiency gains generated, while opponents attack them for the inequalities and narrowing of educational outcomes which result. Terms like 'efficiency', 'accountability', 'stakeholders' and 'incentives' have entered into the language of these policy debates without always possessing the clarity and consistency in use necessary for meaningful dialogue. In explaining our terminology and developing the economic analysis systematically, we seek to make that analysis accessible to all those wishing to examine the nature and consequences of recent market-based reforms of state schooling.

Although the emergence of modern analysis is usually attributed to Becker (1975), a succession of economists, starting with Adam Smith, developed an analysis of education as an investment in human capital. This human capital approach views these investments as directly generating productivity gains and higher earning-power for individuals (Belfield 2000 provides a review). A separate strand of orthodox economic analysis, also developing from Adam Smith, suggests the potential for market forces to efficiently allocate resources between alternative uses. Relying upon the self-interest of producers and consumers can, under certain conditions, lead to socially optimal outcomes. Over the last forty years or so, market choice theorists have used such analysis to justify market-based reforms of state schooling systems. They argue that if enabled to do so, parents and pupils have incentives to choose both the type and duration of schooling which best suits their abilities and the needs of the economy. These incentives are provided by the structure of employment and earnings in the labour market, since human capital theory interprets schooling decisions as predominantly being concerned with maximising anticipated returns to investment. It is contended that where these incentives are strong enough, resources permit and market structures allow, the exercising of consumer preferences in a competitive market can motivate schools to respond to perceived parental needs.

Whether such conditions can be generated in educational markets is currently much disputed (Vandenberghe 1999a). Most educational markets have restricted competition, remain highly regulated and produce multiple outcomes that are difficult to quantify. Furthermore, consumption and invest-ment elements are here closely interlinked, uncertainty and asymmetric information problems abound and equity considerations often appear to conflict with issues of efficiency. These complications have caused many to question the appropriateness of orthodox market-choice analysis in this area, and others to resist all economic analyses of schooling issues. This book focuses on the recent experience of market-based reforms of state schooling in several developed Western economies. We show that the main issue concerns not whether market forces have a role in schooling markets, but how important should that role be and what form should it take. In other words, what institutional arrangements should governments provide for schooling and what is their optimal role in its regulation, funding and provision.

In the following analysis we reassess the economic rationale for increasing the role of market forces in educational decision-making. Initially we explore the general properties of economic analysis and its strengths and weaknesses when applied to the examination of schooling issues. In Section 1.3 we examine the market mechanism in more detail, explaining its operation and how it is supposed to promote economic well being. From this discussion we develop in Section 1.4 the market choice critique of public schooling. Here we identify the processes that are thought, from this viewpoint, to cause under-performance in state schooling systems. After this discussion of government failure in educa-tional provision, in Section 1.5 we turn the arguments around to consider the requirements for the efficient operation of schooling markets and likely sources of market failure. Here we explore the characteristics of schooling which give rise to externalities. It is the presence of externalities, and difficulty in quanti-fying their importance, that complicates any assessment of the need for, and consequences of, market-based reforms.

The role of governments in schooling markets is the concern of Section 1.6. In particular, we examine the determinants of the desirability of state regula-tion, funding and provision of primary and secondary education. Here we concentrate on the factors that have led to the present dominant role of the state in the provision of elementary and secondary education. The fear of signif-icant market failure has so far led to reforms of state schooling that generally fall short of a full-market solution. Emphasis has largely been upon increasing schooling choices and devolving more decision-making powers to individual schools. The term 'quasi-market' has been used to describe the type of market organisation where open enrolment prevails, but government remains the purchasing agent and retains control of curriculum, school entry and exit and the occupational licensing of teachers. We discuss the nature of these quasi-markets in Section 1.7. The penultimate section raises three key questions that our study will have to address. The chapter concludes with an explanation of the structure and content of the remaining chapters.

1.2 Strengths and limitations of the economic analysis of schooling markets

Some critics of market-based reforms of state schooling have tended to equate economic analyses of education with the specific advocacy of those reforms. In part this reflects a further tendency to treat economics as a monolithic discipline with a central tenet that markets always provide the best vehicle for allocating resources. A further reason is that governments sometimes employ economic analysis specifically as a means of gaining acceptability for policies that were formerly politically impossible. As we shall show, economic analysis can indeed be used to justify a market-driven schooling system. However, it can equally be used in support of a schooling system that is funded and provided by the state. While it is true that economic analysis in North America and much of Europe is currently dominated by the neo-classical analysis of market behaviour, alternative economic analysis continues to challenge many of orthodox analysis's fundamental assumptions. Given its current dominance, we focus initially on orthodox neo-classical analysis in our introduction to economic analysis and the assessment of its strengths and limitations.

In his explanation for its invasion into previously impenetrable policy territories, Lazear (2000) points to the rigour and analytic approach of orthodox economic analysis. In particular, he identifies three characteristics of contemporary orthodox economic analysis that have enabled this imperialism. We now apply his arguments to schooling. First, orthodox economic analysis assumes that individuals engage in maximising rational behaviour. While the existence of imperfect competition, transaction costs and social and cultural norms also affect behaviour, orthodox economics assumes that individuals know what they are doing when they make schooling decisions and are therefore maximising 'something'. When that something is specified, a well-defined and predictable response can be derived in the face of any shock. Statistical inference can then be employed to test these hypotheses. Since individuals are assumed to maximise, then at the margin they are always facing trade-offs between alternative decisions. The concept of opportunity costs is central here in specifying these trade-offs. The true cost of any schooling decision is that which must be foregone as a consequence. Hence, choice is at the centre of orthodox economic analysis and the costs and benefits of alternative schooling behaviour are capable of being compared within this framework.

Second, the concept of equilibrium is central to orthodox economic analysis. Observed behaviour is assumed to be consistent with some notion of equilibrium. Individual behaviour can then be aggregated to enable the analysis of the interaction of demand and supply in a schooling market. It is the emphasis upon the properties of this equilibrium, and the process that enables the market to regain equilibrium in the face of shocks, which distinguishes economics from the other social sciences. Third, the presumption of orthodox analysis is that competitive equilibrium in most markets promotes efficiency.

As Hanushek (1997a) points out, orthodox economic analysis of education has already been altering the nature of much educational research, particularly in North America. The quantitative emphasis of economic analysis has led to a much greater emphasis upon observing performance and student outcomes rather than with inputs into the educational process. How such performance should be measured and what outcomes should be prioritised remains the subject of much debate. Hanushek argues that an increased concern with establishing causality in statistical analyses of student performance is a further consequence of the economic approach. A final characteristic that Hanushek points to is the increased emphasis upon targeted incentives to promote favoured educational outcomes.

To illustrate the orthodox economic approach to schooling decision-making and in particular its championing of targeted incentives, we next outline the model of the allocation of an individual's time between alternative uses. This work–leisure model will be used later in this book to analyse parents' choice between alternative schools and the determinants of student and teacher levels of effort. We will here take the specific case of teacher effort levels, which is developed in more detail in Chapter 6. Individual decision-makers, teachers in this case, face a choice of how to distribute their limited time between work and leisure. For simplicity, we here take leisure to include all non-work activities. Given their particular preferences and domestic situation, the nature of their employment contracts, career concerns and the prevailing professional work norms, teachers will choose a combination of work and leisure which maximises their own overall level of satisfaction. That is, they assess the costs and rewards from different allocations of their time and effort in choosing their best combination. This equilibrium position will be affected by shocks – say, an increase in the importance of performance-related pay. In this particular case, the additional financial incentives alters the trade-off between work and leisure at the margin; leisure is now more expensive in terms of income foregone. Rational maximising behaviour therefore leads to teachers substituting additional work effort for leisure, and adjustment is made towards a new equilibrium reflecting the changed environment. Note that if the new incentive payment is just related to part of the teacher's work activities, then they may switch their efforts between different work tasks rather than having to reduce their leisure.

Critics of orthodox economics point to some general limitations of its analysis of economic behaviour. Relating these to the field of education, we can point to the tendency in human capital theory to down-play the importance of cultural, geographical, historical, institutional, political and social factors in influencing individual and collective behaviour in schooling markets (Fevre *et al.* 1999). It is the neglect of these dimensions that cause many to reject the claims of orthodox economists that they are concerned with generating only positive, rather than normative, assessments. One of the main strengths of economic analysis, its ability to abstract and simplify diverse phenomena in different contexts, is here viewed as its main weakness. Collectively these factors mean that individual parents and teachers are often severely constrained in their decision-making. In addition, they often lack the information necessary for them to exercise even that degree of choice left open to them. Once the costs of actually making schooling decisions and the degree of uncertainty of the prevailing environment are also acknowledged, then heterodox economists argue that most individuals in practice exercise bounded rationality (Williamson 1985). That is, rather than display the instrumental reasoning of rational economic man, they tend to display inertia and rely upon simple heuristics when faced with changed environments. Indeed, as Adnett and Davies (1999) argue, once we move away from the narrowest versions of orthodox economic analysis many of the disputes between the economic and sociological analyses of schooling decision-making disappear.

There are two special features of education which pose problems for any economic analysis (Dixit 2000). Firstly, education has multiple outcomes, reflecting the diverse objectives which society and individuals require of schooling. Primary and secondary schooling is designed to develop the basic skills of students such as communication, literacy, reasoning and calculation, whilst fostering their emotional and physical development. In part these skills, personality traits and norms of behaviour are developed in order to prepare students for their future, both as consumers and employees. However, as we shall discuss in more detail in the next chapter, changes in technology and work organisation have blurred the distinction between desired vocational skills and the development of certain favoured personal qualities and characteristics. In addition, schooling involves socialisation in its broadest sense, preparing students for active involvement in democratic society, developing their citizenship skills and promoting active community involvement. Some would extend these objectives of schooling to promote equity and social mobility and combat racism, sexism and classism (Walford 2001). The range of schooling outcomes is much wider than we have so far indicated. Research indicates that education level is strongly correlated to family fertility, health, and household composition (Greenwood 1997) and negatively related to cigarette and drug addiction (Sander 1995) and crime (Behrman and Stacey 1997). Wolfe and Zuvekas (1997) and McMahon (1998) provide surveys of the nature and extent of these non-market outcomes of schooling, and in Chapter 3 we return to a consideration of their importance. Some of these multiple outcomes are jointly produced within the schooling process, whilst others given the limited resources of schools and teachers effectively become substitutes. Thus, for example, requiring schools to spend a greater proportion of the school day on developing literacy and mathematical skills has the opportunity costs of reducing the proportion of the curriculum dedicated to the development of other cognitive and social skills.

The second feature of education that poses problems for conventional economic analysis is the presence of a variety of stakeholders. These attach different degrees of importance to the various schooling outcomes discussed above. Thus parents and pupils, teachers and heads, employers, local and national taxpayers, local communities and society as a whole each have their own goals for compulsory state schooling. Defining 'good' schooling or assessing 'value for money', or more fundamentally defining and measuring the outputs from schooling and comparing school and teacher performance, requires a prior judgement as to what weights are to be attached to individual schooling outputs. Moreover, in changing the nature of government intervention, the role of market forces and the form of school governance, the ability of different groups of stakeholders to influence the composition of schooling outputs is often changed. It follows that assessing the effectiveness of any educational reforms from the viewpoint of economic efficiency is complex. The reforms themselves may alter the weighting to be attached when aggregating and comparing schooling outcomes. An issue we return to in Section 1.5 below.

The complications that these two features of schooling generate for the design, implementation and economic assessment of market-based reforms will dominate much of our following analysis. However, if we are to understand the underlying nature of those reforms of state schooling system, we need to first introduce the basic orthodox economic model of the market mechanism.

1.3 The market mechanism

A market is where providers of a good and service meet those who wish to acquire that good or service. Since Adam Smith, orthodox economics has held that in certain circumstances allowing the forces of supply and demand to freely interact can produce socially beneficial results. A fundamental question in this work concerns to what extent this conclusion holds for education. In order to begin to answer this question, we now provide an outline of the basic economic analysis of market behaviour.

In principle, the interests of those who wish to utilise a good or service, consumers and those who produce it, providers, fundamentally conflict in capitalist societies. Consumers wish to acquire a service of a certain quality as cheaply as possible and providers wish to achieve the highest price possible in the market. However, if both sides have the freedom to make their own bargains then trade will only take place when it is perceived to be mutually beneficial. In a monetary economy, prices will fluctuate to reconcile aspirations on the two sides of the market. In competitive markets individual consumers have, in principle, the ability to exercise exit and voice. If they are unable to acquire the service they require at a price they view as appropriate then they can withdraw their demand and exit the market. It is this potential to withdraw purchasing power that prevents providers from unilaterally fixing the price of their service and the quantity that they will sell. Notwithstanding their ability to influence corporate governance or government regulation, it is their potential purchasing power that largely provides them with influence in the market place. The flexibility of prices in the market, the price mechanism, automatically signals information to providers and consumers, producing incentives for providers and consumers to adjust their behaviour over time. In the modern capitalist society the dominant belief is that reliance on this market mechanism provides an effective system of allocation for most goods and services.

The caricature of the market presented above abstracts from a large number of factors that distort behaviour in real world markets. We concentrate upon five factors that will feature in our later discussion as we begin to consider the applicability of markets to schooling. Firstly, we have assumed that the market is competitive. That is, alternative providers and multiple consumers are to be found in the market place. Where only one provider is present in the market, the case of monopoly, consumers no longer have the power to pick and choose. Only their threat to exit the market altogether constrains the power of the provider to determine both price and quantity. Monopoly or competition amongst a small number of providers, oligopoly, are especially common when we consider behaviour in localised markets. Secondly, we have assumed that consumers are well informed and can make monetary comparisons of the service offered by different providers. This ability to acquire, interpret and influence flows of information in the market is crucial if providers are to be encouraged to meet the perceived needs of consumers at minimum price. Thirdly, consumers have to be able to effectively demand that amount of the service which society believes is the minimum necessary for all to consume. Markets respond not to needs but to purchases, equity plays no role in the pursuit of mutually beneficial trade. If society requires the poor or those who place a low valuation on a commodity to consume a quantity in excess of their current purchases, then mechanisms are needed to supplant or supplement the market. Fourthly, we have assumed that reliance on individual decision-making will promote desirable outcomes. Not only have we neglected the possibility that the pursuit of self-interest may cause spillover effects for other market participants, but also we have ignored the potential benefits from co-operative behaviour and consideration of whether the latter can be sustained in competitive markets. Finally, we have ignored market behaviour over time. Our concern in assessing the desirability of markets is not limited to how successful they are in allocating a given provision between alternative consumers. We are also interested in whether the market encourages quantitative and qualitative improvements over time and whether it provides sufficient incentives for innovation. In other words, we are interested in assessing the dynamic efficiency of markets as well as their static efficiency.

Notwithstanding the logic of orthodox economics summarised above, in most economies markets do not currently allocate schooling. Most governments directly determine minimum educational requirements and provide public primary and secondary schooling for their citizens largely free at the point of delivery. We consider the reasons for the current dominance of public provision later in this chapter. However, we next consider the critique of this dominance, based upon the market analysis developed in this section.

1.4 The critique of public schooling

The market choice critique of state schooling, which developed from the work of Friedman (1955), combines a belief in the potential effectiveness of the market mechanism discussed above with a belief in the intrinsic inefficiency of public provision based upon public choice theory. As Shleifer (1998) explains, the case against the prevailing system of state schooling is not just that governments allow schools a captive market where they have no need to innovate or to respond efficiently, or sometimes at all, to consumer preferences. An important element of the original Chubb and Moe (1988) critique was that state education systems had effectively allowed educational decision-making to be subverted to serve the interests of educational administrators and teachers. In the US, the apparent absence of a relationship between school inputs and student performance, the secular rise in per student teaching and administrative costs and the poor relative performance of schools in metropolitan areas have all been attributed to the effectiveness of teacher unions in determining public policy (Hoxby 1996a; Peltzman 1993).

These aspects of government failure can be given an agency theory interpretation (Rapp 2000). The principal–agent problem arises when a principal (parents, taxpayers or the government in the case of public schooling) delegates some decision-making authority to an agent (heads and teachers). In schooling, as we noted in Section 1.2, we have multiple principals with diverse objectives. For parents the objectives of state schooling may be predominantly concerned with human capital creation, while taxpayers may seek value for money and a level of statutory education where the benefits of a more educated populace offset the costs of providing it. In most state schooling systems parents, taxpayers and other principals delegate responsibility for achieving these outputs to government. Information asymmetries arise since heads and teachers are more knowledgeable about their actual levels of effort and the composition of educational outputs they are seeking to generate. Hence, the agency problem is how to ensure that teachers do not exploit their informational advantages to lower and distort educational outcomes away from those desired by the other stakeholders. Bureaucratic failures also reflect asymmetric information problems. Local providers have little incentive to refrain from spending up to their set budget. They learn that any savings are likely to return to central budget-holders and that their future budgets are likely to be revised downwards. Hence, information flows are distorted and schooling expenditure patterns have a 'ratchet' effect over time (Milgrom and Roberts 1992).

A key argument against public provision of education is the inefficiency of centralisation as a means of addressing these agency problems. Lack of direct accountability results in an over-regulated and non-diversified provision. The different needs of local markets, schools and individual pupils are neglected in favour of a common curriculum and assessment system designed in part to enable the central monitoring of school performance. This provision of standardised state schooling imposes welfare burdens on those parents and students whose optimal level and quality differs from the uniform level. Some will still choose a state school since otherwise they may lose the state subsidy, thus effectively penalising those private schools that are more efficient. Exit and voice mechanisms are either absent or distorted. Attempts to involve parents and other stakeholders in school governance tend to give a voice only to the most active group of parents, who may be unrepresentative of parents as a whole (Chubb and Moe 1988). Commitments to both an occupational licensing system and wage bargaining at the national level for teachers further limits flexibility and prevents the design of effective incentive mechanisms to motivate teachers.

Market choice critics advocate school privatisation, often combined with some system where students can use government-funded vouchers at any school of their choice. Such a combination of vouchers and school choice can be argued to have several advantages over publicly provided schooling (West 1997). First, private schools have more incentive to reduce costs and innovate, potentially leading to both more efficient and higher quality education. Second, private schools will be more able to resist the attempts of teacher unions to distort provision in favour of their members' interests. Finally, competition between schools, both existing and potential, ensures that the 'exit' threat constrains the ability of private schools to undertake quality-reducing cost reductions. Reputational considerations strengthen this market discipline, while the presence of many not-for-profit private schools also curbs the ability of schooling-providers to exploit their market-power.

It is worth noting that there is only a very limited 'model' of educational attainment underlying this critique of public schooling. The market is not necessarily seen as a mechanism for increasing the quantity of resources available to the schooling system. Nor is the market seen as having any major impact on the motivation of parents and students or in increasing participation rates in post-compulsory education. Fundamentally, raising educational attainment seems to rest upon a belief that the performance of schools and teachers can be improved in a market-based system. School choice places greater pressures on schools and teachers to improve teaching as measured by accessible performance indicators. If schools fail to match those of their competitors in the local markets, resources are lost as the school roll declines and teachers' job security weakens. For this threat to be credible, less effective schools need to fear closure and be enabled to make changes that prevent a potential spiral of decline. One problem with reliance on incentive-based improvements to teaching is a fundamental uncertainty about the properties of 'effective' teaching. As we discuss in Chapters 3 and 6, researchers have found it difficult to identify strong teacher effects on pupil attainment. Moreover, as Walford (2001) points out, the market choice argument makes several other implicit assumptions. It views popular schools as 'good' schools and unpopular as 'bad' ones. It assumes that popular schools wish and are able to expand, and that their expansion does not threaten their effectiveness. We now systematically examine the propositions of the market choice approach in the following section.

1.5 Schooling markets

1.5.1 Requirements for an efficient schooling market

A common starting point in defining productive efficiency in schooling markets is that output is maximised for the given utilisation of resources. Employing this limited definition, efficiency can only be improved if more output is achieved for the same resources or alternatively if the same output can be achieved for less resource use. One way of addressing such internal efficiency considerations is by cost-effectiveness analysis, where costs are related to outcomes. The main problem with such analysis is how to measure the latter. As we have emphasised, most educational programmes produce a range of outputs and it appears arbitrary which specific measure of these should be chosen.

Attempts to operationalise a more sophisticated use of the term 'efficiency' have been a cause of some confusion. We build upon the classification used by Hoxby (1996b). She argues that the ultimate function of an educational system is to create an environment that induces people to make socially optimal investment decisions. Within this framework, she argues that equity is about ensuring that this standard of optimality is applied to all groups, regardless of family background or wealth. The problem of allocative efficiency, whether society is making best use of its resources, concerns the standard, type and amount of schooling provided, whilst productive efficiency concerns minimising the costs of that provision (the 'value for money' or 'cost-effectiveness' dimension). According to the market critique, the absence of market forces and the behaviour of self-interested pressure groups caused homogeneous and, in relation to the resources provided, mediocre schooling throughout the state system. The system had failed on each of the efficiency and equity criterion identified above.

What is missing from this more refined treatment of efficiency is a recognition of consumption outcomes from schooling and a discussion of 'dynamic efficiency' – that is, performance over time. One of the weaknesses of conventional economic analysis is that it concentrates upon static efficiency. The preoccupation of much orthodox analysis is with the equilibrium properties of different forms of market organisation. However, as we explain in the following chapter, the motivation of most governments initiating educational reforms has been a concern with the ability of their existing educational system to respond to a changing economic and social environment. Governments have been predominantly concerned with raising the standards of educational attainment and promoting curriculum changes to reflect changing economic and social needs and aspirations. The ability of a system to promote innovative behaviour, to monitor its consequences and encourage imitation if justified, are all key features of the schooling system which governments wish to create. Hence, it is in terms of the impact on dynamic efficiency which our analysis of market-based reforms will be largely based.

Applying the conventional economic analysis of markets developed above, then, there are three main sets of conditions that are necessary if market forces are to promote a socially optimal level of educational provision. Firstly, parents and pupils need to have a choice of schooling and access to the appropriate information to assess alternative provision, together with an ability to change schools should circumstances require. Thus, following our discussion in Section 1.2, they need to have access to information on each of the multiple schooling outcomes that they value. Even if we limit these outcomes to the investment emphasis explicit in the conventional economic analysis of human capital, the constituents of 'appropriate information' are both complex and numerous. Unlike most consumption decisions, investment decisions require information about the future consequences of the decision taken. Since it is the role of the labour market in this framework to ensure that the educational needs of the economy are reflected in the structure of labour market earnings, pupils/parents require information about the labour market consequences of their different schooling options.

Different schooling decisions also imply different costs for pupils and their families in terms of travel and effort and different risks of non-completion. These costs and risks again need to be assessed in comparison with the expected current consumption benefits and the lifetime labour market income associated with the alternative potential schooling attainment levels, where the latter comprise academic, vocational and personal skills and qualifications. To even begin to estimate the probability distribution of the latter, pupils/parents need information about their absolute and relative position in the ability range and comprehensive data on the past performance of every school in each of these areas. These issues are developed further in Chapter 3.

A second precondition for markets to generate socially optimal outcomes is that consumer preferences are efficiently communicated to schools who are able and motivated to respond. In most markets consumer preferences are communicated through purchasing decisions with firms able to adjust prices and output to maximise their profitability. How to mimic such mechanisms in schooling markets, if the government retains the purchasing role, has led to much discussion about the advantages of vouchers (West 1997).

As we discuss in more detail in Chapter 3, it is not clear what is the appropriate way to model the objectives that motivate schools in markets. A pupil's education is a joint product, dependent upon the contribution of several teachers, the prevailing school's culture and contextual factors, such as peer groups. It follows that the degree of co-ordination and the efficiency of intra-organisational behaviour are critical determinants of schooling outcomes. Successful schools are likely to be those that achieve the right balance between co-ordinating individual teachers' activities and respecting their professional autonomy (Vandenberghe 1999b). Levin (1996) argues that this optimal balance has five key attributes. First, schools must be clear about their objectives, which must be both agreed and accepted by all participants. Second, teachers and heads must be offered incentives, pecuniary or otherwise, which are related to their success in meeting these objectives. This requires that the agreed objectives must be measurable. Third, information systems within the school must be designed and utilised to encourage systematic assessment of current practices and innovations. Fourth, schools must continually evolve to reflect their changing economic and social environment and the particular requirements of their current pupils. Finally, schools must be able to choose the most efficient teaching technology within their budget constraints. A key question, addressed in Chapters 7 and 8, is therefore whether these attributes can be encouraged by market-based reforms and associated changes in school governance structures.

The third set of conditions necessary for markets to produce socially efficient outcomes requires that consumer preferences are themselves consistent with social welfare maximisation over time or that the regulatory regime adjusts market behaviour to achieve this outcome. These requirements raise issues concerned with the objectives of parents and pupils in schooling markets and whether they internalise into their decision-making all the consequences of their behaviour. Those aspects related to the presence of spillovers and externalities are addressed in the following section. A more detailed discussion occurs in Chapters 3 and 5.

1.5.2 Market failures and schooling

The conclusion that more competitive schooling markets can promote the public interest rests upon certain assumptions about the behaviour of parents, schools and government. We now need to explore the nature of potential schooling market failures (circumstances where the market will fail to produce optimal outcomes). Apart from equity considerations, our discussion above suggests several types of market failure that may be present in schooling markets: – ill-informed and non-rational consumers; inadequately and inappropriately motivated providers, and the presence of externalities. We now consider these individually.

Consumer behaviour

There is ample evidence from other markets that when consumers are faced with complex decisions they rely upon simple signals and employ heuristics which generate systematic deviations from that behaviour implied by conventional economic analysis (Conlisk 1996). As Levin (1991) argued, schools are too complex to portray their quality effectively to parents and pupils. Most parents make infrequent, but closely spaced, schooling decisions and the consequences of those decisions are only revealed, if at all, in the long term. Moreover, education is an 'experience good' in that the costs of identifying the quality of provision are higher before admission than after pupils and parents have spent time at the school. There are also significant switching costs should pupils and parents wish to change schools. In such markets, Klemperer (1987) has shown that consumers are reluctant to exercise their 'exit' threat and consumer preferences may be less effective at influencing school behaviour.

Mainstream economists are beginning to acknowledge that the failure of the labour market to provide cheap and/or appropriate signals to educational decision-makers may lead to greater reliance upon peer group and role-model behaviour (Pratten *et al.* 1997). Key educational decisions, such as those influencing staying-on rates and applications for higher education, may therefore be subject to bandwagon effects rather than the incremental changes implied by conventional economic analysis. Market failures are not merely associated with the investment nature of educational decision-making. Consumption motivations may further weaken the link between parent and pupil preferences and social welfare maximisation. Recent work by Frank (1997), synthesising psychological and economic research indicates that consumer satisfaction depends heavily upon their consumption relative to other consumers. Thus individual payoffs from schooling decisions may differ sharply from the benefits to society. As Ball (1993) argued, exclusivity may itself be desired by participants in schooling markets, hence parents may be willing to pay a premium to buy a house in the catchment area of a 'good' school, but unwilling to fund collectively the levelling-up of standards. We discuss the implications of this positional demand for schooling in Chapters 3 and 5.

School behaviour

Where schools face little existing or potential competition, they are not subject to significant market pressures and may have little incentive to respond to consumer preferences. Naive applications of market analysis ignore two important characteristics of schooling markets: they are local and a clear hierarchy amongst current providers exists. The degree of actual competition in schooling markets reflects the locational mobility of parents and schools and the extent of economies of scale in schooling provision. In many local markets, schools have substantial monopoly power with high barriers to entry preventing new entrants. That means that the degree of contestability in such markets is often low. Thus, in many local markets there are no, or very weak, entry and exit threats to encourage efficient school behaviour. However, technological developments and changes in labour market behaviour may be beginning to challenge such inertia. These forces have already caused major changes in access to schooling at the tertiary level with the growth of distance learning and intensive study (Heyneman 2000).

As we have noted, the market choice critique sees increasing parental and pupil choice as a mechanism for raising quality. Less effective schools have to improve or be eliminated from the market. A credible exit threat is more likely in a school system with over-capacity in many local markets. As Walford (2001) points out, the British quasi-market reforms were initiated at a time, the 1980s, when there had been a fall of 9 per cent in the school-age population. Although some schools had been closed, the resistance of parents had often prevented local authorities from reducing overall capacity in line with the fall in demand. In part therefore, the 1988 Education Reform Act was designed to provide a mechanism for rationalising local provision. Increased school choice would clearly identify the 'bad' schools, the closure of which could be justified, and the overall quality of the surviving schools would therefore be higher.

The existence of an, often well-established, hierarchy amongst local schools also constrains their response to market-based reforms. Local market leaders with excess demand for their places may have little incentive to improve their own performance. Even without improvements in their effectiveness, they can expand market share and benefit further from any scale or scope economies and positive peer group effects (discussed in the following section). Those schools lower down their local hierarchies face the prospect of losing market share, especially amongst the more able pupils in the local cohort. Even the most efficient amongst them will therefore have difficulty in maintaining over time the absolute level of attainment of their pupils. We discuss the consequences of such processes below and in Chapters 3 and 8.

The presence of transaction costs within the educational process may be a further source of market failure. Transactions-costs economics views organisations as a web of contracts rather than just a structure for the transformation of inputs into outputs. In schools there are formal and implicit contracts between governors, managers, teachers and students. If we wish to understand how schools work we must, according to this approach, understand the factors which induce teachers and students to regard a contract as worthwhile. Crucially this involves understanding their perception of the likely outcome of the contract. They are assumed to be self-seeking, but not fully informed, hence the assumption of 'bounded rationality'. Acquiring knowledge is costly and risky as the individual may be ill equipped to acquire all the information relevant to a decision. As professional knowledge and skills are costly to acquire they become valuable assets, but specific to the contexts in which they are valued. This 'asset-specificity' means that professionals face a strong incentive to maintain circumstances in which their assets keep their value and to be cautious about changes that threaten the value of their existing knowledge and skills. Following Williamson (1985), House (1996) sets out the implications of the assumptions of bounded rationality, opportunism and asset specificity for the contracting process (Table 1.1).

Brown (1992) draws attention to the difficulties in monitoring teachers' output, given problems with measuring certain outputs, their joint supply and

Table 1.1   Attributes of the contracting process

Rationality	Opportunism	Asset specificity	Implied contracting process
Unbounded	Yes	Yes	Planning
Bounded	No	Yes	Promise
Bounded	Yes	No	Competition
Bounded	Yes	Yes	Governance

Sources: House 1996: 7; Williamson 1985: 31

the practical difficulties in observing the process of teaching. Hence, teachers' contracts are written in terms of inputs rather than outputs. However, in England benchmarked attainment data and lesson observation have now become routine aspects of school life (discussed further in Chapter 7), arguably leading to a substantial alleviation of these problems. Competition becomes inappropriate if there is asset specificity because the primary interest of parties to contracts will be to protect their current assets. In particular, they will develop relationships with contracting partners that they will seek to exploit. Evaluating different types of reform, House (1996) concludes that the probability of success for national standards and testing programmes will be undermined by opportunism (grade inflation) and performance incentives will be undermined by bounded rationality (managers and teachers will have insufficient knowledge to generate trust and confident monitoring). The examples of education reform reckoned by House to implicitly acknowledge the existence of bounded rationality, opportunism and asset specificity are remarkably similar to those advocated by Levin above. In particular, he emphasises the importance of a community of teachers and parents working together to establish goals and to develop their understanding of the process of education.

Externalities

Society benefits from increased education comprise more than just the higher earning power that accrues to the educated individual. Externalities or spillovers occur in schooling markets since the decisions of parents and schools influence the well-being of those not a party to the original decisions. Where these, say, beneficial consequences to others are not internalised in the original decision-making, then unregulated markets would generate socially sub-optimal outcomes. For example, modern theories of economic growth emphasise the benefits of a more educated workforce in raising the rate of success, and therefore the level, of research and development, resulting in a faster rate of productivity growth (see the discussion in Chapter 2). Along similar lines, other economists have argued that economies which lack an adequate supply of vocationally educated and skilled workers may generate insufficient incentives for employers to create or sustain high technology production (for example, Snower 1996 and Acemoglu 1996). A consequence is that economies can get stuck in a 'low-skill, bad-job' equilibrium, whereas seemingly similar economies maintain a 'high-skill, good-job' equilibrium. A common element of these approaches is that relative earnings in labour markets may provide inadequate signals to individual educational decision-makers. In such circumstances we cannot rely upon schooling reforms based upon strengthening consumer power to produce socially desirable outcomes, even when the latter is measured solely in terms of international competitiveness and economic growth.

As Hoxby (2000) points out, school choice can allow students to self-sort in a manner that may either benefit or impede the learning of some students. Since the self-sorting of parents and pupils is motivated by maximising private allocative efficiency, that is their own welfare, it may lead to poor social allocative efficiency. The existence of peer group effects causes some externalities to occur during the process of education itself. For example, able, well-adjusted pupils create positive spillover effects for their fellow pupils and their teachers. In particular, the knowledge a pupil assimilates at school appears to depend directly upon the ability and behaviour of their classmates. For example, Feinstein and Symons' (1999) results support the 'parents and peers' theory of educational attainment. Parents select the peer groups of their children in ways associated with their social class, educational background and family structure. Peer group factors together with parental involvement in their child's education, rather than other background variables, appear to largely determine educational attainment. It follows that given heterogeneous pupil ability and peer group effects, the pattern of allocation of individuals across different schools influences aggregate educational attainment (Vandenberge 1998). A free schooling market, since it fails to internalise these externalities, may therefore have 'good' peers sorted in a way that they are not in contact with the students who would benefit from them most. We return to this possibility in Chapters 3, 5, 6 and 8.

We have now identified the nature of the government and market failures that may be found in schooling markets. The key question therefore concerns which combination of regulations, governance structures and incentives minimises the welfare losses from government and market failures in schooling markets. Accordingly we now examine the nature and consequences of government interventions into schooling markets.

1.6 Government intervention in schooling markets

Education does not have the attributes of what economists call a public good. In other words, it is a service that is both appropriable and divisible. As such, education can in principle be left fully to the market. Indeed, in a world containing no sources of schooling market failure, equity considerations apart, market-based reforms must improve overall performance. However, our discussion of both government and market failures above indicates that no general conclusion can be made as to the optimal degree of government involvement in education. Moreover, the theory of the second best explains how in the real world of imperfect markets, even movements towards more competitive behaviour cannot be assumed to be beneficial.

In general, equity considerations may require some minimum mandatory years/levels of education to be required of all children, whilst capital market imperfections may also necessitate government funding for such requirements to be met. The presence of externalities also provides a rationale for welfare-improving government intervention, though not necessarily for public provision. As to government involvement with curriculum, schooling funding and teacher accreditation and pay, then economic theory provides no clear universal rules.

We now discuss the role of government intervention in schooling markets in more detail, distinguishing between interventions related to regulation, public funding and the public provision of primary and secondary schooling.

1.6.1 Regulation of schooling

A common element of regulation in schooling markets concerns the minimum age at which pupils can exit secondary schooling. Society seems to view compulsory schooling as a normal good, since the general tendency over the long run has been for the amount of compulsory schooling to increase. Such movements may reflect underlying views on the marginal social benefits and costs of such changes, though rarely have governments relied explicitly upon economic arguments to justify the extensions they have introduced.

We have previously discussed the extent of imperfect information in schooling markets. These imperfections give rise to two separate reasons for governmental regulation of schooling. Firstly, in order to protect consumers from opportunistic providers government may enforce a common curriculum and provide a centralised inspection service. Since poorly informed consumers are unable to identify the quality of schooling provided, contracts with suppliers are incomplete and unenforceable. Where reputation effects are weak or subject to inertia, providers can therefore exploit this information asymmetry to provide a low quality service. Governments with their superior access to information can in principle write and enforce more complete contracts with schooling providers. This may include provisions regarding the details of curriculum (discussed in Chapters 4 and 8), or a requirement that only licensed teachers may be employed and determining the requirements to obtain that licence (discussed in Chapter 6).

A second information problem concerns schooling outputs. In the absence of external exams, schools set the standards which students seek to attain. These standards effectively determine the effort levels required of both teachers and students. The overall efficiency of the system will depend upon how assessments are set, the form of the assessment used and the level of proficiency required for success. In the absence of government regulation, teachers and students may have a mutual interest in setting low standards. For example, if median student ability is lower than the mean ability, the student body may press for standards to be lower (Costrell 1994). Since they wish the adjustment not to harm their employment prospects, grade inflation may result. Governments may therefore require a system of external examinations and the construction and publication of performance indicators that enable comparisons between alternative providers, issues we address in Chapter 7.

US debates on educational reform have recently focused on policies that would make educational standards more homogeneous across schools. Bishop (1996, 1997) and others have developed the case for Curriculum-based External Exit Exams (CBEEEs). As we explain in Chapter 7, this is largely based on the resulting improved signalling to the labour market of relative academic achievement. The absence of mandatory CBEEEs has been argued to contribute to a large variation in school quality in the US. Somanathan (1998) develops this argument to show that where informational asymmetries prevent employers observing the quality of school attended by an applicant, greater school diversity can lead to inefficient human capital decisions. CBEEEs can correct this inefficiency, since they improve information flows and reduce the distortions favouring college entry. However, as we show in Chapter 8, CBEEEs in quasi-markets are also likely to influence the pattern of demand for schooling and may in conjunction with peer group effects distort the distribution of schooling outcomes in a local market.

A further area of government intervention is centrally determined pay for teachers, which is common in developed Western economies. One rationale for its dominance concerns relative bargaining power. Individual schools lack the managerial resources and market power to negotiate freely with teachers who are usually nationally organised. Additionally, centralising wage determination enables the government to target both turnover and initial teacher-training intakes. The principles that governments should employ in designing the structure of pay for teachers are discussed in Chapter 6.

1.6.2 Public funding of schooling

The case for public funding of education rests upon the desirability of intervening on the demand side of the schooling market. It therefore depends upon the specific equity and market failure considerations that can be addressed through intervention on this side of the market. We identify four areas of market failure that may justify such intervention.

First, our discussion above introduced the possibility of ill-informed consumers. The full consequences of schooling decisions are revealed only gradually over time and may be particularly difficult to forecast for those parents unable to use their own experience. Hence, differences may exist in the ability to assess returns to schooling investments between 'educated' parents and those whose own educational investments were low. Governments have access to superior information on the returns from schooling investments and may therefore exploit this information asymmetry to guide individual and family decision-making by enforcing a minimum school leaving age and funding compulsory schooling. In addition, improving the quality of information flows can reduce the uncertainty and risk facing ill-informed decision-makers.

A second concern is the possibility that capital market imperfections may distort the pattern of demand in schooling markets. The absence of a forward market in labour requires investors in human capital to rely either on their own or their family's finances or borrows from financial institutions. The illiquidity of human capital and the diversity of its financial returns to individuals make financial institutions more wary of lending for this category of investment. Any additional risk premium required for lending on schooling investments creates a gap between the borrowing and lending rates in such capital markets. In this case, the children of wealthier parents will have a greater ability to fund potentially profitable investments in schooling and there exists a rationale for government intervention. In the UK, an example of such intervention is the Education Maintenance Allowance, a means-tested benefit payable to young people who stay on in full-time education past compulsory schooling. Alternatively, loans may be provided on preferential and/or socially redistributive terms, as again practised in the UK for those entering higher education.

A further reason for public funding of primary and secondary schooling concerns the positive externalities generated from such investments. As we have argued above, the benefits generated from schooling do not just accrue to the parents and pupils, hence at the margin a free market would generate a level of provision where social benefits still exceeded social costs. More generally, a society may have a collective desire for greater educational opportunity than a free market would provide. The electorate may charge that government should promote equality of opportunity in schooling markets regardless of the consequences for narrow allocative efficiency, a proposition shared by both traditional and 'third way' social democrats.

Finally, subsidising the demand for schooling from general tax revenue may have two further rationales. Government support of education may be a desirable example of promoting compulsory saving as well as investment. It may be that myopic consumers would otherwise be unable or unwilling to fund future desired human capital investments. Similarly, since schooling is a labour-intensive process, its efficiency may rise more slowly over time than the economy's norm. This means that its relative price will increase. Government funding may therefore enable an inter-generationally equitable contract of education provision in the face of an increasing relative resource burden (Belfield 2000).

Theoretically, in order to determine the optimal government subsidy of education, social rates of return need to be calculated. This is normally viewed as requiring an initial estimate of the earnings premia to educated workers and then expressing it as a rate of return on costs incurred. Such private rates of return then need to be revised to incorporate transfers and the net costs borne by taxpayers. Externalities need to be expressed in monetary terms as do any government failures resulting from the subsidy. The difference between social and private rates of return for different groups in society can, in principle, also be used to determine the appropriate degree of government subsidy across these groups. In practice, the inability to provide accurate aggregate social and private rates of return to schooling precludes the fine-tuning of the targeting of government educational subsidies. Additionally, the realities of retaining political power in a democracy encourage governments to respond to median voter preferences and special interest groups. The interaction of diverse costs and concentrated benefits often resulting in the vocal middle classes especially benefiting from the provision of public funding.

Any public funding of schooling requires additional tax revenues that will cause welfare losses by changing relative prices and distorting decision-making in the economy. In addition, any government funding of non-public goods will generate deadweight and displacement effects. The former occurs, for example, where subsidised students would have been willing to undertake post-compulsory schooling even without the subsidy. While displacement effects occur when subsidised students merely displace others from the limited places available on an education programme. The availability and administration of public funding may also weaken the incentives for schools to be both technically and allocatively efficient.

A further issue concerns the interaction between education and taxation policies. Once individuals have made their investments in human capital then a hold-up problem exists in that governments could raise the tax rate on the returns to schooling. One solution to this time consistency problem may be the public provision of schooling, the topic of the following section.

1.6.3 Public provision of schooling

A key question concerned with market-based reforms is whether state schools should dominate educational provision. Notwithstanding the critique developed in Section 1.2 above, there are a number of reasons why the government may be able to offer schooling more efficiently than the private sector. Shleifer (1998) has produced a summary of the conditions in which government provision might be preferred, which we now relate to schooling:

- where innovation is relatively unimportant, since the absence of market incentives and hard budget constraints encourages inertia;
- where reputation effects are weak, since consumer choice is less effective in rewarding the successful and punishing the failing schools;
- where non-contractible deteriorations in schooling quality are likely due to cost-cutting by private providers, since the market would here under-supply education.

Whilst this list provides a useful starting point, there are number of factors specific to the schooling market which must also influence the choice between private or public provision.

Gradstein and Justman (2000) develop an economic rationale for state schooling based upon the accumulation of social capital. They argue that one advantage of state schooling is that it instils a common cultural norm and set of ethical values in the population. Developing civic virtues from an early age reduces future enforcement costs of compliance with those norms and values. Uniform state schooling in a common culture also generates network externalities, which lower economic transaction costs, and stimulate aggregate economic activity. Differences in customs, language or religion could, in the absence of uniform schooling, reduce the efficiency of production and exchange. Finally, common state schooling promotes social cohesion, reducing tensions between different population groups and avoids wasteful rent-seeking activities.

Gradstein (2000) provides a further rationale for public provision. A common problem with government financing and/or provision of private goods and services is that typically the time horizon of their decision-making is short-term, related to the electoral cycle. This problem is related to a further one: time-inconsistency. For example, government may announce policy decisions which influence the future behaviour of teachers, trading-off higher salaries against the desired changes in teacher behaviour. However, once teacher behaviour has changed they often have incentives to renege on the higher salaries and allow the relative pay of teachers to fall. Similar considerations concern their funding of education through taxation. Gradstein argues that it is just this inability of a government to commit credibly to future levels of taxation that, perversely, explains the widespread phenomenon of uniform public schooling. It is parents' fear of future high redistributive taxes that causes them to under-invest in their child's human capital in a private schooling market. Government provision of schooling provides a solution to this under-investment.

Brown (1992) provides an explanation for the inability of private schools to compete effectively with state schools in the US based upon the economics of risk and uncertainty. He argues that since parents all seek a similar provision in terms of curriculum and socialisation, private schools have few niches to exploit. Most that do survive offer a characteristic unavailable in the public sector – such as religion or responding to idiosyncratic demands. The reason for this outcome is that parents are initially uncertain about the ability and career preferences of their children and wish to avoid premature specialisation that restricts future options. This argument may be linked to the existence of economies of scale and standardisation in gathering information and organising provision. Together, these factors may prevent private providers from effectively competing with public schools in many local markets. However, Brown, in seeking to explain US schooling decisions, neglects a key feature of certain European systems. The idiosyncratic demands which private schools may satisfy may be largely based upon income or positional considerations. The demand for private schooling may be a demand for exclusivity and a rejection of the concept and practice of equality of opportunity.

The motivation of teachers provides a further rationale for public provision. Francois (2000) argues that workers such as teachers can be motivated by a 'public service motivation'. This induces them to provide effort out of concern for the impact of their work on the community as a whole. To the extent that private schools cannot induce such altruistic behaviour amongst teachers, then public provision effectively lowers the cost to taxpayers of schooling provision. The existence of such non-pecuniary benefits to teachers also affects the efficient structure of pay. Imitation of market forces, by increasing performance-based elements or the introduction of public–private partnerships, may reduce the 'gift' which teachers are prepared to make to further communal welfare. Analyses of these propositions form a major part of our discussion in Chapters 6 and 7.

Given the costs to society of unemployment and social exclusion, government provision of schooling may enable a bundling together of targeted policies. In the terms of 'third-way' jargon, state schooling may facilitate 'joined-up' government initiatives. Public providers are more likely to be able to co-ordinate their behaviour with local social services and health providers who are also in the public sector and share a common work culture. In both England and Scotland, recent government policies have favoured such multi-agency responses to the promotion of social inclusion, an issue we explore further in the following chapter.

Though all of the above factors may contribute to the dominance of public provision, our previous discussion indicates that a degree of competition from alternative providers may still be beneficial. Several American studies have analysed whether competition from private schools improves student performance in neighbouring public schools (for example, Dee 1998 and Hoxby 2000). In general, these studies find a positive relationship between the degree of competition from private schools and the high school graduation rate of neighbouring state schools. Though importantly for our later discussion, Hoxby finds that greater competition from neighbouring state schools also improves student outcomes. Using Czech and Hungarian data, Munich and Filer (2000) analyse the response of state schools to greater competition from private and religious schools. They also find some evidence that state schools slightly improve the quality of educational inputs and significantly improve the quality of their graduates.

1.7 Quasi-market reforms: an introduction

Most market-based reforms of state schooling still retain a central agency which allocates funding and tries to impose constraints on: the quality and variety of schooling offered, the ability of schools to expand or contract, and the structure of decision-making within schools. Chapter 4 provides a discussion and categorisation of the details of recent reforms. The high degree of regulation retained can be viewed as responding to the diversity of purchasers and providers in schooling and the asymmetry of information between them, which together preclude a more contractually based system of controlling standards (Challis *et al.* 1994).

Currently, the UK has a quasi-voucher system in which parents and pupils exercise choice and with money following pupils under essentially an age-weighted, pupil-number formula. Little formal information is generally available to schools about consumer preferences apart from pupil registrations. The increase in inter-school competition following the creation of quasi-markets itself reduces cross-school co-operation and creates further information asymmetries (discussed in Chapters 7 and 8). For most schools it follows that discovering the preferences of existing and potential consumers is expensive in a quasi-market structure; much more accessible are the preferences of government and their regulators.

The quasi-market process may even distort the information on preferences that is available to schools. As explained in Chapter 5, reforms that strengthen market forces make schools more responsive to the perceived needs of the more visible and potentially mobile consumers. This bias, when combined with unit funding, may limit the ability of school managers and government to cross-subsidise between different groups by allocating resources on the basis of their judgements rather than those of consumers. Whilst this may result in equity problems (Edwards and Whitty 1994), it may also be inconsistent with dynamic efficiency.

In the absence of a price for schooling, quasi-markets encourage parents to respond to measures of the quality of schools' outcomes. Choosing an appropriate measure is problematic, since these schooling outcomes are necessarily uncertain and disparate (e.g. average level of academic outcomes, distribution of academic outcomes, vocational preparation, socialisation, citizenship). Yet, as explained above, consumer behaviour in all markets often relies on the application of simple heuristics. Parents will tend to base their decision-making on one or two key signals which provide partial, biased, information about the full set of outcomes with which they are, in principle, concerned. However, providers only have an incentive to provide information that they believe will encourage consumers to demand their service. Information on quality based on criteria that can be applied to all providers more commonly results from government intervention or the activity of consumer groups. Therefore, it is not surprising to find the government acting on behalf of parents and pupils determining the measures of quality which schools must disclose. An inevitable consequence of this government intervention is a partial sublimation of diverse parental criteria of quality by a uniform government criterion.

In England and Wales, experience gained from the regulation of privatised utilities encouraged the application of competition by comparison policies (Vickers 1995) to the schooling market. The government sponsored the compilation and publication of school performance tables that currently consist largely, see Chapter 7, of measures of the proportion of pupils obtaining good passes in national curriculum based exams at ages 16 and 18. As we record in Chapter 5, school performance tables have now become an important influence in parental decision-making, a finding consistent with US evidence that consumer choice is highly sensitive to relative test scores (for example, Murray and Wallace 1997). In our detailed analysis in Chapters 7 and 8, we assess whether reliance on average unadjusted examination results obscures information and is inferior to value-added measures of pupil attainment.

1.7.1 Some initial questions

Schooling quasi-markets are recent phenomena and it should not be surprising that at the end of our initial analysis we are left with a range of unanswered questions. We now raise three interrelated key questions which the analysis in the following chapters will seek to answer. First, is rewarding success and penalising failure appropriate mechanism for schooling markets? Second, will an increased use of incentives harm beneficial co-operation both between and within schools? Finally, will market-based reforms inevitably lead to increased polarisation?

Should resources be re-allocated away from 'unsuccessful' schools?

Market forces can promote efficient behaviour when effective incentives are created for agents to promote social welfare. They are less successful in raising welfare when some agents have substantial market power or when efforts are not reflected in rewards. Market-based reforms of schooling markets should ideally ensure that incentives are generated which encourage all schools and teachers to raise educational value-added. Agreed performance indicators to assess the extent of 'success' in schooling markets have to be constructed and publicised, if the market mechanism is to be successfully employed.

The difficulties of promoting entry and exit in local schooling markets and constraints upon the ability of 'successful' schools to expand create complications. With open enrolment and formula-based funding, the quasi-market rewards success through reallocating resources to expanding schools. However, it is not clear that in schooling markets the marginal net benefits from additional expenditure on expanding schools exceeds that for declining schools. Indeed, the conventional economic logic of diminishing returns suggests that under these constraints, resources should be reallocated to the weaker schools. In several of the quasi-market systems 'failing' schools are indeed allocated additional funding, being closed only in extreme circumstances. Such perverse incentives have no place in the market choice model given their effects upon dynamic efficiency, but their survival suggests that there are compensating benefits which conventional market theory has neglected.

Does the increased use of incentives have to reduce co-operation?

In a market economy, governments can use their powers to tax and subsidise to stimulate changes in market behaviour at the margin. As the schooling market has developed these policy instruments have become more popular. For example, targeted financial incentives have been effective in the UK in raising the number of entrants into teacher training and they may also become important policy instruments for influencing demand at the margin. Research on the initial effects of Education Maintenance Allowances in England and Wales (introduced in Section 1.6.2 above) suggest that they have encouraged an additional 5 per cent of young people from low income families to stay in full-time education and reduced significantly their drop-out rates.

Market-based reforms have often sought to strengthen incentives for individual schools and teachers to improve their relative performance in local schooling markets. One way to achieve this outcome is to co-operate with other schools and teachers only when the benefits from such actions are distributed in one's own favour. The logical consequence of such selectivity is that beneficial co-operation between schools largely disappears within a local market. Information flows deteriorate, inertia and duplication increase and the overall quality of decision-making falls over time.

A similar process can occur within schools, when individual performance-related pay is introduced (Chapter 6 below). As we noted in Section 1.2, rewarding teachers in this way encourages them to reallocate their time and effort. They are encouraged both to neglect those aspects of their duties that are not monitored and to no longer internalise the consequences of their behaviour for fellow teachers and overall school performance. Hence the benefits gained from increased motivation need to be measured against the costs of reduced co-operation.

Is increased polarisation inevitable?

Increasing parental choice and inter-school competition appears to produce forces which encourage the segmentation of schooling markets by social class and ability (Chapters 5 and 8 below). On the demand side, the cultural capital of parents appears to be influential in determining their ability to exploit the additional powers given to more active consumers. Similarly, providers become more sensitive to the perceived tastes of the marginal, active consumers. In addition, competition by comparison encourages individual schools to cream-skim the more able pupils in the local market. Thus, irrespective of the optimal mix of ability dictated by peer group effects or any preference for social integration, market-based schooling systems become more polarised. A key concern is whether state school systems can be reformed in ways that generate higher levels of educational attainment and avoid the undesired consequence of increased polarisation.

1.8 Plan of the remaining chapters

Tyack (1990) argues that 'reform periods in education are typically times when concerns about the state of the society or economy spill over into demand that schools set things right' (p.174). Accordingly in Chapter 2, we examine the economic and social context within which contemporary schooling markets operate. We identify the overall level of educational expenditures and their typical composition in developed economies. We assess the impact of education on economic growth and an economy's competitiveness. We also examine the emergence of the 'knowledge-based' economy and consider its significance for the school curriculum. This chapter also examines the links between education and discrimination, inequality and social exclusion.

In Chapter 3 we review the microeconomic analysis of schooling, addressing more systematically many of the issues introduced in this chapter. We examine the behaviour of parents, pupils, school managers and teachers and the nature of the process of schooling. This review encompasses both theory and evidence. Initially we concentrate upon the choices which parents and pupils make in schooling, analysing both the consumption and investment objectives that determine their behaviour. We then examine the motivation of administrators, school managers and teachers, again using many of the concepts and analyses introduced in the present chapter. Finally, we examine the process of education, considering in more detail the outcomes of schooling and the relationship between inputs and those outcomes. We investigate the difficulties in identifying the contribution of teachers and schools to educational outcomes and the evidence concerning the importance of peer group effects. In Chapter 4 we examine the nature of the market-based reforms introduced in recent years in several developed economies. We classify those reforms into five categories: funding; open enrolment; teacher training and pay; local school management and information; and monitoring. We assess the similarities and differences between national reforms of school funding and open enrolment, providing a more detailed description of the recent development of the state schooling system in England and Wales.

The remaining chapters of the book assess the consequences of those reforms, again paying particular attention to the case of England and Wales. In Chapter 5 we analyse how parents and pupils have responded to increased school choice. Employing the analytical framework developed in Chapter 3, we reassess previous studies of school choice in quasi-markets. In particular, we are concerned to review the extent to which parent and pupil behaviour has been consistent with the analysis of the market mechanism outlined above. Chapter 6 considers how quasi-markets have affected teacher training and remuneration. We address the arguments concerning the need for occupational licensing and accreditation of teachers, but the main part of the chapter assesses the arguments for, and consequences of, increased incentive pay. Concentrating upon recent reforms in England and Wales, we try to identify the nature of the potential benefits and likely dysfunctional effects from increasing incentive payments in professional labour markets like teaching. In Chapter 7, we review the changes to school governance, monitoring and performance management that have been associated with the quasi-market reforms. Initially we examine the consequences of the decentralisation of managerial decision-making to individual schools. This is followed by an analysis of the various experiments in England and Wales to promote diversity of provision in local markets by introducing an element of institutional competition. We then contrast such policy initiatives with more recent ones that attempt to promote higher educational attainment by encouraging co-operation between local providers. The remainder of this chapter considers how performance monitoring has developed in quasi-markets. It analyses the consequences of publishing school performance tables and how the failure to report performance adjusted for a school's intake and resources has distorted market behaviour. In Chapter 8 we bring all of our analyses together to examine how schools have responded to the new challenges provided by the quasi-market reforms. In addition to surveying previous research we make use of our own studies of school behaviour in two local schooling markets in England. We concentrate upon the impact of quasi-markets on three areas: productive efficiency, the distribution of educational benefits across individuals, and the diversity of outcomes generated by the school system. Chapter 9 contains our conclusions.

2 Education and the economy

Examining the context of schooling markets

2.1 Introduction

The dissatisfaction felt by many Western governments with the performance of their public schooling system towards the end of the last century partly reflected a concern that existing and future economic and social challenges were not being adequately responded to by that system. From the 1970s it was believed in much of Europe and North America that slowdowns in economic growth and losses in international competitiveness were partly the result of failures in the schooling system (Adnett 1997). Similarly, the growth in labour market inequality, predominantly wage inequality in the US and employment inequality in Europe, was partly attributed to a schooling system that was failing those towards the bottom end of the ability range. In this chapter we explore the broader economic and social context of schooling systems in developed countries. The underlying motivation for this review rests upon two issues. First, to investigate the extent to which changes in the economic and social environment were responsible for the introduction of market-based reforms of state schooling. Second, to identify those environmental factors that may influence the outcome of those reforms.

The dissatisfaction with the performance of state schooling also reflected policy makers' loss in confidence in two key propositions, commonly used as a basis for educational and social policy in the second half of the last century. First, that the extension of general subsidies for investments in human capital could effectively tackle poverty and labour market discrimination. Second, that sustained economic growth would automatically generate sufficient 'trickle-down' effects to promote social inclusion and prevent widening income inequality. The collapse of the conventional wisdom based upon these two propositions has led a fundamental rethinking of social, educational and training policy amongst both neo-liberal and third-way analysts. In Europe, shared concerns about the consequences of increased globalisation and the emergence of the 'new economy' have led to major changes in these policies. At the Lisbon and Nice Councils of Ministers in 2000 there was agreement of the need for fundamental education and training reforms which would promote European leadership of the 'knowledge-based' global economy (Adnett 2001).

Budgetary pressures in many Western countries at the end of the twentieth century generated internal pressures within governments for schooling reform. In the US doubts about the sustainability of federal government deficits in combination with taxpayer revolts at local and state level, focused policy makers concern on the apparent irreversible rise in educational expenditure. Real public expenditure on elementary and secondary education in the US rose three times faster than GDP since 1890. Hanushek's (1994) analysis of this rise identifies three factors as being mainly responsible: rising teachers' salaries, declining pupil–teacher ratios and rising non-instructional staff costs. In Europe, governments funding the costs of mass unemployment came under pressure to comply with the strict budgetary requirements set by the convergence criteria for membership of the European Monetary Union. These constraints were partly offset by the windfall gains from the end of the Cold War. The latter moderated the impact of fiscal consolidation on the non-defence areas of government spending, including the public schooling systems.

In the following sections we address these issues and assess their influence on the nature and impact of market-based reforms. In Section 2.2 we present international comparisons of expenditure on education and assess long-term trends in its relative size and composition. We also investigate the determinants of the optimal level of government spending on education and whether there has been a decline in schooling productivity across OECD countries. In Section 2.3 we consider the evidence on the contribution of education to the aggregate economic performance of an economy. Initially, we summarise the evidence concerning the private returns to schooling emphasised by the theory of human capital. We then assess the evidence of the impact of an economy's level of education on its economic growth. In this discussion we concentrate upon developed economies. We question whether the current popularity of endogenous growth theory with its increased importance attached to government-funded schooling is based upon adequate empirical foundations. The general paucity of evidence concerning the economy-wide effects of education has led to some economists questioning the legitimacy of the dominant role of the human capital model. In the penultimate part of Section 2.3 we develop the rival screening and status-conflict theories, assessing whether they are more consistent with labour market behaviour. This section concludes with an examination of the role of education in sustaining national competitiveness. In particular, we assess the extent to which increased globalisation has made international capital and technology flows more sensitive to the human capital embodied in a particular nation's workforce.

Section 2.4 expands this discussion to directly incorporate changes in technology over time and the resulting changes in the pattern of labour demand. We briefly review the nature of the 'new economy' and assess its significance for the content and duration of compulsory state schooling. In particular, we examine how organisational changes are influencing employers' demand for labour and hence affecting their desired combination of schooling outputs. This leads on directly to a discussion in Section 2.5 of the recent growth of labour market inequality and the extent to which this reflects increasing and more diverse returns to schooling investments. In the next two sections, we extend this analysis to discuss education's role in reducing labour market discrimination and promoting social inclusion. Finally, we bring together the various components of this chapter to delineate the nature of the economic and social environment within which schooling markets have been introduced.

2.2 Government spending on education

2.2.1 The underlying economic principles

Fashions change in economic analysis and the current infatuation with sustainable fiscal policy and credible policy rules have radically changed the context within which governments make spending plans. The former concern has normally led governments to formulate their spending and taxation plans so as not to cause government debt to rise as a proportion of GDP over time. The emphasis upon credible rules concerns the perceived need for policy makers to commit themselves to a specific long-term sustainable fiscal policy strategy. Together the general acceptance of these principles has led to the abandonment of discretionary fiscal policy and produced a more stable, if more restrictive, budgetary environment within which a government's educational expenditure is determined. For example in the UK, a Comprehensive Spending Review now determines individual departments' spending levels for a five-year period.

Contextual factors have also contributed to the adoption of fiscal consolidation at the end of the last millennium. In the US, concern with the sustainability of federal deficits was a major factor, as was the failure of voters to support propositions further raising state educational expenditures. In Europe the consequences for public finances of population ageing, persisting high rates of unemployment and the convergence criteria for Monetary Union created further pressures for tighter controls of public spending. Currently, the macro-economic mission of all national fiscal policy makers is to respect some solvency conditions for public finances, subject to being consistent with a monetary policy targeting low and stable inflation (Price 2000). The associated microeconomic mission is to set taxes and spending at their optimal levels. Since both taxes and government spending distort the market behaviour and generate externalities (discussed in Chapter 1), the determination of their optimal level is problematic. Typically, governments currently make a distinction between their consumption and investment expenditure. For example, in 1997 the incoming Labour Government in the UK set itself a 'golden rule' with respect to the government's budget. Over the economic cycle it would only borrow to invest, not to fund current spending. In addition, that government adopted a 'sustainable investment rule'. This requires that public sector net debt as a proportion of GDP be held stable and at a 'prudent' level, again over the cycle.

This present dominant concern to achieve fiscal stability has two major consequences for the determination of government spending on education.

Firstly, as we noted in Chapter 1, education generates both consumption and investment benefits. To an extent therefore the division of a government's education spending between these two components is arbitrary. Secondly, as several critics (see Price) have pointed out, any rule, such as the golden rule, will be deficient if it prevents social investments in education where the social returns exceed the opportunity costs of that investment. The role of government borrowing should ultimately be to smooth out consumption, not only over the cycle but also between generations. The latter role is particularly important in the case of public expenditure on education, given the presence of capital market imperfections that may prevent some individuals financing their optimal rate of human capital investment.

2.2.2 International comparisons of expenditure and outcomes

As we have explained above, the interactions between current fashions in economic analysis and other environmental factors generated a climate of fiscal consolidation in both North America and much of Europe. The consequence has been a general tightening of the controls on government spending on schooling. In Chapter 1 we raised the issue of the rationale for government funding of schooling, given that education generates higher lifetime incomes for private individuals. Apart from equity and risk and uncertainty considerations, the main justification was that education produces positive externalities. We concluded that in the absence of public subsidies, many individuals would under-invest in schooling.

In the modern global economy with capital and technology mobility increasing, simple economic analysis would suggest that two trends in government expenditure on education are likely to emerge:

- convergence on similar expenditures on schooling amongst economies of similar economic structures and levels of development
- a rise in overall spending per student, reflecting higher family wealth, higher marginal returns to schooling (both to individuals and society) and the consequences of schooling being a labour-intensive activity.

Are these expected trends emerging amongst developed countries? As always, international comparisons are fraught with dangers and we rely heavily on two authoritative sources in drawing our comparisons. Even so we should note that not only are there wide differences between individual OECD countries, but these differences are not always stable over time. Most developed countries spend between 5 and 7 per cent of GDP on education. In 1997 the average expenditure in OECD countries was $3,769 per primary pupil, $5,507 per secondary student and $10,893 per tertiary student (OECD 2000). Public funding accounts for on average 91 per cent of total school expenditure in these countries, with direct public expenditure on educational institutions ranging from under 4 per cent of GDP in Greece and Japan to a high of nearly 7 per cent in Sweden. Public spending on education as a percentage of GDP has stabilised or declined slightly in OECD countries since 1970 (Martin 1998), partly reflecting demographic factors.

Even within the European Union there are large differences in educational expenditure per pupil. For example, in 1997 Luxembourg spent nearly five times the amount spent in Greece in educating a secondary level student (European Commission 2000). There is some evidence that wealthier countries choose to make educational expenditure a higher priority, though different priorities in allocating that expenditure are also a significant cause of national differences. In most EU countries expenditure per pupil increases in line with age (the Netherlands has the steepest progression), though in Denmark the expenditure per student hardly differs between primary, secondary and tertiary levels (European Commission 2000).

The initial *European Report on Quality of School Education* (European Commission 2000) suggests that there is less evidence of a convergence in the quantity and quality of educational outputs. Exploiting this source, we initially consider participation in pre-primary education, between the ages of 3 and 6. In France and Belgium the figures for 1996/7 indicate that virtually all children of this age range attended an education-orientated institution. In other EU member states – for example, Greece and Finland – a child in this age range would on average spend half as long in a comparable institution. At the other end of the age range, for the EU the 1997 Labour Force Survey indicates that of those aged 22 about 71 per cent had successfully complete upper secondary education. The national figures ranged from over or around 80 per cent in Belgium and the Nordic member states to around 60 per cent and below in Italy, Portugal, Spain and the UK.

Qualitative international comparisons of education are perhaps even more difficult to make than quantitative ones. This difficulty reflects the diversity of national education systems and the weaknesses of international indicators of the levels of educational attainment. Currently we have data available from the Third International Mathematics and Science Study (TIMSS) conducted in 1995, supplemented by an initial EU report providing sixteen 'quality' indicators which is to be periodically updated (European Commission 2000). The first results from the OECD Programme for International Student Assessment (PISA) are available from autumn 2001. Both the TIMSS mathematics and science results suggest large differences even between EU countries. For example, at seventh grade, Belgian students got 65 per cent of their mathematics questions correct, while in Portugal the students scored just 37 per cent in the same test. National differences within the EU were generally less in science, though again, whilst they were comparable to the performance of US students, they were significantly below that of Japanese students. The International Adult Literacy Survey provides comparative data on the ability of workers to understand and use printed information in the workplace. It found large national differences in the mean and distribution within the three domains of literacy skills: prose, document and quantitative. For example,

Sweden had typically a quarter of its population classified in the lowest category while the US and UK had around a half in this category. Indeed, of those recent US secondary school graduates who do not gain a higher qualification, 60 per cent have low literacy compared with just 10 per cent in Finland. The OECD (2001) concludes that while increased public spending does not always produce strong performing national systems, those countries performing well on most indicators are among the highest spenders.

The TIMSS data also indicates a widening gap in student performance within countries. For example, on average the dispersion of results on mathematics achievement is larger as students enter their secondary school than in their early elementary school years. Once again, however, there are considerable differences in the growth of this disparity between OECD countries. The consequence is a large variation in attainment levels of a given cohort. For those in their early teens, even in the middle half of the population, the lowest performing students would have to study for several years to catch up with the best.

There is some evidence that is supportive of our second proposition. In almost all countries expenditure on education has increased faster than national wealth in recent years (OECD 2000). Given demographic trends these figures also indicate increases in per pupil expenditure. In OECD countries about 60 per cent of working-age adults have attained at least a qualification at upper secondary level, a proportion that is continuing to increase as each cohort of entrants to the labour market attains progressively higher qualifications. A widely used measure of the stock of human capital is the average number of years of schooling completed by the adult population. Martin (1998) suggests that the average years of schooling in the adult population in OECD countries increased by about 2–3 years in the last three decades. In the UK, Spain and Portugal this increase was achieved in just the first six years of the 1990s. A comparison of the attainment of the population aged 25–34 with that aged 55–64 in the OECD shows that the proportion who do not complete secondary education has been shrinking, especially in those countries with lower levels of educational attainment (OECD 2000). Notwithstanding these improvements in educational attainments, evidence reported by Martin suggests that the average private rates of return to upper secondary education are still high in OECD countries, averaging over 15 per cent.

Comparing over-time changes in the total expenditure on education per pupil and the performance of students in standardised achievement tests can generate measures of schooling productivity growth. In labour-intensive services where technological advancements are relatively low, Baumol (1967) pointed out that the relative price of such services would tend to rise over time. Gundlach *et al.* (2001) find that in a sample of OECD countries between 1970 and 1994 there was a negative relation between changes in the quality of schooling output and changes in the relative price of schooling. This suggests that especially in those countries with the highest increase in the relative price of schooling, Australia, France and Italy, the decline in schooling productivity may have been relatively large. The source of any such general decline in schooling productivity has yet to be identified, though public choice theorists have sought to blame the absence of competitive market pressures (Pritchett and Filmer 1999).

Across OECD countries, education is still largely a mainly public enterprise, yet in many countries it involves a substantial and growing component of private financing. In those OECD countries that provide data, the private sector is the source of 20 per cent of aggregate expenditure on educational institutions. In Chile, private sector expenditure almost matches the contribution of the public sector. In the US, this private spending largely originates in households, though in Germany private enterprises provide the major share. In the UK, expenditure per pupil in private schools is approximately three times that of state schools (Dutta *et al.* 1999) largely reflecting a much lower pupil–teacher ratio in private schools. In Chapter 6 we discuss in more detail international trends in the composition and remuneration of the teaching workforce.

2.3 Education and economic performance

2.3.1 The private returns to schooling

In Chapter 1 we explained that the orthodox economic analysis of education is based upon human capital theory. This theory postulates that private educational decisions are sensitive to the anticipated rates of returns from such investments. That is, decision-makers compare the opportunity costs of particular schooling opportunities to the expected differential lifetime income flows associated with that schooling. There are a number of problems to be overcome in trying to estimate the size of the rate of returns to schooling investments (summarised in Belfield 2000). We now summarise the most recent findings. For most Western developed economies the evidence suggests that the gross rate of return to a year's additional schooling lies between 5 and 10 per cent (Ashenfelter *et al.* 1999 and Blundell *et al.* 1999). For example, Dearden (1998) estimates that for the UK the rate of return to an additional year of full-time education is between 5 and 7 per cent for men and 8 to 10 per cent for women. These are averages for the population as a whole and, as discussed below, returns differ according to qualifications gained. More evidence on the role of education can be gained from studying those workers who have acquired either more or less education than their jobs require. Several studies – for example, Daly *et al.* (2000) – find that those with surplus education received a wage premium and those with deficit education suffered a wage penalty. These findings support the view that productivity on any job is affected by the level of education the worker brings to that job.

Education provides not only an initial advantage in the labour market but also a permanent advantage that increases over time. That is, more educated workers get higher returns to experience (Brunello and Comi 2000). Both literacy and numeracy have highly significant effects on earnings, though the former appears to work predominantly through its effects on educational attainment (Dougherty 2000). Harmon and Walker (2000) find that the returns to the quantity of schooling in the UK are large in comparison with those to quality. Controlling for ability and peer groups, their results suggest that private schooling generates no effect on wages. They also find that elective state schooling has no effect on wages conditional on the quantity of schooling. However, there is a large positive effect on the quantity of education for high ability students attending a grammar school and a large negative effect for all children in secondary modern schools relative to comprehensive schools.

2.3.2 Education and economic growth

While these findings suggest that additional schooling appears to be on average highly beneficial for individuals, of more fundamental concern to governments' budgetary decisions is whether additional schooling benefits an economy's rate of economic growth. Human capital theory models education as predominantly enhancing labour inputs and thereby raising labour productivity and output. Modern endogenous growth theory postulates that, in addition, growth externalities are generated from schooling investments. According to this approach, both the rates of technical innovation and the size and speed of learning-by-doing benefit from an increase in the mean level of schooling of an economy's population (Aghion and Howitt 1998).

There is some supportive evidence for these causal arguments, but, as Martin (1998) reports, it is not overwhelming. Across OECD countries there is a positive but insignificant correlation between public spending on education and productivity levels. There is a stronger and statistically significant association between educational attainment, proxied by average years of schooling, and productivity, but not for literacy scores. Early attempts to measure the contribution of education to economic growth utilised a growth accounting framework that related growth of inputs to output growth. Taken together these studies indicated that education could have an important effect upon economic growth (Dutta et al. 1999). More recently, regression studies have displaced growth accounting techniques following, in particular, the study by Barro and Sala-I-Martin (1995). The study by Bils and Klenow (2000), for example, suggests that an extra year of schooling has been associated with a 0.3 per cent faster annual growth rate. However, they conclude that overall, schooling can explain less than a third of the empirical cross-country relationship. There are severe data problems in such studies and Topel's 1999 survey concludes that while micro studies provide a fairly precise range on the private returns to schooling investments, little is still known about the social returns to that schooling.

Econometric studies indicate that measures of educational attainment are significant determinants of growth in OECD countries, though the estimated coefficients are not always robust. In particular, distinguishing between the contributions of changes in the quantity and quality of schooling remains unresolved. One alternative approach is to investigate directly the contribution of cognitive skills to differences in growth rates. Hanushek and Kimko (2000) find that mathematics and science scores are strongly related to international differences in growth, apparently through their effect on productivity differences. However, their estimate of this effect looks implausibly large: one standard deviation increase in mathematical and science skills leading to a 1 per cent increase in the average annual growth rate. One further aspect of the relationship between education and economic growth concerns the role of inequality. If capital market imperfections constrain private investment in human capital then we would expect high rates of return from additional investments in schooling by the poor. Persson and Tabellini (1994) find some supporting evidence. They conclude that greater state schooling reduces inequality and inequality is harmful to economic growth.

2.3.3 Stratification and the private and social returns to schooling

The generally weak evidence concerning the nature and size of the macroeconomic effects of education is open to another interpretation to that of orthodox analysis so far assumed. The relationship between schooling and earnings that lies at the heart of human capital theory is claimed to be independent of the impact of ability and cultural capital. It assumes a functional view of schools as organisations of socialisation that instil knowledge, attitudes, values and skills which are then rewarded in the labour market. An alternative approach, especially popular amongst sociological researchers, views schools as organisations of stratification (Rubinson and Browne 1994). This approach argues that the social-class background is the single most important determinant of students' educational achievements and aspirations. According to this approach, schools' key role is to select, certify and allocate, a role that need not necessarily assist productivity or economic growth.

These stratification or allocation models have had a peripheral impact on the economics of education, predominantly in the form of the sorting (signalling or screening) approach, surveyed by Weiss (1995). This approach argues that investments in schooling have little direct influence on productivity, but instead provide signals of ability or preferred personal characteristics to potential employers. To illustrate the difference, consider how to interpret the finding of Andrews *et al.* (2001) that skill preferences, skill destinations and labour market outcomes are primarily determined by examination performance. According to the human capital approach, an individual's expected economic returns to schooling, and therefore their demand, is based upon their absolute investment in schooling. However, in sorting models, schooling is correlated with unobservable productivity differences that predate schooling decisions. Employers make inferences about these productivity differences from an individual's schooling choices and outcomes. Hence this sorting behaviour encourages a positional demand for investments in education.

According to the status-conflict theory or credentialism, often grouped with sorting models, wage differences are independent of productivity differences and education need have no effect upon productivity. The main activity of schools is to teach and certify students in particular status cultures which consist of values, preferences, vocabulary and sociability rather than technical job skills. According to this approach, increases in absolute levels of educational attainment merely induce higher educational entry tariffs to be applied to the 'good jobs', perpetuating social inequalities. The status-conflict theory is consistent with the claimed failure of education and training to eliminate wage gaps for black workers in the US (Rubinson and Browne 1994). Additionally, as Levin and Kelley (1994) point out, it is also consistent with the observation that unemployment has become more education-dependent over time.

Within the broad screening approach, social returns to educational expenditure will be low. Increased provision largely redistributes wealth, whereas subsidies for education encourage over-investment in human capital. Empirical studies of the relationship between education and earnings, surveyed by Weiss (1995) and Topel (1999), whilst generally rejecting credentialism and supportive of human capital approaches, rarely completely reject the importance of sorting considerations. However, there is some limited evidence to suggest that 'over-education' may already be significant in developed economies (for example, Borghans and de Grip 2000). Indeed, Sloane *et al.* (1999) conclude that nearly a third of British workers were over-educated for their employment. In terms of the social returns to education, the key distinction concerns whether the increased employment of higher educated workers in jobs at lower levels reflects a bumping-down or upgrading process. Bumping-down occurs as a result of the excess supply of the higher educated, implying low marginal social returns to additional levels of schooling. Upgrading occurs when technological change or changes in consumer preferences raise the education level required for a given job. Robinson and Manacorda (1997) analyse recent changes in occupational and educational structure of employment in the UK. They conclude that the increased holding of qualifications over time simply results in employers raising the educational requirements for an occupation. In contrast, Green *et al.* (1999) find little evidence of widespread qualifications inflation; they find at both ends of the occupational spectrum a rising demand for skills in Britain. However, they find that the increased demand for more educated and skilled labour has not produced uniformly higher returns to education. It appears that the type of education in terms of skills acquired and curricula studied are important in determining returns, rather than just the level of educational attainment.

2.3.4 Education and competitiveness

Globalisation, particularly the growth of economic integration, trade and capital mobility, is commonly interpreted to have increased the importance of labour market performance in maintaining national competitiveness. It is argued that the prosperity of national producers and the ability to attract and retain foreign direct investment has now become more sensitive to the maintenance of a competitive unit labour cost (Greenaway and Nelson 2000). As a 1998 British Competitiveness White Paper explained:

> In the global economy, capital is mobile, technology spreads quickly and goods can be made in low-cost countries and shipped to developed markets. British business has to compete by exploiting capabilities which competitors find hard to imitate. The UK's distinctive capabilities are not raw materials, land or cheap labour. They must be our knowledge, skills and creativity ... which help create high productivity business process and high-value goods and services.
>
> (Department of Trade and Industry 1998: 6)

These sentiments were echoed by the European Council of Ministers in their 2000 meetings in Lisbon and Nice. In the modern global economy the key requirement, they argued, was to move up-market and escape the fierce price competition in the markets for goods with low technical specifications. By adopting a 'high-spec' strategy, quality and customising products partly replace price–cost competition and sustain the 'good jobs/high skill' economy. Increases in the general level of schooling attainment, particularly amongst the less able, can assist the speed at which a country's workers adjust to these changing patterns of demand (Greenaway *et al.* 2000). The role of schooling in promoting this process in the context of the 'knowledge-based' economy is the topic of the following section. Section 2.5 considers the extent to which these developments require targeting a raising of levels of educational attainment amongst the less able groups.

2.4 Education and the 'knowledge-based economy'

To design appropriate policy responses to achieve and maintain competitiveness within the high skill sectors of the global economy requires an understanding of the nature and extent of the new skills demanded and their relationship to schooling. Keep and Mayhew (1999) argue that policy makers often conflate at least two radically different categories of skills. First, skills of manipulation and analysis originating from abstract theoretically-based bodies of high-level knowledge. Second, skills based upon tacit knowledge and related to personal characteristics and psychological traits rather than acquisition of theoretical skills and knowledge. In the past, 'skills' were often treated as solely of the former category and the emphasis was upon a combination of educational qualifications, 'hard' technical skills and knowledge, and a variety of forms of manual dexterity and spatial awareness. Reflecting in part the growth of service sector employment, recently the common usage of 'skills' has evolved to encompass an additional range of key skills. These new components include: use of IT, problem-solving, and teamworking. Keep and Mayhew argue that increasingly employers are embracing an even wider usage, with 'skills' now including the second category above, that is, personal characteristics and psychological traits such as appearance and motivational skills. We now investigate the processes causing these changes.

For much of the last hundred years, competitive success for firms has been based upon Fordism, that is production characterised by the extension of the division of labour, product standardisation and mass production. The need to co-ordinate production led also to the division of labour in management, with firms creating managerial pyramids in which middle managers, conventionally organised into functional departments, were answerable to specialist senior executives. The current industrial revolution is threatening to make these types of organisational structures inefficient. Following Lindbeck and Snower (2000), we can identify four separate but interrelating forces that are generating this revolution.

Changes in machinery

Advances in capital equipment – flexible, programmable machinery; computer-aided design (CAD), and multi-purpose machine tools – have reduced the costs of small production runs. For business organisations to exploit these opportunities, their employees need to be able move rapidly between production tasks (multi-tasking)without lowering overall productivity.

Changes in human capital

As we have noted above, in all developed economies the median student is leaving the educational and vocational training systems at a later age and with higher levels of attainment. This increased personal human capital is creating employee demands for a more varied and stimulating work environment. It follows that the increased demand for multi-skilled workers can potentially be matched by an increase in the supply of workers able and willing to perform in multi-tasked roles. Traditional occupational and functional barriers are accordingly being relaxed as employees fulfil multiple roles in their organisations.

Changes in information technology

Computerised data systems enable up-to-date information to be accessible to all workers and managers. Production, marketing, human resource and financial information are now available to all, rather than being contained within functional divisions. Decision-making can now be decentralised to small teams of employees producing a flatter organisational structure and enabling the introduction of 'lean production' (keeping inventories low) and 'just-in-time production' (reducing the stocks of components).

Changes in consumer preferences

As material living standards rise, consumers are increasingly demanding customised products and service. Firms respond by shortening production runs and offering greater product variety, continually improving quality and targeting new market niches. Over time, competition between firms is increasingly based upon product specifications and delivery and payment terms.

With growing international trade and rising mobility of capital and technology, individual countries cannot isolate themselves from these global trends. This current industrial revolution is dramatically changing the organisational structure of businesses. Schooling systems need to evolve to assist this revolution and ensure that all labour market participants share the productivity benefits of these changes. Reich (1991) has propounded the following three-fold occupational typology for this 'new economy':

i   high-level symbolic manipulators and analysts;
ii   production workers (a declining number over time);
iii interpersonal services workers (an increasing number over time).

While each of these groups requires skills, their requirements are very different and policy responses based upon a general increase in the level of education and training provided may be misplaced. In order to determine the appropriate policies we need to be able to project the relative size of these three groups over time. For example, if we expect the interpersonal services to grow the most rapidly, requiring lengthy compulsory schooling and promoting a target of high academic qualifications for all would appear to be an unsuitable response (OECD 2001, ch. 4). Thus, adjusting schooling provision to respond to the needs of the 'knowledge economy', raising the potential for invention and innovation, could lead to more concentration of educational resources on those already highly educated. Alternatively, in order to produce the new technology, exploit it as both workers and consumers, and prevent growing social exclusion we may need to place an emphasis upon raising the basic cognitive and social skills of the less educated.

Further elements of the 'new economy' create additional needs to those identified by Reich. Greater lifetime mobility between occupations and employers and greater entrepreneurial and consumer skills also have to be addressed by the schooling system. As argued above, the modern business organisation requires a knowledgeable, adaptable and flexible workforce. The great majority of entrants into the labour market need to have a broad base of knowledge rather than great depth in one subject area. That knowledge needs to be 'transportable', that is, applicable to a wide range of jobs, tasks and business organisations. The greater emphasis on team production also increases the importance of social and people skills – skills that enable an individual to promote team productivity (OECD 2001, ch. 4). Educational systems, such as that in the UK, which encourage early specialisation and neglect the development of social and people skills, are increasingly at odds with these developments. This has led, as we report in Chapter 4, to several attempts to broaden the upper secondary curriculum in England and Wales. Similarly, an occupation-based system of initial on-the-job training, such as traditional apprenticeships, is likely to be less supportive of the new organisation than one based upon task and job rotation and lifelong learning. The greater flexibility of modern workers increases the incentives for organisations to poach trained workers from other firms rather than contribute to the investment costs of training their own workers. Such failures in the training market also need to be targeted by governments if national education and training systems are to effectively support the development of the modern business organisation.

To summarise, technological and organisational changes are altering the desired characteristics of workers. The required 'skills' of entrants into the labour market now incorporate not just a range of technical skills, theoretical knowledge and competencies but also traits and personal attributes. This makes assessing the appropriateness of any schooling system much more problematic than in the past. Differentiated and even divergent demands for skills are inconsistent with the setting of simple outcome targets based upon a single measure of academic attainment (see Chapter 7). These developments also raise a question concerning the ability, and desirability, of schooling systems promoting particular personal attributes and traits. This question re-emerges in our following discussion of an associated issue: the relationship between schooling outcomes and the growth of labour market inequality in Western economies.

2.5 Education and labour market inequality

One key consequence of the processes discussed in the previous sections has been greater labour market inequality in developed Western economies. The new labour market for skills raises the real wage paid to high-skilled and highly educated workers. At the same time, the decline in the relative demand for low-skilled and less educated workers has either resulted in a sustained fall in their relative wages, as in the US, or a higher incidence of unemployment as in Europe (Katz and Autor 1999). Across OECD countries, school-leavers without an upper secondary qualification can expect to earn about 20 per cent less in mid-career than a leaver who has completed that qualification, and 50 per cent less than a university graduate. In addition, they will initially spend twice as long unemployed as a graduate would and, over the course of their career, between four times (males) and ten times (females) longer out of the labour market (OECD 1998).

In the UK, Machin (1998) shows that the switch in demand towards the more educated has been sufficient to increase the wage differential earned by more educated workers by around 30 per cent since the mid-1970s, notwithstanding the large increase in their relative supply. Taken together, this indicates that the supply of 'good jobs', or at least those that pay a premium to educated workers, has increased as average schooling investments have increased. In the US, the rise in wage inequality was not just due to wage increases for the highly educated, real earnings of males who had only achieved high school graduation and with just 1–5 years experience fell by 27 per cent between 1979 and 1995 (Freeman 2000). Blau and Kahn (2001) find that the greater dispersion of cognitive test scores in the US plays some part in explaining its higher wage inequality. Though higher returns to human capital and cognitive performance are quantitatively considerably more important. Francesconi *et al.* (2000) argue that an associated consequence of this bias in technological change has been to raise the equilibrium rate of unemployment for the less educated. Nickell (1998) points out that in certain economies, such as the German, the less skilled workers have managed to avoid these tendencies and have experienced a sustained increase in their real wages. Indeed, German men in the bottom wage decile seem to earn around twice as much as American men in a similar position. The less educated German youths also have higher employment rates than their American counterparts (Blau and Kahn 2000a).

It is now clear that there are multiple causes of this decline in the demand for less-educated labour. The globalisation process – in particular, the increased mobility of capital and technology – has led to a rapid outsourcing of labour-intensive stages of production to the low labour cost economies of Eastern Europe and Asia. The knowledge-based economy has also displaced less educated workers from those stages of production retained in developed Western economies. The growth of e-commerce and internet use in general threaten to extend this process to many service sector jobs (Autor 2001). Further, institutional changes have contributed to this trend. The decline of trade unions who have traditionally compressed wage structures and, especially in the US, the slow adjustment of minimum wages have been further factors in reducing the wages of the least skilled workers in developed economies.

Most analysts currently view the technological developments discussed in Section 2.4 as the dominant cause of this increase in labour market inequality (Wood 1998), though Haskel and Slaughter's (2001) study re-establishes the importance of trade effects. In part this change in the composition of employment may be endogenous, reflecting a country's distribution of schooling attainment. Nickell (1998) attributes the success of the German economy in resisting increasing wage inequality to the ability of its schooling system to sustain high levels of performance by those in the bottom half of the ability range. Such arguments can be related to the type of model developed by Acemoglu (1999), where a steady increase in the proportion of graduate entrants eventually changes the composition of jobs through the effect on skill-complementary technology. Brunello and Comi (2000) suggest that not only the level of schooling, but also the design of labour market institutions and educational systems, influences wage inequality. They find that European countries without corporatist labour market institutions and comprehensive secondary education tend to have more pronounced earnings growth by education.

The appropriate response to this trend, especially in terms of the schooling system has generated many debates. Heckman (2000) suggests that there is a need for a fundamental rethink in Western countries about the way in which socially useful skills embodied in persons are produced. Policies too often focus on cognitive skills as measured by IQ tests or qualifications rather than communication skills, social adaptability and motivation. Heckman argues that the current preoccupation with formal schooling is based upon two popular misconceptions. Firstly, a failure to appreciate that learning is a lifetime affair and that much of this takes place outside of schools. Families and the environment, especially pre-school, are crucial determinants of educational success and much learning occurs informally outside of educational institutions. Secondly, undue reliance is placed on achievement tests and cognitive skills in assessing the overall success of a schooling system. While there is some evidence, as we have noted above, that returns to cognitive skills have increased over time, such a narrow focus neglects the full array of non-cognitive skills and motivation necessary for economic success. Heckman claims that while early intervention programmes do not alter IQ, when suitably constructed they can substantially raise the non-cognitive skills and social attachment of participants. Similarly, Heckman argues that the early human capital analysis made a false dichotomy between human capital and innate ability that has influenced much thinking up to the present. He argues that the evidence indicates that, in the early years, schooling can raise ability, while that additional ability creates a further demand for schooling as the pupil progresses through the schooling system.

Taken together, Heckman argues, these misconceptions have distorted schooling policies. He points out that the investment in human capital required to restore the real earnings of American unskilled workers to levels of twenty years ago would be prohibitively expensive. His preferred policy prescription is to concentrate resources on the very young amongst high-risk groups and improve their basic learning and socialisation skills. Several US experiments indicate the advantages of targeting policy at the pre-school years of severely deprived children in disadvantaged environments (Heckman 2000). Concentrating resources here generates higher returns to the government since there are fundamental dynamic complementarities to be exploited. Learning begets learning and skills acquired early make later learning easier and promote further productivity and earning increases. There is also some evidence of positive spillover effects to the younger siblings of participants (Garces *et al.* 2000). In contrast, targeting marginal reductions in pupil–teacher ratios or increases in HE participation rates are less effective since these dynamic benefits are largely absent.

2.6 Education and labour market discrimination

Both equity and efficiency considerations require that public schooling systems should foster equality of opportunity. To the extent that post-entry discrimination persists in the labour market, then schooling should at least attempt not to contribute to that discrimination. While the desire for education to promote social justice at least dates from the introduction of universal schooling a century ago, some of the recent trends discussed above have raised the importance of this ambition. The growth of importance of human capital in knowledge-based economies is tending to exacerbate existing skill-based inequalities and 'digital divides'. The growing recognition of the need for life-long learning in this new economy may be a further cause of polarisation as the degree of active learning in adulthood is strongly related to success in initial schooling. Finally, the weakening of social bonds – for example, the higher rates of family break-up and growth in the number of lone parents – has increased the risks of social exclusion. Taken together these factors suggest that in modern societies the distribution of education and lifelong learning can have profound effects on social equity. A recent report from the OECD (2001) concludes that educational outcomes amongst children from poor or less educated families, ethnic minorities and children with disabilities have not converged on those from more privileged groups in recent years. Only amongst one less privileged group has convergence occurred. In all OECD countries over the last three decades, the proportionate rise in educational attainment at both upper-secondary and tertiary level has been greater for women than for men. We now concentrate upon examining the impact of this convergence on gender discrimination in the labour market.

In most developed economies the achievement of gender equality in participation rates in post-compulsory schooling, including higher education, has been associated with increasing gender equality in participation in the workforce. The latter has most recently been associated with an increase in the employment rate of women with children. However, despite the increasing gender balance in the workforce, occupational segregation and a significant gender pay gap are still evident, most especially for women with children (Blau and Kahn 2000b). Similar pay gaps are found for minority racial groups and certain other groups of workers. To the extent that such wage gaps do not reflect differences in productivity characteristics, their presence distorts behaviour and lowers overall efficiency. Thus, apart from equity considerations, there are efficiency gains from the schooling system reducing discriminatory differences in the labour market.

The raw gender pay differentials have continued to narrow in recent decades in most developed economies. For example, in the UK between 1980 and 1998 the female–male hourly earnings ratio increased from 64 per cent to 80 per cent for full-time employees (Office for National Statistics 1998). Joshi and Paci (1998) suggest that the considerable improvement in the educational qualifications of full-time working women has been responsible for a major part of the decline in the difference in pay between men and women. Harkness (1996) found that whilst the narrowing of the skills gap had contributed to this, differences in male and female returns to those characteristics accounted for about 90 per cent of the remaining gender earnings gap for full-time workers.

The gender pay gap persists alongside a 'family gap', i.e. a gap in pay between women with children and those without. Waldfogel (1998) noted that whilst mothers were earning 64 per cent of men's hourly pay, non-mothers were earning 84 per cent. That part of the gap associated with mothers being less educated and less able than childless women had fallen significantly, whilst that due to the pay penalties associated with part-time work and lost work experience had increased. In summary, family status appears to account for approximately half of the current gender wage gap, with most of the remainder being associated with the shorter experience of the average female worker and their lower returns to that experience.

As we have noted, a clear positive relationship exists between pay and education: pay rising for both men and women with the attainment of each successive level of qualification. In OECD countries rates of return to schooling are on average higher for women than for men (Martin 1998), and relative female earnings are higher amongst the most educated groups (OECD 2001), though Italy and some Nordic countries are exceptions. For example, though on average women graduates earn less than male graduates, this gender gap is less than that for those with lower education qualifications (Blundell *et al.* 1999). The higher rate of return to women graduates indicates that, when compared with non-graduates, the gender wage gap is smaller and female graduates are more likely to take shorter career breaks. Thus, it appears that the labour market provides greater incentives for women to increase their level of educational attainment.

The question remains as to why in OECD countries the impact of educational qualifications on earning is typically greater for women than for men. Kuh *et al.* (1997) suggest that because of career interruptions, due to child-rearing, on-the-job training and work experience contribute a smaller part of women's human capital. Hence, potential employers may rely more heavily on educational qualifications as a marker of individual potential. However, progression in many occupations depends upon a continuous full-time career path. Dex *et al.* (1998) found that women who exhibit the most continuity in employment across childbirth were highly educated and that their career progression was therefore much less affected by family formation. Dex *et al.* found that graduates were five times more likely to be employed six years after becoming mothers than those with no qualifications. In addition, Macran *et al.* (1996) found that the better educated were more likely to delay childbearing. Thus, as we noted above, in addition to its positive effect on earnings, higher education is also an important factor in determining women's employment patterns: graduates taking shorter career breaks and being more likely to work full-time (Blundell *et al.* 1997). Across virtually all OECD countries, the level of educational attainment has a stronger impact on expected years of employment among women (OECD 1998). Higher educational attainment thus provides incentives for women to maintain a labour market profile of continuous employment when raising children, which in turn creates the necessary conditions for women to maximise their career potential and lifetime earnings (Rubery *et al.* 2000).

The foregoing analysis of wage and employment patterns of women with children suggests that increased schooling investment is one of the most important ways in which women can protect themselves against the negative labour market consequences of family formation in later life (Sommerland and Sanderson 1997). The benefits which increased schooling brings to the relative position of women in the labour market are underestimated if inter-generational effects are neglected. Research suggests that strong role-model effects are present. Blundell *et al.* (1997) found that for females it was whether their mothers, but not their fathers, had experience of HE which had a positive influence on their entry into HE. This finding is supported by Dearden *et al.* (1997), who conclude that mother's education is more important than father's education in influencing the achievement of daughters. Swaffield (2000) concludes that the professional or skilled employment of mothers directly influences the labour market aspirations of their daughters. Kuh *et al.* (1997) suggest that women with the best-educated mothers achieve a significant earnings advantage. Women whose mothers received a further or higher education earned significantly more than their peers did. This again suggests that these mothers may have provided a career role model or had high expectations for their daughters that influenced their daughters' aspirations and achievements.

These findings of important family and environmental affects on the level of educational attainment and the economic returns to that attainment are also of concern to our next topic. The possibility of inter-generational transmissions of inequality lies at the heart of discussion of the role of education in promoting social inclusion.

2.7 Education and social exclusion

Welfare to work schemes have become popular in North America and Europe as a means of breaking cycles of social and economic deprivation. However, by themselves the extension of low-paid employment, even with tax incentives, may not be sufficient to break inter-generational cycles of social exclusion. Empirical research has established the importance of family background and the local environment on educational attainment. In particular, there is much evidence of a strong link between the earnings of parents and those of their children. This link seems to be especially strong in the UK where Dearden *et al.* (1997) suggest that 33 year olds in 1991 had inherited up to half of the relative earning power of their fathers in 1974. Education seems to play a key role in this relationship, with Dutta *et al.*'s (1999) modelling of the link between class and education suggesting that equal access to human capital investments would much reduce the inheritance of social class.

Social exclusion appears to reflect a cycle of individual and family disadvantage conferred by lack of family wealth and parental occupational and educational success. Gregg and Machin (2000) find that economic and social disadvantages faced during childhood have a strong influence on the subsequent degree of economic success of British individuals. Dolton *et al.* (1999) provide evidence for the UK that negative attitudes to school and higher levels of truancy are associated with lower staying-on rates in post-compulsory schooling, even when accounting for educational achievement. Dearden (1998) finds some evidence that those with less taste for education may actually have higher average marginal rates of return to education than the population as a whole. These arguments are consistent with Heckman's (2000) findings in his review of recent programmes aimed at increasing early childhood investments for targeted groups. High quality early childhood interventions targeted on disadvantaged groups appear to have lasting effects on learning, social skills and motivation and often yield large pay-offs to society. From a similar perspective, Dolton *et al.* conclude that schools need to be differentially resourced according to the needs of their pupils.

As levels of typical affluence increase, the discussion above suggests that the material and knowledge requirements for full participation in society also increase. Education equips individuals with skills in communication, critical evaluation and a greater ability to learn. Developments in the prevalence of information and communications technology and in the complexity of external economic and commercial pressures suggest a need for both increased and refocused schooling to maintain levels of social participation (Flores and Gray 2000). In turn, these higher education levels may lead society to create more complex, less accessible, forms of interaction which bring greater satisfaction at the expense of the social participation of those with lower levels of education. For example, the learning which contributed to the development of e-mail, the internet and mobile phones can be reasonably regarded both as a source of economic growth and as enabling greater social interaction for a wide section of society. Studies suggest that schooling can play an important role in reducing digital divides that threaten to create new sources of social exclusion. The OECD (2001) has shown that there are substantial differences between social groups in the access which students have to computers at home. In some developed countries with a relatively low home access, access to computers in schools is more favourable.

2.8 Conclusions

We have identified a number of economic and social factors that caused Western governments to reconsider the performance of their educational systems. The long-term trend is for total expenditure on education per citizen to increase. At a time of fiscal consolidation in many developed economies, this growth alone was probably sufficient to generate questions about the effectiveness of government expenditure in this area. However, there were further factors that contributed to the widespread re-assessment of educational policies. The process of globalisation was increasing the sensitivity of a country's relative economic performance to the skills and knowledge of its workforce. At the same time, changes in technology and the organisation of work were creating demands for new workforce skills and competencies. In combination these latter two forces were radically reducing the demand for less skilled workers and raising the premiums earned by the more educated groups in developed economies.

Advances in the understanding of the economic and social effects of schooling were a further stimulus to policy reform. Improvements in data and its analysis enabled a consensus to be reached about the large private returns to schooling. Greater understanding was gained about the sources of differences in attainment levels amongst the school population. Targeted increases in levels of educational attainment were established as potentially effective devices for reducing labour market discrimination and promoting social inclusion. Further factors were responsible for the performance of primary and secondary education becoming the focus. In the US, this was largely the result of the perception that though the mass higher education system was world class, educational attainments during compulsory schooling were lagging behind international standards. In Europe, the persistence of high unemployment, rising dependency ratios and the promotion of social cohesion were the major causes for this focus.

We have seen how a range of diverse factors encouraged many Western governments to consider the need for a fundamental reform of their state schooling systems. As these developments coincided with resurgence in the influence of neo-liberalism on governments in the US, UK and elsewhere, market-based solutions were an apparently inevitable outcome. In the following chapter we develop our economic analysis of schooling market behaviour before describing, in Chapter 4, the main reforms that have been implemented.

3 Parents, pupils, schools and teachers

The microeconomics of schooling

3.1 Introduction

The outcomes of market reforms in education are determined by the interplay between the preferences of parents and teachers, the nature of the process of schooling and the incentives created by market structures and regulation. We introduced our economic analysis of schooling markets in Chapter 1 and in the previous chapter we have outlined the general economic and social environment within which reforms have been developed. In this chapter we concentrate on parents' and pupils' preferences and the nature of the schooling process. In so doing, we lay some theoretical and, to a lesser extent, empirical foundations for the following chapters. In particular, we prepare for our analysis of empirical evidence of parental choice in Chapter 5 and schooling market behaviour in Chapter 8.

In Section 3.2 below, we develop theoretical foundations for the analysis of parental choice. In this section we consider the implications of orthodox economic theory for the study of parental choice and the consequences of relaxing key assumptions with regard to the treatment of the household as the decision-making unit, uncertainty and the formation of expectations. We follow this theoretical review with summaries of research evidence on educational choice in two contexts: post-compulsory education and zonal allocation of places in state schools. These two contexts allow us to examine some aspects of demand for education both in terms of quantity and quality. Many countries allow students to choose the number of years they remain in full-time education. Parents and pupils may increase their consumption of education through adding to the number of years spent in full-time education or by increasing the quantity of education received at a given point in time. The latter might be achieved by paying tutors for additional support outside of school hours or by taking advantage of additional services offered by the school. There is relatively little data on this second option for increasing the quantity of education consumed and we therefore concentrate on decisions to continue with post-compulsory education. Through these two contexts we begin a review of research evidence on school and college choice, which is taken forward in Chapter 4 and completed in Chapter 5. In Chapter 4 we consider choice of school in relation to different forms of governance, particularly with respect to private and religious schools. In Chapter 5 we concentrate on school choice in the context of quasi-market reforms that have been introduced in recent years.

Section 3.3 of this chapter follows a similar format to Section 3.2 in so far as we begin with the application of orthodox economic theory to the production of schooling outcomes. Orthodox economic theory leads to the representation of the school in terms of production and cost functions and we first consider the specification of these functions before examining evidence provided by econometric studies. In the second half of Section 3.3 we relax the rationality assumptions required for the predictions of orthodox theory and consider the behaviour that might be expected if schools are not holistic decision-making units and if they operate under conditions of uncertainty. This provides a context for a review of the school effectiveness research that explores the implications of the managerial as opposed to resource inputs on schooling outputs. In Section 3.4 we present our conclusions.

Throughout this chapter our aim is to review a range of evidence and discuss the way in which alternative theories account for this evidence. The evidence we use is not restricted to recent studies of market processes in schooling. Evidence, for example, from studies of student choice at the end of compulsory schooling can tell us something about the way choices are exercised and the impact these choices may have. Whilst we might expect market reforms to impact on the way in which choices are exercised, we should also expect to provide explanations for choice under market reforms that are consistent with explanations of schooling choices in any context.

We utilise evidence that has been gathered by researchers employing different theoretical bases and contrasting methodological assumptions. Research in economics on parental choice has focused on inferring preferences from the outcomes of schooling decisions, the latter being analysed through econometric studies. This contrasts with much sociological enquiry which has paid most attention to the process of choice, frequently using ethnographic methods. Yet this dichotomy does scant justice to the variety of work that has been carried out in each discipline. For example, theoretical perspectives developed by economists such as Leibenstein and Frank relax some of the key assumptions of orthodox economics about the process of choice and draw upon evidence from psychology. A substantial body of statistical work on the outcomes of educational choices has also been carried out by sociologists. In Chapter 1 we noted the consequences for the predictions of the impact of markets on schooling outcomes of alternative assumptions about the knowledge that decision makers possess, the way this knowledge is generated and the objectives or habits that drive behaviour. In many ways the important differences between research surveyed in this chapter are more strongly related to these assumptions, than to distinctions between the methodology employed by the individual social science disciplines.

Two important assumptions have shaped the way that we have approached the tasks outlined above. First, we assume that no single theoretical perspective has an exclusive claim on the 'truths' concerning the nature of educational choices and processes. We hope that those who are strongly committed to one perspective will find the points of comparison of sufficient interest to overcome any frustration with ideas and evidence derived from theories that they find fundamentally unsound. Our second assumption is a corollary of the first. We assume that agreement between evidence that derives from contrasting theoretical perspectives is more compelling than evidence derived from a single perspective. Our interest in presenting a diversity of perspectives lies not in attempting to discover some fundamental unity, but in noting points of agreement and disagreement and identifying the principles on which these are grounded.

3.2 Choosing an education: parents and pupils

In this section we review competing theories of parental and pupil choice and consider two contexts for educational choice that are pertinent to our interest in the choice of school. Explanations of educational choice may be divided into theories of individual and social decision-making. Whilst orthodox economic theory assumes that the decision-making is a process within the individual, the work of writers such as Leibenstein (1950) and Frank (1985, 1997) shows how a social 'frame of reference' may be employed within an economic perspective. Within sociology, the theory of individual decision-making is referred to as Rational Action Theory (Hatcher 1998) and this contrasts with theories of social and cultural transmission associated, for example with Bourdieu (1990). The distinction between individual and social decision-making is not simply a matter of economics vs. sociology. Theories of decision-making may also be distinguished on the basis of whether the information required for decisions is assumed to be known, accessible but costly, or partially unknown and subject to speculation. Theories of individual decision-making are prone to assume that information is known or accessible as this facilitates the calculation of costs and benefits to the individual. Theories of social decision-making are more prone to assume that information is partially unknown. This provides a rationale for reliance on cultural norms, and fashion leaders who provide decision-makers with the confidence that they are making the right choice.

School choice pre-dates the introduction of market reforms. By and large, these reforms have been introduced in place of zoning systems that allocated school places on the basis of neighbourhood 'catchment areas'. This system presented parents with the option of choosing the location of their home on the basis of the school they wish their child to attend. In understanding the effect of market reforms we must consider the effect of superimposing open enrolment upon existing patterns of parental choice and school location. Parents and students have also been faced with a choice at the end of compulsory schooling. In England and Wales, this choice has largely consisted in choosing between continuing studies at the local school or transferring to a college of further education. Evidence from studies of these choices provides insights into the behaviour of parents and students that can inform our understanding of the effect of market reforms. We reserve our consideration of two other areas of choice, between private and state schools and between secular and religious schools, to Chapter 4. There we concentrate on the implications of different forms of governance for schooling market behaviour.

3.2.1 Consumption and investment demands for schooling

Before considering the process of choice we must identify the factors that will be considered by the chooser. We noted in Chapter 1 that schooling produces multiple outcomes and we now depict these in terms of a utility function:

$$U^E = f (C^E, I_p, I_s, I_f)$$

Where U^E is the utility or benefit that is derived from schooling, C^E is the stream of consumption benefits whilst attending the school, $I_p, I_s,$ and I_f are streams of investment benefits derived after the individual has left the school. These benefits from education have to be compared with the opportunity costs of education in terms of lost leisure and any direct costs and lost income from work. The investment benefits have been divided into productivity gains (I_p), socialisation gains (I_s) and personal fulfilment gains (I_f). Productivity gains to the individual will be experienced in terms of future earnings and greater freedom to choose between preferred occupations or to choose between income and leisure. Socialisation gains for the individual will be experienced in terms of ability to participate in a wider selection of social networks and greater probability of entry into high status networks. The context of school choice is, as we shall see, particularly important for this outcome. Parents seek a schooling that will prepare children to enter the culture and associated social networks which they perceive as appropriate to their family. In doing so, they may well take a view of desirable schooling that contrasts with views of others who seek an overtly multicultural schooling for their children. Personal fulfilment gains will be experienced through an increased ability to participate in a wider range of sporting, cultural and artistic activities and increased satisfaction from such participation. As Fevre *et al.* (1999) point out, one implication of the distinction between investment and consumption demand for education is the behaviour of the student as a learner. It may be very different according to whether they have chosen the education on the basis of current or future expected benefits.

We noted in Chapter 1 that orthodox economics assumes that future earning power predominantly reflects the impact of schooling on productivity, rather than through returns from social networking or other channels. Specifically, the dominant human capital approach claims a causal link between absolute investments in schooling and earning power through the influence of knowledge and skills on productivity. However, studies of compulsory and post-compulsory education indicate the importance of other benefits from schooling. For example, the youth trainees interviewed by Banks *et al.* (1992) indicated that they perceived the satisfaction they gained from their college-based training exclusively in the form of current benefits. It may be, of course, that these trainees subsequently derived earnings benefits from their training of which they were presently unaware. However, schooling choice will be driven by perceptions of benefits, whether they are accurate or not.

Amongst the opportunity costs that will influence educational decisions are: search costs in gathering relevant information; transport costs incurred in getting a child to an out-of-neighbourhood school; the cost of foregone income through supporting a child in education beyond 16; and tuition costs in the form of parental and pupil time, private tutors and books. For a given level of schooling, these costs will be a higher proportion of the income of parents with lower incomes. Where capital markets are imperfect it therefore follows that there may be an unequal ability to finance these costs.

The estimation of expected investment benefits is particularly problematic for parents and students. Parents can confidently predict that the average student will gain a substantial earnings premium from continuing in full-time study beyond compulsory schooling and that obtaining higher qualifications will make this more likely. However, they are less able to predict what kind of schooling and the mix of investment outcomes that will best suit their child. This will be particularly so where, say, the impact of the 'new economy' is rapidly changing the structure of educational premiums. As we noted in Chapter 1, this uncertainty provides a rationale for parents to avoid early specialisation in their child's curriculum. A broad curriculum keeps future options open and allows parents and pupils to delay specialisation in study until the aptitudes of the child and the structure of rewards have become clearer. We now consider how the process of choosing between these options is portrayed by theories of individual and social choice.

3.2.2 Theories of individual choice

Orthodox economic theory assumes that parents and children make rational and well-informed decisions to maximise their utility. Being well informed, parents are able to accurately predict future streams of benefit that will follow each choice and they can, therefore, make their decisions with confidence. Parents are able to attach accurate probabilities to streams of expected future benefits and they will choose the option that will maximise their private welfare, given their attitude to risk-taking. Following the work of Becker (1967, 1975), it has also been standard practice to view the educational choice of parents and pupils as based solely on investment benefits in terms of higher productivity. In this section we examine the implications of viewing educational choice from both the perspective of investment and consumption behaviour.

Application of the orthodox economic theory of educational choice yields a number of important predictions. First, it suggests that if parents are free to choose between a number of schools offering the same curriculum, they will choose the school that will lead to the greatest increase in their child's future productivity. Second, they will identify the comparative advantage of their child in terms of the skills and aptitudes required by different occupations and, given the opportunity, they will choose a school that has a special expertise in developing those capabilities that the labour market rewards more generously. Third, in choosing between institutions parents will evaluate the additional benefits offered by an institution relative to the additional costs that they will incur. However, as parents will vary in the weight they attach to their children's education, some parents will be motivated by small differences in school performance, others will only be influenced by substantial differences in school performance. Fourth, parents will accurately assess switching costs in making their choice of school. Students develop friendship bonds with their peer group that provide important current benefits. They may also contribute to levels of attainment in so far as positive peer group effects operate through social support and collaborative learning. Students also develop an understanding of school and teacher expectations that enables them to operate more successfully in the environment of a particular school. However, since orthodox theory assumes that the risk of significant change in school quality can be accurately assessed, this can be incorporated in parents' choice.

Fifth, parental choice will be systematically related to parental income, parental assessment of the child's aptitude and the parents' time preference and attitude to risk. The effect of income alone is unclear. Higher income makes it easier for parents to incur search and travel costs, but if these costs are experienced in the form of parental time then the opportunity cost for higher income parents is greater. However, if the effect of schooling on productivity varies positively in proportion to initial ability, parents of more able children have a greater incentive to incur additional costs through choice of a better school. Schools may also specialise in adding value to the attainments of a particular segment of the ability range. Either of these cases will make it more likely that there will be a social pattern in the type of parent choosing each school. Parents with high time preference will value current benefits and costs much higher than distant benefits and they will give less weight to the additional earnings that may accrue in the future as a result of attending a higher performing school. Sixth, if the child's educational outcomes are positively related to the ability of the peer group, all parents have an incentive to choose a school that offers an able peer group. This will create a dynamic advantage for any school that initially has a higher ability peer group. We consider this possibility in more detail in the second section of this chapter.

Finally, the theory of rational individual choice also makes predictions about the effect of introducing open enrolment in place of a zoning system (discussed more fully in Chapter 8). The introduction of open enrolment in place of a zoning system allows parents to live in a neighbourhood that is distant from the child's school whilst bearing the additional transport costs that will ensue. They may prefer the type of housing or the local amenities in one neighbourhood and school in another. Proponents of market reforms have fixed on the implications of this change for parents whose choice of neighbourhood is restricted by their income. With this restriction removed, it may be argued, parents on lower incomes are more able to express their ideal choice of school. In a zoning system, parents on higher incomes are more likely to consider schooling quality as a factor in their choice of neighbourhood as their higher income allows them to consider a much greater range of neighbourhoods. Thus, on the introduction of open enrolment, these parents will be much more used to thinking in terms of 'active school choice'. In the first years of the introduction of open enrolment this might lead to an observation that parents from higher income groups are more pro-active in their exploitation of market opportunities. According to Gorard (1999) this is precisely what is observed in practice. Knowledge of differences between schools is valuable for parents in a zoning system, but this knowledge only has value in so far as schooling quality is important for neighbourhood choice. Parents for whom this will be the case have an incentive to develop their knowledge of different schools through their network of social contacts. The introduction of open enrolment allows them to exploit this knowledge in new ways.

A second implication of the introduction of open enrolment is that choice of school incurs transport costs. Increasing distance between the home and chosen school incurs costs for the parents in terms of payment for travel and time spent supporting travel arrangements, and incurs costs for the child in terms of time spent travelling. Households with higher incomes are more able to bear financial costs and may consider schools more distant from their home. However, households where all adults are in full-time employment may also find it difficult to bear the time costs of supporting travelling arrangements for their children.

Open enrolment may also result in an increase in search behaviour by parents. Any form of school choice, whether operating through a zonal system or through open enrolment, imposes an information gathering cost on parents considering their child's schooling. However, there are several reasons why we might expect search behaviour to be greater in an open enrolment system. First, parents who are only able to afford low-cost housing are now able to consider schools in high-cost neighbourhoods that were previously out of their reach. Second, we might expect parents to be more interested in school choice as their children approach critical ages related to school transfer. In a zonal system, parents need to gather information on schools before they choose where to live. In a quasi-market, detailed data gathering can be delayed until children reach an age when schooling begins or they need to transfer to another school. Any tendency for the quality of each school to change over time will reinforce the incentive for parents to seek data on school quality at these critical periods. Third, in a zonal system school choice is only one aspect of neighbourhood choice and, assuming that parents have a finite budget for search costs at any particular time, gathering data on schools competes for time with gathering data on other amenities in parents' priorities.

There are a number of differences between these systems that bear on the impact of the six predictions considered above. Parents choosing a higher performing school in a zonal system incur additional costs through higher house prices, whilst in an open enrolment system parents may choose either to buy a house near a high performing school or incur additional transport costs in sending their child to an out-of-neighbourhood school. The effect of school quality on house prices should, therefore, be lower in an open enrolment system. In the absence of peer effects on schooling outcomes, open enrolment will reduce cost constraints on parental choice if transport costs are less than the house price premium to be paid to live in the catchment area of a higher performing school. If the children of high-income parents are more likely to be academically able and there are positive peer effects, then it is much more likely that the house price premium will greatly exceed transport costs. In addition, if schools have a restricted ability to expand their intake, open enrolment is likely to be constrained by school capacity and this is likely to be the case in higher performing schools. Parents must therefore take into account how these schools will allocate places when they are oversubscribed. The potential effects of changes in school size in an open enrolment may also be a factor in parental choice. As we shall see later in the chapter, school size is related to discipline and curriculum breadth, both of which may be considered important by parents.

We now consider theories of individual choice that do not assume that choosers are fully informed about the implications of their choice. Given that research is not able to provide definitive assessments of the impact of school characteristics on the quality of outcomes, it becomes difficult to argue that parents make rational choices in the sense just described (Manski 2000). If parents and students are not fully informed, we argued in Chapter 1 that their rationality may be described as 'bounded', and this has several consequences for educational choice. Parents may have limited information about the impact of different types and duration of schooling on academic outcomes for their child, and they may be yet more uncertain of the effect of these outcomes on their child's lifetime opportunities. For example, parents and pupils may not be aware of the relative difficulty of different subjects they might choose or the impact of achievement in different subjects for future labour market income (Fitz-Gibbon 1999). They may be uncertain about the differential effectiveness of different schools for different kinds of student (as reported, for example, by Goldstein *et al.* 1993). Likewise, they may be unsure about which curriculum areas are strong in each school and how that corresponds with their child's aptitude. For example, in comparing schools' results, Goldstein *et al.* (1993: 43) report that 'there is little relationship between English and maths performance'. Uncertainty about future benefits may also discourage lower SES (socio-economic status) parents' educational investment. As parental background influences the probability of academic success independently of a child's ability, parents with less financial and cultural capital are discouraged from educational investment. Parents with lower incomes and lower financial capital may be less confident about their future employment status and their ability to sustain education expenditure during a period of unemployment. In addition to being more dissuaded by the uncertainty of future benefits, parents from lower SES are more likely to have a high time preference: placing much higher value on immediate benefits and less on future benefits. This follows from the likelihood that these parents will have spent less time than higher SES parents in full-time education and evidence that more schooling lowers time preference, reducing the drive for short-term benefits (Maital and Maital 1977; Leigh 1986; Becker 1996). Consequently, for these reasons, parents from lower SES may be making rational decisions when they do not encourage their children to take academic options or stay on in full-time education.

An aspect of parental choice in the face of uncertainty that has received considerable attention in the sociological literature is the ability of parents to analyse available information. Bowe *et al.* (1994a) convey this problem through referring to their field notes following observation of a school open evening for parents

> I began to look back at other open evenings and realized that making sense of such an experience is bound to require considerable analytical powers as well as the capacity to process huge amounts of sensory data ... There is a strong sense of sensory overload, of trying desperately to ascertain the meaning of an activity or display or perhaps letting it all flow by and hoping it will make sense.
>
> (Bowe *et al.* 1994a: 40)

The ability of an individual to interpret information depends on their processing ability and their familiarity with the images and language in which the information is conveyed. Systematic differences in parents' abilities and familiarity in relation to school processes will therefore result in systematic differences in parental choice. In particular, we may expect parents who are better equipped to interpret school data to be more discriminating and to be less likely to make systematic errors in exercising their choice. 'Those parents who possess the cultural capital which enables them to "read" the signs and images are clearly better placed to take advantage of the educational market' (Bowe *et al.* 1994a: 43). The cultural capital referred to here consists of acquired knowledge and understanding that is accumulated through personal experience of the education system and participation in social networks. If schooling success (as measured in terms of qualifications and number of years of full-time education) conveys an ability to interpret educational markets more accurately, then cultural capital helps educational success to be passed down from generation to generation. The evidence discussed later in this chapter suggests that academic achievement is closely related to parents' socio-economic status. Hence, cultural capital provides a second reason why we would expect parental choice to vary according to parental background.

This argument applies principally to parents' ability to interpret information about school effectiveness. The formation of parents' assessments about their child's potential and the benefits that will ultimately accrue from different schooling choices may be more significant. The uncertainty that parents face in comparing the expected benefits of alternative schooling choices provides a rationale for regarding their choice as partly social.

3.2.3 Theories of social choice

In this section we first examine the reasons for believing that parental choice of school will be dependent on their social context. Whilst much of this reasoning depends on the assumption of uncertainty, there are also reasons to regard schooling decisions as a 'social choice' even in the absence of uncertainty. Having reviewed these arguments we then consider the impact of social contexts on the relationship between choice and outcomes in schooling. We concentrate on arguments concerning the status of education as a positional good in section 3.3.2.

We can identify three distinct aspects of uncertainty which create the potential for different types of social reference. First, the benefit an individual expects from any commodity may be determined not so much by the commodity's characteristics as by the way in which consumption positions the individual in relation to different social groups. In Baudrillard's (1998) terms, consumption expresses a desire for social meaning. The self-image of parents and pupils may be significantly affected by their educational choice and there is substantial empirical evidence (for example, Easterlin 1995 and Solnick and Hemenway 1998) indicating the general importance of relative standing in consumer behaviour. Leibenstein (1950) identified three types of effect: a 'Veblen effect' when consumer demand for expensive goods and services is influenced by the impression made upon other consumers; a 'bandwagon effect' when demand is positively influenced by the number of other consumers purchasing it; and a 'snob effect' when willingness to pay reflects exclusivity. Second, parents may be uncertain about the mix of outputs aimed for by each school and the effectiveness of schools in achieving these outputs. This uncertainty may lead them to rely on the signals provided by the preferences of other parents. Third, parents may be uncertain about the future benefits that will follow from their children's achievements and this may again lead them to follow the preferences of other parents. In these latter two cases, parents may rely on their observations of the preferences of other parents in their social group to provide an indicator of the most sensible choice. Reliance upon the signals provided by a reference group of parents has been referred to by a number of researchers in terms of parents' perceptions of what is 'normal for people like us'. In the words of Hodkinson *et al.* (1996: 148) preferences result from 'the socially constructed and historically derived common base of knowledge, values and norms for action that people grow into and come to take as a natural way of life'. The degree of uncertainty faced by parents varies according to social class and particularly in relation to educational background. Education provides a cultural capital and the social networks a social capital on which parents may draw upon in making schooling choices.

Even if parents experience little uncertainty in their decision-making, they have an incentive to make their choices dependent on the choices of other parents. This dependency arises from the effect of the pupils' peer group on educational outcomes. If parents believe that peer groups exert a substantial influence on the level of benefits that arise from schooling then they will seek a school that has been chosen by a particular type of parent, deepening the dependence of parental preference on the decisions of other parents (Manski 2000).

We return to the social context of schooling choice in Section 3.3 when we consider the effects of parents' schooling choices on the benefits from schooling derived by other parents and pupils. We further develop our analysis of parental choice through a review of evidence in Chapter 5, but before leaving the subject we examine two contexts for educational choice which shed further light on decision-making by parents and pupils.

3.2.4 Choosing post-compulsory education

Students in the UK complete their compulsory education at the age of 16. They then choose whether to remain in full-time education and, if so, the kind of institution at which to study. Most continue at the school where they completed their secondary schooling and, of these, the majority follow an academic route. However, a significant minority moves to study at a college which caters exclusively for post-16 education and which offers a greater range of vocationally orientated programmes. We now consider two aspects of choice at 16: whether to continue in full-time education and choice of institution at which to study. Evidence suggests that these choices are significantly influenced by parental background, local economic conditions and the school attended during compulsory education.

Most students claim sole responsibility for choice of post-compulsory education. (Foskett and Hesketh 1997). However, the strong and lingering influence of parents remains, effectively framing the way in which students view their options. This effect has been identified by studies of students' experience of post-compulsory education (Banks *et al.* 1992) and the decision-making process (e.g. Lauder *et al.* 1992; Foskett and Hesketh 1997; Hemsley-Brown 1999), although it is reduced by the growing influence of the immediate peer group to which the student belongs. The impact of social class on post-16 decision-making is confirmed by econometric studies (Micklewright 1988; Cheng 1995; Bennett *et al.* 1997). The influence of social class may operate through the financial capacity of families to support children continuing with their full-time education. Armstrong's (1997) Northern Ireland evidence can be interpreted in this light. He found that children with parents in work and children with no or few siblings were more likely to stay on in post-compulsory schooling. However, this interpretation is contested by evidence that once social class has been accounted for, household income has no effect on the decision to stay on in 16–19 education (Micklewright 1988, and Bennett *et al.* 1997). A study of progression into higher education in Australia (Williams and Carpenter 1991) also suggests that income effects are modest whilst parental expectation and student self-concept exert a strong significant effect on the probability of students of similar ability continuing into higher education. The sociological studies of Reay (1996) and Maguire *et al.* (1999) also suggest that students' expectations of 'what is normal for people like us' play the crucial role in these decisions.

Cheng (1995) and Armstrong (1997) investigate the effects of the school and economic environment. Armstrong found that a 10 per cent increase in an individual school's GCSE results led to a 3 per cent increase of staying-on rates, after controlling for the effect of the young person's own GCSE results. Students' post-16 choices also reflect local labour market conditions. Cheng found that local unemployment was negatively correlated with post-16 participation in England and Wales, whilst Armstrong found that unemployment in Northern Ireland was negatively correlated with staying on in further education but not correlated with staying on in school. Current levels of unemployment are more likely to influence students who anticipate earlier entry into the labour market (not continuing into higher education). In the mid-1980s in England and Wales students at 16 faced clear financial incentives to study A levels or BTEC qualifications, but no financial incentives to study on intermediate level vocational programmes (Bennett *et al.* 1997). According to Whitfield and Wilson (1991) the growth of youth training significantly depressed school staying-on rates. Where careers advisers exert more influence, students are more likely to stay on in full-time education (Witherspoon 1995; Howieson and Croxford 1996). However, given the increase in the participation rate in 16–19 education, labour market changes and recent policy initiatives, this situation may have changed.

Students actively considering moving to another local school or college are likely to face significant transaction costs, largely associated with the costs of search and switching. In order to assess alternative providers, information needs to be collected, collated and then analysed. Some information is available at low cost – for example, reliance on friends and family knowledge and experience – but more formal search – for example, attending meetings – will be more expensive, particularly in terms of time. Hemsley-Brown (1999) found that students often relied on printed information and experienced difficulties in comparing colleges and schools in relation to independence and work ethic. These problems may explain why parents remain the most important source of information for students (Witherspoon 1995). Students who choose a College of Further Education are also more likely to refer to careers advisers as having been helpful and are less likely to refer to parents as a source of advice (Keays *et al.* 1998; Mangan *et al.* 2001).

To these costs need to be added the costs of changing school or college, the switching costs. These costs are likely to be largely associated with the need to develop new social relationships and behaviour patterns and they encourage students to make similar choices to their peer friendship group. Keays *et al.* (1998) found that the most frequently cited factor in post-16 choice of students staying on in school sixth forms was 'wanting to stay somewhere familiar' and Thomas (2000) reports evidence of strong peer group effects, especially for females. Friends' decisions were found to be much less important to students who move to a College of Further Education than those who stay at the school to continue their 16–19 education. This latter finding may reflect the impact in this study of the majority of young people who stay on at their existing school. Finally, as a majority of students in state education attend a local school, a move to another school or a College of Further Education, with a larger catchment area than a typical school, is likely to incur increased transport costs. Students attending a school sixth form are far more likely to cite proximity to home as a factor in their choice of post-16 institution (Keays *et al.* 1998). Recognising this further cost disincentive to moving, CFEs may provide free or subsidised transport (e.g. Maguire *et al.* 1999).

In summary, in the absence of compensating benefits from moving, transaction costs, particularly switching and transport costs encourage most students to remain at their present institution.

3.2.5 Choosing schools through choosing where to live

Administrative systems that allocate school places according to where pupils live present parents with a joint housing–schooling decision. In so far as the range of public services vary in quality according to residential area, choice of school is one aspect of a general process known as Tiebout choice (Tiebout 1956; Starrett 1981). Hoxby (2000) provides a full account of the theory and evidence of Tiebout choice in schooling. In theory, choice of neighbourhood will depend not only on parental income, but also on parents' valuation of schooling and their preferred mix of educational outcomes, prompting an increase in private allocative efficiency. Parents who prefer to pay higher prices for houses in the neighbourhood of higher quality schools are free to do so. In addition, schools may attract to their neighbourhoods parents with a particular mix of preferences. This self-sorting by parents can raise social welfare as parents choose neighbourhoods with schools that produce their preferred mix of outputs. Social allocative efficiency may not increase, however, if this process leads to strong segregation by ability and returns to peer effects (discussed in more detail below) are diminishing. This allocation mechanism may also produce a distribution of benefits from schooling that may be regarded as inequitable. Further, as the overall pattern of school enrolments is not affected by these aspects of parental choice, there may be no incentive for technical efficiency, unless school income is directly related to local tax income which is in turn based on property values.

Hoxby measures the effect of choice in a zonal system in the US by comparing the educational and earnings outcomes of students in locations that have different levels of concentration of schools between which parents may choose. She finds that academic results are 1.4 grades higher, and income at age 32 is 15 per cent higher, for children attending schools in densely populated areas with many competing schools, compared with schools serving isolated districts where parents have no effective choice. She also finds that an increase in Tiebout choice lowers per-pupil spending and this entails a strong association between Tiebout choice and school productivity. Households with a greater Tiebout choice are also less likely to choose private schooling. This has important implications for policy as parents who choose private schooling are less likely to support tax increases to finance public schooling. She also finds that the effect of Tiebout choice 'are not significantly different for lower-income and higher-income families' (2000: 1229).

Other empirical evidence from the US and the UK is broadly consistent with this analysis, and we now report three findings from these studies. First, in choosing a neighbourhood, parents de facto choose a peer group for their child. In a study of two urban areas in England, Conduit et al. (1996) find that socio-economic characteristics of the school neighbourhood account for between 40 and 60 per cent of variance in school examination results. As we shall see later in this chapter, the ability of the peer group is one factor affecting the child's educational outcomes. Parents who believe this to be the case will seek a neighbourhood that provides a peer group that will have the most positive impact on their child's education. Second, a school with a good reputation for adding value to children's attainment will attract parents to a neighbourhood. Exploring the combined effect of these two factors, a US study by Black (1999) found that a 5 per cent increase in primary school test scores led to an increase of 2.1 per cent in the marginal resident's willingness to pay for a particular type of house. Dee (2000) finds that additional per-school state spending in the US led to a significant increase in house prices. For state schools in England, Rosenthal (2001: 10) estimates a much lower level of responsiveness for the average purchase. Given a mean dwelling purchase price of £72,000, 'households are willing to pay close to £450 more to buy dwellings whose nearest GCSE performance is this much (5 per cent) higher'. Third, if some neighbourhoods are served by a local school whilst others are not, we may observe the importance to parents of proximity to a school in their choice of neighbourhood. Bogart and Cromwell (2000) compared house prices in local neighbourhoods in one US district before and after a change in zones that closed schools in some neighbourhoods. They found that the presence of a local primary school increased neighbourhood house prices by 10 per cent whilst the provision of a school bus service increased house prices by 2.5 per cent.

Overall, this evidence confirms the belief that zonal systems of allocating school places will lead to sorting of families according to income and educational preferences, with this process operating through house prices. Hoxby's evidence suggests that if school income is related to house prices through local taxation, then Tiebout choice will raise school efficiency when parents are able to choose between a large number of alternative schools in an urban area. The effects of the introduction of open enrolment will be superimposed on these existing patterns. Moreover, some degree of neighbourhood choice as an aspect of school choice is likely to persist in an open enrolment system. Parents who choose a neighbourhood close to their preferred school gain benefits in reduced transport costs. Bogart and Cromwell's (2000) study suggests these may be quite significant to parents. Using data collected after the introduction of open enrolment in the UK, Hammond and Dennison (1995) report that 19 per cent of parents surveyed claimed that school choice has influenced their choice of home. However, it may be that most of these parents had bought their present home before the introduction of open enrolment.

3.3 The process of education in schools

In the Section 3.2.1 we noted the diversity of schooling outcomes in terms of consumption and investment (productivity, socialisation and self-fulfilment) benefits. In this section we examine the production relations between these outcomes and we extend the analysis of outcomes to include externalities that arise from schooling choice. In the first part of this section we also consider some problems to be overcome in the measurement of school effects on these outcomes. Thereafter, in the following section, we summarise more detailed evidence about the production of schooling outcomes. This can be divided into intake effects, resource effects and management effects.

The characteristics of the pupil intake vary from one school to another and these characteristics have a powerful impact on outcomes. This impact may be divided into the effect of parents and peers. The socio-economic and educational background of the child's parents is strongly associated with their schooling outcomes, but the characteristics of the peer group with whom they are educated can have an independent and significant effect. The effect of schools on outputs may be divided into resource effects and management effects and the former may be further divided into quantity or quality effects. An increase in the quantity of resources may be experienced through an increase in the teacher–pupil ratio and an increase in quality of resources through an improvement in the capability of new entrants to the profession. Either of these might be achieved by an increase in the value of resources committed to schooling. Outputs might also be increased through higher resource productivity following, for example, a change in the dominant teaching style. The orthodox economics view of production traditionally stopped at this point. However, if production takes place in the context of uncertainty about production processes and outcomes, then we must also be interested in the way management effects schooling outcomes. Management style, organisational structure and incentive structures may affect outcomes through, for example, the deployment, motivation and professional development of teachers.

3.3.1 Production relationships between schooling outcomes

The precise nature of the production relationship between outcomes is important because we need to know the extent to which these outcomes are in joint or competitive supply. If they are jointly supplied then increasing the output of one outcome will automatically increase the output of another. However, if outcomes are in competitive supply then schools must choose the emphasis that they will give to each output. Chubb and Moe's (1990) critique of state schooling assumes competitive supply, such that schools that seek to achieve a range of outcomes face 'goal confusion' having to switch resources between alternative purposes. We now consider relationships between each of the outcomes we have identified.

Consumption and productivity outcomes would be in joint supply if increasing the happiness of the child at school automatically leads to an improvement in their learning. Studies of the human brain have suggested just such a link. However, learning in school takes place in a social setting and the complexities of this context introduce many other factors beyond the individual that affect happiness and learning. Hofman *et al.* (1999) present evidence from a study of primary children which identifies three aspects of teaching (concentrating on the 'basics', strong formal school rules, and regular monitoring of student achievement) which are associated with higher achievement in mathematics but a lower sense of well-being at school. We need to be careful in interpreting these results as the aspects of teaching identified could be responses to children's happiness at school and their aptitude for mathematics. Shann (1999) reports school level data for four US middle schools and finds that students at the schools with higher levels of academic results report positive social behaviours more frequently and antisocial behaviours less frequently. Shann interprets this result as indicating

> an important synergy between an emphasis on academics and a culture of caring (that) may be needed to promote optimal achievement. One without the other is not insufficient. Students need to feel that their teachers care about them, want the best for them, and are interested in their success, before students will give their full effort.
>
> (Shann 1999: 409)

One of the schools studied by Shann 'seemed to have a law-and-order environment', but achieved lower academic results than the most 'caring' school. One of two schools achieving low academic results 'placed greater priority on support services for their students whereas teachers in the high achieving schools called for more emphasis on academics' (*ibid.*: 410). The contrast between the findings of Hofman *et al.* and Shann suggests that firm conclusions on the relationship between consumption and productivity outcomes would be premature. However, we may note at this stage that the importance of consumption benefits of education have been relatively neglected in the economics of education. As detailed in the previous chapter, most individuals spend a considerable part of their life in full-time education and whilst they may not consider their time at school 'the best years of their life', their net consumption benefits from schooling will form a significant part of their lifetime welfare.

There are reasonable grounds for presuming a relationship between consumption benefits and socialisation. Patterns of student behaviour in relation to absenteeism, discipline, weapons possession and the availability of drugs may affect students' happiness at school and the development of their view of 'normal behaviour'. According to Shann (1999: 392) 'an atmosphere of "fear and disorderliness" is both formative and summative of the culture in many troubled urban schools'.

The production relationship between productivity and socialisation benefits is equally uncertain. In so far as these outcomes are addressed by different parts of the curriculum (such as lessons in personal and social education or lessons in mathematics) we might expect these outcomes to be in competitive supply. However, socialisation is also the product of the school's social organisation and the norms that govern daily life in the school that may contribute to academic learning as well as to socialisation outcomes. Pupils who have learnt to show greater respect for each other should be more ready to listen to and learn from their peers. However, as socialisation outcomes are rarely measured on a systematic basis it is difficult to investigate the substance of these possibilities. Personal fulfilment may also be positively related to productivity in so far as achievement at school allows students a greater choice of occupation. However, personal fulfilment derived from appreciation of and participation in artistic, cultural and sporting activities may be unrelated to productivity if these aspects of an individual's interests and achievements are not drawn upon in their employment. Schooling that concentrates on 'the basics' may do so at the expense of benefits to the individual in terms of personal fulfilment once they have left the school. At present, policy is formed without the benefit of clear evidence about these production relations and this entails considerable risks in terms of predicting the effects of policy change on welfare and the composition of schooling outcomes.

3.3.2 Schooling and consumption externalities

So far we have not considered externalities created through the production and consumption of schooling outcomes. Production externalities arise inter alia from peer group effects and consumption externalities arise from the effect of schooling outcomes for one individual on the well-being of others. In this section we focus on consumption externalities and we consider production externalities in Section 3.4.2. An individual suffers a negative consumption externality when a good or service bought by someone else reduces the satisfaction they get from their own purchases. Conversely, they gain a positive consumption externality when the purchase of a good or service by someone else increases the benefit they receive from their own purchases. We now examine the circumstances that may lead to either of these events. First we consider negative externalities which arise if education is a positional good.

The analysis of positional goods found in the work of Hirsch (1976) and Frank (1985, 1997) employs a theory of decision-making as social choice; Ancil and Hakes 1991 and Ackerman (1997) provide reviews. As Mason (1998) points out, both Hirsch and Frank viewed demand for positional goods and services as being consistent with standard economic theory's assumption of the rational pursuit of self-interest. However, in conventional economic analysis the utility gained from a good or service is an increasing function of its present and future consumption. For Hirsch, the utility gained from education depends in part upon both the absolute and relative levels 'consumed', with many consumers seeking status based on exclusivity or scarcity. These latter consider-ations lead to positional competition, where one parent's attempt to improve their child's relative position encourages imitation from other parents. In the case of the pure positional good, the private benefits resulting from additional acquisitions by one parent are completely offset by the negative externalities borne by other parents.

The desirability of positional goods, according to Hirsch (1976), reflects their absolute scarcity and/or sensitivity to social congestion or crowding. Schooling is clearly not subject to absolute restrictions, the very short run excepted. If some individuals increase their demand for schooling it is always possible to build another school, employ more teachers and buy more educa-tional technology. Similarly, it would appear to be always possible to create more 'good' schools according to conventional absolute definitions of 'good'. Neither critics of the school improvement agenda (e.g. Gewirtz 1998) nor those questioning whether quality is resource-dependent (e.g. Hanushek 1996b) argue that the quality of schools' outputs is immutable or predetermined. Hirsch's argument that positionality may also reflect 'social scarcity' appears more rele-vant to education.

Hirsch's argument presumes that a fixed social structure provides a limited number of positions of status to which individuals may aspire. Access to these positions depends on quality of education received relative to other individuals. An individual's investment in education to achieve higher social status will create a negative externality in terms of actual experiences attainable by others. Moreover, parents' attempts to improve their child's relative position encour-ages imitation, and can result in both low private and social marginal returns to increases in the resources devoted to schooling.

The positional analysis developed by Frank (1985, 1997) focuses on consumption benefits and the negative externalities created by the impact of one individual's consumption on the perceptions of others. In Frank's analysis each individual's consumption behaviour affects the frame of reference which others use to evaluate their own consumption behaviour. He argued that this frame of reference effectively becomes a public good influencing the subjective well-being generated by individual behaviour. The uncoordinated decisions of individual parents cannot produce an optimal output of this or any other public good. In his analysis of 'local' status, individuals are largely concerned with within-group comparisons. He argued that position is particularly important when choosing for one's child and educational decisions were identified as an example where interpersonal comparisons were particularly important. In the context of local schooling markets, Frank (1997) argued that the tendency for families to seek to buy houses closer to 'better' schools reallocates family expenditure away from retirement savings and inflates certain house prices without raising social welfare.

A more optimistic view of positional competition is provided by Congleton (1989) who points out that the social desirability of status competition depends crucially upon the net size of the externalities or spillover effects generated. Transferring Congleton's argument to the schooling market, what matters overall is whether those demanding highly ranked education for their children, have the effect of raising or lowering the general quality of education in society. There is a case to be made for expecting each of the private outcomes (consumption, productivity, socialisation and personal fulfilment) to be associated with a positive externality. Children who are happier at school (consumption benefits) are more likely to provide a positive environment for their peers. The potential for high productivity that students develop at school is likely to benefit work colleagues who may learn from working with that individual or may benefit from the increased productivity the individual brings to a work-team. Moreover, an increase in the supply of educated workers raises the probability that an employer can fill a vacancy for a 'good' job. As a consequence more 'good' jobs are created. As Snower (1996) has argued, national differences in the exploitation of such trading externalities can account for observed differences in the proportion of 'good jobs' in an economy's labour market. In the case of personal fulfilment outcomes, children who develop their capability to participate in or appreciate sport or art may provide pleasure for others through their skill or their participation. However, the strongest case for externalities arising from schooling outcomes is most likely to be made for socialisation outcomes. Individuals who are less likely to engage in 'anti-social behaviours' (such as theft or assault), more likely to devote time to voluntary activity for their community and more likely to contribute critically to the development of communities will generate benefits for others. Indications that education does in fact yield positive externalities can be found in a number of studies discussed in the previous chapter.

We conclude, therefore, that contrary to the arguments of Jonathan (1990) and Ranson (1993) consumption externalities are not inevitably negative. At worst, net externalities have only a small negative effect on the sum of educational outcomes and at best might have a considerable positive effect. Available evidence does not allow a stronger conclusion at present. We now turn to measurement of school effects on educational outcomes.

3.3.3 Measuring the effect of inputs on educational attainment

The outcomes of schooling are not easily measured. Productivity may, in competitive labour markets, be proxied by earnings, but it is difficult to isolate the effects of schooling and adjust for differences in tastes and working conditions. Estimating enjoyment of culture or participation in society raises more

fundamental problems. Criminal records and participation in voluntary chari-
ties may be treated as related to the latter, but such measures are more likely to
provoke discussion on what it means to participate in society than they are to
shed light on schooling outcomes. Developing measures of pupils' happiness at
school are even more problematic.

Research generally utilises data that are widely available: years of schooling,
academic attainment and attendance. However, these variables do not match
our specification of schooling outcomes very closely. This is not too severe a
problem if all schooling outcomes are in joint supply, but as we have seen, there
are good grounds for doubting that this is the case. If we accept that schooling
outcomes are, to some extent, in competitive supply then difficulties in accurate
measurement of these outcomes create information problems for parents and
planners. We return to these problems in Chapter 7. Bearing in mind these
reservations, in this section we review evidence that assumes that academic
attainment is *the* measure of schooling outcomes. In doing so we acknowledge
that academic attainment may be taken as an indicator of future productivity,
ability to enjoy culture and quality of future participation in society.

The academic output of schooling is the value added to a pupils' attainment. Where reliable measures of pupil entry and exit attainment exist the
difference between the two can be interpreted as the value added and variations in value added can be compared across schools. Data of this kind usually
rely on test scores in mathematics and language or mathematics and science (as
in the TIMMS data set discussed in the previous chapter). Use of these data
presumes a strong correlation between pupil attainment in these 'core' subjects
and their attainment in other aspects of the curriculum (e.g. modern foreign
languages, history, art). In the absence of these data, exit attainment might be
proxied by the number of years spent in full-time education and entry attainment might be proxied by the socio-economic status of parents (e.g. Bennett *et
al.* 1997). Schools in England and Wales are encouraged to review their
achievements using an even cruder measure: the proportion of children eligible
for free school meals (FSM) (a practice reviewed in Chapter 8). This is used as
a proxy for SES that is, in turn, a proxy for entry attainment. One feature of
the introduction of the National Curriculum in England and Wales has been a
considerable increase in the data available to estimate progress in pupils'
attainment.

Once a measure of schooling output has been chosen, it remains to choose
inputs, variables to be used to measure those inputs, and a statistical procedure
for estimating the effect of those inputs on educational output. In commenting
upon methodological issues in this procedure we draw heavily on Vignoles *et al.*
(2000). We organise our summary by first outlining two commonly cited problems and we then outline alternative statistical approaches to resolving these
problems.

The first problem is how to specify the model of the transformation of inputs
into outputs. There are two aspects to this problem. The model ought to be
derived from a theory of teaching and learning. In particular, we might expect a

model to identify theoretical relationships between independent variables that may be taken into account in testing for effects of inputs on outputs. Multicollinearity can lead to misinterpretation of the effect of independent variables, as Fortune and O'Neil (1994) argue in relation to the effects of parental background and peer effects. The omission of key variables and the misattribution of their effects is the most severe problem. Vignoles *et al.* cite a number of studies (Carroll 1963; Walberg 1985; Creemers 1994; Reezigt *et al.* 1999) which they regard as having modelled relationships between inputs and the process of learning in ways that minimise this problem. These studies develop a model in which learning depends on: aptitude, ability to understand instruction, perseverance, opportunity and the quality of instruction. This consistency helps the growth of a coherent body of evidence. In addition, the model ought to recognise the institutional structure within which inputs are transformed into outputs. That is, the attainment of pupils will be affected not only by the resources of a school, but also by its institutional management and the characteristics of its other pupils. The effect of a smaller class, a more highly qualified teacher or the adoption of a particular teaching method will depend on the institutional context in which they are applied. That is, data on educational inputs and outputs are hierarchical (Goldstein 1995). Mancebón and Bandrés (1999) also argue that the cumulative nature of the learning process and the contribution to learning of experiences outside schooling should be included within the model. By the cumulative nature of learning we refer to the way in which the development of understanding (and particularly in the level of thinking skills) of the pupil affects the speed at which they can develop further. For example, the grading scale employed by the National Curriculum in England and Wales assumes that initial attainment will influence rate of progress, expecting that a 7 year old achieving level 1 attainment will on average attain level 2 by age 11, whereas a 7 year old attaining level 2 would be expected to attain level 4 by age 11.

A second problem arises from the endogeneity of independent variables. Some of this endogeneity is removed once the model is specified in terms of added value. However, the value added by one school may be higher than that of another because it has been chosen by higher SES parents who are better able to support the learning of their children. Endogeneity may also be caused by parents of more able children being more likely to choose an able peer group for their children (Evans *et al.* 1992). However, this effect is likely to vary according to context for parental choice and a UK study by Feinstein and Symons (1999) finds no evidence of endogeneity of this kind. Conversely, the level of resources and pupil attainment may appear to be negatively correlated if managers of a schooling system allocate higher per-pupil levels of resources to schools and classrooms with a disproportionately high number of children with learning difficulties (Goldstein and Blatchford 1998).

Single level OLS regression methods run into difficulties associated with both of these problems. They take no account of the hierarchical nature of the data and they also struggle with the endogeneity problem. The problems of endogeneity may be reduced by the use of simultaneous equations or instrumental variables as long as sufficient appropriate instruments (which affect resources but not learning outcomes) can be found to solve the equations. For example, Hoxby (1998b) uses demographic trends and externally imposed class limits to identify random changes in class size. The problem of hierarchical data may be overcome by the use of a multi-level model (Goldstein 1995). The model could be specified to identify 'cluster' effects at the class, school and local education authority level, although estimates using multi-level models are frequently restricted to the two levels of the pupil and the school. In these cases the variation in pupil outcomes is made dependent on variation between pupils and variation between schools. As intra-unit (within class, school or LEA) correlation increases the results from a multi-level model will increasingly diverge from an OLS estimate as the latter underestimates the standard error and falsely rejects null hypotheses that the coefficient on the explanatory variable is zero.

A quite different approach to estimating the relationship between educational inputs and outputs is provided by frontier estimation models and data envelopment analysis (DEA) in particular (Mancebón and Bandrés 1999; Bradley *et al.* 1999). This approach has the advantage of identifying those schools that are using their resources most efficiently and provides a measure of the extent to which other schools are falling short of this measure. Mancebón and Bandrés suggest that DEA is an appropriate tool for analysing effects on educational outputs because DEA does not require the data to adapt itself to a pre-ordained functional form, allows for local flexibility and choice in objectives, and copes well with absence of prices. However, Vignoles *et al.* (2000) cite a number of technical problems with the approach, particularly related to the problem that the data employed is not entirely reliable.

3.3.4 Intake effects

Family background

It is well known that a large part of the variation in pupil attainment can be accounted for by family background. Educational attainment varies significantly with socio-economic background (Willms 1986; Haveman and Wolfe 1995), the number of siblings (Hanushek 1992) and (in the Netherlands) according to strength of religious commitment (Dijkstra and Peschar 1996). It is not unusual for the proportion of variation in pupil attainment to be accounted for by family background to be as high as 75 per cent (e.g. Goldhaber and Brewer 1997). This type of finding appears worldwide, in developing countries as well as OECD countries (Lee and Barro 1997), although its extent varies. For instance, family background explains a much smaller proportion of variation in pupil attainment in East Asia than elsewhere in the world.

The family background effect may be due to inherited ability, consistency of social norms between home and school, the provision of a good environment for learning, specific support and interest provided by the parent or the effect of parental aspirations. If behavioural norms and values encouraged by teachers are similar to those experienced at home, children are more likely to feel comfortable at school and more able to interpret expectations and instructions. Parents with higher levels of education are likely to earn more and to place greater value on the benefits of education for their own children. As parents' income increases they are more able to afford to provide their children with space at home for learning, books and private tutors. Some parents are more able to support their children's learning and some parents may prefer to devote more of their time to this support. Feinstein and Symons (1999) include teachers' estimates of parental interest in their estimation of the determination of educational attainment. They find that this variable has far more impact on attainment than does socio-economic background. Indeed, they conclude that the majority of the SES effect observed in other studies may be accounted for by a combination of parental interest and peer group effects. In a study of Australian students, Williams and Carpenter (1991) find that parental aspirations explain a small but significant proportion of student achievement and that they are a large significant factor in explaining the likelihood that students will continue into higher education.

This evidence suggests that at least part of the parental effect may be responsive to targeted policies. If parents are encouraged to develop higher aspirations for their children and are enabled to give them greater support, then children's attainment will increase. This lends support to policies to improve home–school liaison. There is also evidence that parental employment affects children's attainment. Using a comparison of the attainment of siblings who are not twins, Ermisch and Francesconi (2000) estimate the impact of the mother's employment whilst children are between 0 and 5 years. They find that if mothers are working full-time during this period there is a 7–9 per cent reduction in children's attainment, with a smaller, but still significant, effect if mothers are working part-time.

In order to investigate the effect of religious commitment on educational outcomes in the Netherlands, Dijkstra and Peschar (1996) construct a variable they call 'Christian worldview' on the basis of parents' answers to questions concerning belief in key doctrines. They find a significant positive effect of a Christian worldview that amounts to half a year of learning gain between extreme values of this variable. However, this could result from a stronger compatibility between home and school for religious parents, given that the majority of schools in the Netherlands are affiliated either to the Protestant or Catholic church.

Peer effects

A student's peer group affects the outcomes of their schooling in a number of ways. First, collaboration with peers affects the learning process (Johnson and Johnson 1994). When students co-operate in learning they challenge, prompt and support each other, leading to improvements in learning outcomes. We might expect students' capacity to support each other's learning in this way to be influenced by their ability, although a well-known study by Barnes (1976) illustrates how a more able student can benefit from working with a less able student. Second, peer groups establish cultures of expectation that may limit or extend what a student had previously thought they were able to achieve and will shape students' attitude towards the process of schooling. One aspect of this culture of expectation concerns the student's self-esteem. Students placed in a high ability stream may conclude that they are highly esteemed, with the reverse effect operating upon students placed in a low ability stream. The effect of students' expectations and self-esteem on their learning is strongly attested in the psychological literature. Amongst many studies of this characteristic of peer groups the work by Willis (1977) is amongst the most often cited. Third, the peer group can influence teacher expectations and the teacher's ability to respond to individual differences even when they are noted. For example, a study by Savage and Desforges (1995) shows how a group of primary teachers responded to children in a similar way even though they were able to identify differences between their needs and abilities. Fourth, ability grouping may affect the allocation of teachers to classes with consequences for pupil attainment. Betts and Shkolnik (2000) found that more able students tended to be educated by teachers with higher levels of qualification, whilst less able children were taught by less experienced teachers in schools that grouped students according to ability and by more experienced teachers in schools which did not. Finally, homogeneous groups of students might be easier to teach, although this may be dependent on teaching strategy. Heterogeneous groups may pose particular difficulties for teachers who rely heavily on a didactic approach. An illustration of the interaction between teachers' preferred style and the impact of streaming or non-streaming is given by Robertson *et al.* (1998).

Consequently, we should expect to observe peer effects operating at school and class level. At school level we would expect peer effects to be mediated through the culture and general expectations within the school and at class level we would expect peer effects to be mediated through the expectations of teachers and the process of teaching that they adopt. The strength of this mediation will depend on other factors affecting the culture and organisation of the school and the style of teaching. If attainment is positively related to the ability of the peer group we would expect to find that schools and classes segregated by ability lead to higher than expected attainment of the more able and lower than expected attainment of the less able. If it is easier to teach homogeneous classes we would expect segregated schools and classes to secure higher levels of attainment than non-segregated schools and classes.

Given these reasons to expect peer effects in teaching we need to consider the overall implication of these effects for schooling attainment. In particular, we need to know whether an able child gains as much from being educated with other able children, as does a less able child from being educated with more able children. If returns to peer effects are constant then shifting from all-ability to segregated schooling affects the distribution of benefits from peer effects, but it will not affect the overall average level of academic attainment. However, if returns to peer effects are diminishing then a switch from all-ability to segregated schooling will lead to a net decline in average academic attainment. It follows that if the introduction of schooling markets causes peer effects to be distributed less evenly across schools, then aggregate as well as individual attainment may be affected.

The effect of a student's peer group has been studied in terms of the academic ability and socio-economic background of the peer group. Summers and Wolfe (1977), Henderson *et al.* (1978) provide evidence of positive peer group effects with respect to ability, whilst Kerckhoff (1986) and Robertson and Symons (1996) also provide evidence of socio-economic background effect. Positive constant returns to peer group are found by Hoffer (1992), positive increasing returns to peer group are found by Argys, Rees and Brewer (1996) and positive peer effects with diminishing returns by MacPhail-Wilcox and King (1986) and Feinstein and Symons (1999). Henderson *et al.* (1978) found strong evidence and Robertson and Symons (1996) found weak evidence of an ability peer effect for primary children that exhibited diminishing returns. Studies of the impact of the socio-economic background of the peer group suggest that this effect emerges in secondary, rather than primary education. Willms (1986) finds a pronounced effect for secondary school pupils in Scotland, yet Bondi (1991) found no such effect for Scottish pupils at primary level.

3.3.5 Resource effects

In recent years a key debate in the economics of education has concerned whether there is any significant relationship between the level of educational resourcing and educational outcomes. Orthodox theory assumes that increasing the inputs into the production process can usually raise output. In the case of schooling, popular clamour for smaller class sizes and more teachers echo this assumption. However, if the quantity of one input were fixed we would expect diminishing returns to increases in other inputs. Moreover, if the fixed input exerts a very strong influence on final output, returns may diminish sharply. It is well known that pupils' initial ability accounts for a major part of their educational achievement and estimates of school effects on educational attainment typically suggest that schools account only for between 10 and 20 per cent of the variance in pupil attainment. It seems probable then that unless schools employ very different levels of resources we would find, at most, that the level of resources accounts for a very small proportion of the variance between schools. In England, central government sets a target figure for spending per pupil in different parts of the country. For primary schools in 2000/2001 this figure varied from £3,701 in one inner city borough to £2,190 in one rural borough, whilst for secondary schools the variation was from £5,138 to £2,799 (TES 2001b). This target spending is calculated on the basis of anticipated unit cost differences arising from issues such as teacher recruitment and the proportion of children with special needs. Variations in school funding based on assessments of this kind make the task of disentangling the effect of resources on attainment more complex. In this section we look at two aspects of school resourcing: the relationship between resources per pupil and educational outcomes and the relationship between school size and unit costs. From a policy point of view providing more resources and increasing the efficiency with which those resources are used are alternative routes for a government seeking to raise educational outcomes. Given the macro context we described in Chapter 2, there is an inherent attraction for governments in policies that do not increase overall government spending. Education reforms introduced in England and Wales by successive UK governments were predicated on a belief that there was substantially more scope for efficiency gains than for gains from increased resource levels. A similar stance is echoed in the policies of other Western governments (e.g. New Zealand) that have stressed the benefits to be gained from education reform. In the following two sections we review the evidence of the impact of resource levels on outcomes and then consider the effects of changes in school size. A policy of open enrolment makes variation in school size, and the threat of such variation, a key incentive for schools to raise educational outcomes. We therefore need to assess the significance of such changes in size for school costs and outcomes.

Resource level

An increase in funding per pupil may be used to increase the quantity and/or quality of resources. More teachers or learning support assistants may be employed or the quality of recruits into the profession may be increased and more experienced staff retained. Both possibilities are reflected in data on spending per pupil, whilst studies of actual resources deployed may distinguish between these two effects. On the basis of reviews of previous studies, Hanushek (1986, 1996b, 1997b) has concluded that spending per pupil has no effect on attainment, but this review has been criticised on a range of counts (Hedges, Laine and Greenwald 1994; Kremer 1995). In addition, some subsequent studies (e.g. Fortune and O'Neil 1994; Card and Krueger 1992, 1996; Lee and Barro 1997) provide evidence of the effect of per pupil spending on attainment. Fortune and O'Neil, in their study of school districts in Ohio and Missouri, find a significant relationship between spending and attainment once a certain threshold is exceeded. Fortune and O'Neil speculate that (at 1994 costs) additional spending per pupil needs to be at least $700 a year for any difference to become apparent. On the basis of a review of meta-analyses of the effects of resources on outcomes, Vignoles *et al.* (2000: 36) conclude that '"positive" results of some meta-studies can at best be taken as indicative rather than conclusive'.

Teacher inputs to education have been measured in terms of the proportion of resources accounted for by spending on teachers and through measures of teacher quality. Spending on teachers is measured through the pupil–teacher ratio. A lower pupil–teacher ratio should lead to higher pupil attainment if this results in a higher quality of teacher–pupil interaction that is focused on developing pupils' understanding and attainment is measured in terms of level of understanding rather than accumulated knowledge. Evidence of the effect of class size is inconclusive. Meta-analyses by Glass and Smith (1979) and Hanushek (1989) indicated no overall relationship between class size and attainment. A majority of the studies reviewed by MacPhail-Wilcox and King (1986) indicated a negative relationship and a similar conclusion emerges from a smaller review by Blatchford and Mortimore (1994). A study of sixth form classes in England by Fielding (1995, 1998) found that larger classes were more cost effective.

Amongst the factors making it difficult to detect any relationship between class size and pupil attainment is the relationship between pupil ability and class size. Class sizes in the UK and US tend to vary positively with student ability. This is shown in the UK by the NCDS data (Feinstein and Symons 2000) and in the US by Betts and Shkolnik (2000). A study by Krueger (1999) avoids this endogeneity bias through a random experiment conducted in Tennessee between 1985/86 and 1988/89. He found that children in smaller classes did significantly better (5–8 percentage points) than their peers in larger classes, with these benefits accruing more strongly to pupils from poorer and minority households. This finding is consistent with other recent studies of the effect of class size (Hanushek *et al.* 1998; Angrist and Lavy 1999), but Hoxby (1998b) finds no evidence of a relationship between class size and attainment in a study of Connecticut schools. Vignoles *et al.* (2000) conclude that the evidence suggests that smaller classes have a small positive effect on educational outcomes, but that this is insufficient to justify the additional cost of reducing current class sizes.

One possible cause of variation in results from studies of class size is the dependence of outcomes on teaching style. If the teaching style is didactic and relies heavily on structured programmes we may expect the relationship between class size and outcome to be very small. Where teaching style is based on interactions between the teacher and individual pupils or small groups there is more reason to expect to find a relationship between class size and outcomes. Evidence of the dependence of these results on the form of teaching is provided in the study by Glass and Smith (1979). They found that in small classes where teaching was individualised, pupil attainment was higher.

Evidence suggests that teacher quality (intake and retention) does respond to pay (Murnane 1991; Ballou and Podgursky 1997a). If teacher quality has a significant effect on pupils' outcomes, teacher pay provides a mechanism through which market effects can impact on educational quality (an argument we examine in Chapter 6). The importance of variations in individual teacher quality in explaining educational outcomes is suggested by the variation in attainment across subjects within secondary schools (Schagen 1999). This outcome is hardly surprising given that the dominant form of education entails an individual teacher in the classroom with a class of pupils. Teacher quality has been measured through qualifications, years of experience, verbal achievement scores and salary earned. Whilst it is plausible to expect experience and qualifications to affect teacher quality, it is far from clear whether these effects would be linear or strong. Teacher effectiveness might be expected to rise with experience in the early years of teaching as new staff develop their skills. However, the grounds for assuming that this process of learning and development continues throughout teachers' careers are less clear. Belief in the importance of teachers' academic qualifications is apparent in teacher-training policy in England. One publicly reported measure of the quality of training institutions is the proportion of trainees possessing a First or Upper Second Class Honours degree. More direct measures of teacher quality are potentially available through the processes of monitoring and inspecting teaching. In England and Wales school inspections grade individual lessons observed, but this information is not made public (see Chapter 7).

A review of evidence of teacher effects by King and MacPhail-Wilcox (1994) finds that a majority of studies identify relationships between teachers' verbal attainment, years of experience and salary and pupil attainment. A study by Card and Krueger (1992) and a meta-analysis by Hedges *et al.* (1994) find strong effects of teacher quality on pupil attainment. Lord (1984) and Hanushek *et al.* (1998) find that more experienced teachers exert a positive effect on outcomes. Monk (1994) finds evidence that teachers' subject knowledge and training in pedagogy exert a positive effect on pupils' attainment. However, statistical evidence of the effect of teachers' education on pupil outcomes is restricted to the benefits to mathematics attainment of teachers' own mathematics education (Goldhaber and Brewer's 1997). The Hay McBer report (DfEE 2000) commissioned by the DfEE in England found no relationship between teachers' experience and education and teacher effectiveness. Vignoles *et al.* (2000: 51) conclude that 'there is some robust evidence that teacher experience and teachers' salaries have significant effects but that teachers' education levels (with the exception of teachers with qualifications in mathematics) do not'. However, the same survey concludes that 30 per cent of the variation in pupil progress can be attributed to teachers' skills, professional characteristics and classroom climate. This emphasis (though not the scale of impact) is consistent with Goldhaber and Brewer (1997) who also found that teacher's behaviour and techniques might be more important than their experience or education.

We are ultimately interested in whether market processes can affect the development and distribution of these skills that are held to promote pupil learning and the distribution of small, cost-inefficient classes. We consider the role of market incentives in developing teacher effectiveness in Chapter 6. Schooling markets may influence the distribution of more effective teachers through the salaries and working conditions they are able to offer. Combining the evidence on class size and teacher effects on pupil learning suggests an interesting tension for schools. If teacher effects outweigh class size effects there is a financial incentive for schools to offer higher salaries (through more posts of increased responsibility even within a national system of pay bargaining) to attract more highly skilled teachers. They can pay for the higher salaries by increasing class size. This should lead to an improvement in pupil attainment. However, the potential for increasing class size will be constrained by parental demand. If parents believe that class size is more important than teacher skill (which they can observe less easily), they will trade off the improvement in average attainment against increases in class size. If highly skilled teachers are, on average, attracted by working conditions and more able pupils are easier to teach, then schools with a high proportion of more able pupils will enjoy a virtuous circle. They will find it easier to attract teachers who will add more value to pupils' learning. We extend this analysis in Chapter 8.

Schooling markets may affect the distribution of small classes through the combined effect of low enrolment and a school's efforts to maintain a broad curriculum. A school facing a falling roll may seek to maintain a broad curriculum either to comply with regulations (as in the case of the National Curriculum in England and Wales) or to stem the fall in parental demand. The evidence on class size effects suggests that schools following this strategy will not gain any significant benefit in terms of rising pupil attainment.

School size

As we noted in Chapter 1, two factors that have an important bearing on the potential impact of market forces on schools are (1) the capacity of schools to change their resource levels to accommodate short-run changes in enrolment and (2) long-run relationships between school size, costs and schooling outcomes.

The ability of schools to increase enrolment depends on the existence of spare capacity or the capability to increase capacity. Schools may operate with spare capacity in their classroom accommodation and other physical resources or in their staffing levels. In principle, capacity may be increased in the short-term by hiring portable classrooms and new staff. In practice, these possibilities will be constrained by government regulation and the prevailing market for teachers.

The size of a school may have an impact through costs, outcomes or both. Until fairly recently (Lamdin 1995), studies of school cost functions and studies of school effects on pupil attainment have developed as separate bodies of research. In fact, even within the latter group of studies there is little cross-reference between production function studies carried out by economists and the school effectiveness literature. Smaller schools are likely to face higher long-run average costs in so far as they (i) carry a proportionately higher administrative burden; (ii) are required by regulation or parental preference to provide a broad curriculum; (iii) require teachers to cope with a wide range of responsibilities with little opportunity to develop specialist skills, and (iv) avoid grouping pupils of different ages in the same class. The broad curriculum constraint has more impact in secondary schools where subject specialists are employed for each part of the curriculum. This effect is pronounced in 16–19 education in England and Wales where a broader range of subjects is offered at a high level of specialisation to a smaller cohort than in 11–16 compulsory education. The different age constraint is more relevant in primary schools where the strategy of combining classes of pupils of different ages is more common, particularly in rural schools. Very large schools may also face increasing average costs due to the managerial problems created by the size of the institution. The maintenance of communication between staff adds to costs (through need for administrative staff and senior management time), but the key factor seems to be the problems in managing pupil behaviour (Haller 1992).

Studies of school costs in different countries have usually sought to examine cost per child (rather than cost per level of outcome). These studies have concluded that there are significant economies of scale as school size increases and that average size of existing schools is well below that optimum on cost minimisation grounds. From a study of 38 Canadian schools over three years (mean size 400–450), Kumar (1983) concludes that average costs decline proportionately with size and that the optimum school size is 800–1100. However, Kumar also finds that his estimation of average costs is not stable across the three years or across different types of school in the sample. Smet and Nonneman (1998) find that average costs would still be declining if secondary schools in Flanders were three times their current average size. Merkies (2000) estimates an average cost function for Dutch elementary schools that suggests an optimal size of 450, but with only modest cost savings as size increases beyond 200. Lamdin (1995) finds a modest (-0.22) correlation between school size and expenditure per pupil in Baltimore elementary (primary) schools with an average size of 469.

There are a number of reasons why we might expect small schools to produce higher levels of pupil attainment for a given ability of intake. Interactions between students, teachers and managers are more easily organised and the quality of these interactions ought to bear directly on pupil attainment. Low quality interactions may lead to pupil indiscipline and low school efficiency. Evidence of a negative relationship between school size and pupil behaviour in US schools is given by Fowler and Walberg (1991) and Haller (1992). If returns to the peer group are positive and diminishing, small primary schools that group together pupils of different ages might also benefit from peer group effects in so far as older children positively influence the learning of younger children. However, the more specialised resources that larger schools are able to employ might also have a positive effect on pupils' attainment so the a priori case is far from clear cut.

Evidence on the effect of school size on pupil attainment is available through studies in many countries over a wide time period. Reviewing US evidence in 1991, Fowler and Walberg conclude that small elementary schools have a positive effect on student achievement and satisfaction. However, other studies in the US and elsewhere (Michelson 1972; Brown and Saks 1975; Luyten 1994; Lamdin 1995) find no effect of size on attainment whilst Sander (1993) finds a positive effect. Recent evidence from Bradley and Taylor (1998) suggests that pupils' attainment in England has a non-linear relationship with school size. They estimate that average pupil attainment is maximised in 11–16 schools with an enrolment range between 900 and 1,500 and in 11–18 schools with an enrolment range between 1,200 and 1,800. The majority of English schools are currently smaller than these 'optimal' size ranges.

School size has routinely been included as a variable in statistical studies of school effectiveness. One problem facing researchers is that school size in primary education is strongly correlated with school location. Rural schools tend to be smaller and if school location is included as a separate variable it tends to pick up all the effect that might otherwise be attributed to school size. For example, Bondi (1991) finds no evidence of school size on the attainment of primary pupils in Scotland.

As argued by the Audit Commission (1996), the viable size of sixth forms depends on the range of courses on offer. Institutions that offer a narrower range of courses can afford a smaller sixth form, although they report that 58 per cent of school sixth forms in England and Wales had fewer than 150 students on roll, calling their financial viability into question. The range of sixth-form courses offered by many schools requires cross-subsidy and the growth of GNVQ (see Chapter 7) has tended to increase this range still further.

3.3.6 Management effects

School management might affect outcomes through the choice of inputs, the choice of outputs or the processes by which outcomes are generated. These choices may reflect overt decisions made by a headteacher or a governing body. However, it is also possible that the choice of inputs, outputs and processes in a school is the outcome of an evolving professional culture, which the school leadership can influence but not fully control. Our concern in this section is with any output effects from the way in which the school is run, whether the school operates like a 'rational planning model' (see Chapter 7) or whether strategy develops in a more emergent fashion. A considerable body of evidence on the relationship between school management and educational outcomes has been developed through the 'school effectiveness' research programme and this literature provides the evidence summarised in this section.

Through large-scale statistical studies and small-scale case studies, a body of evidence has been developed suggesting a number of management factors that influence (primarily academic or productivity) outcomes. We begin this section with two summaries of this evidence (Table 3.1).

Factors (1) and (2) in Table 3.1 can be seen in terms of 'input mix'. Involving parents or students takes teachers' time that might have been used in direct instruction of pupils. However, this involvement increases the total resources being devoted to the child's education. If this involvement leads to parents providing more encouragement or support to their child's learning, then this increase in resourcing could be considerable. If parent and student involve-

Table 3.1 School (management) factors affecting pupil outcomes

	Mortimore (1993)	Creemers and Reezigt (1996)
(1)	Parental involvement in the life of the school;	Policy on parental involvement
(2)	Student responsibilities and involvement in the life of the school	
(3)	Academic press and learning – teacher intervention focused on learning rather than administration	Focus on basic skills/learning time
(4)	High expectations that present an appropriate challenge for students' thinking	High expectations
(5)	Systematic use of rewards and incentives for pupils and teachers	Orderly environment and school climate
(6)	Monitoring student progress	Monitoring of student progress/evaluation
(7)	Strong positive school leadership	School educational/administrative leadership
(8)	Joint planning and consistent approaches towards students	Consensus and co-operation between teachers

Sources: Mortimore (1993); Creemers and Reezigt (1996)

ment leads to an increase in the child's motivation, the effective level of inputs is increased further. In fact, a number of the items (4, 5, 6) may bear upon the child's motivation, suggesting that this aspect of adjusting the input mix is crucial. It is interesting to note some aspects of input mix that are missing from the surveys summarised in Table 3.1. There is no reference to the use of information and communications technology and no reference to learning support assistants. The level of variation in use of these inputs appears to be insignificant for school effectiveness.

Rows (3) and (4) in Table 3.1 can be interpreted in terms of choice of outputs, although there is some suggestion of difference between the two categories in row (3). Whilst a focus on 'learning rather than administration' suggests a choice between pupil outcomes and bureaucracy, a focus on 'basic skills' suggests an emphasis on one part of the curriculum rather than another. Neither of these categories suggests an emphasis on investment in productivity outcomes rather than consumption, personal fulfilment or socialisation, contradicting Chubb and Moe's (1990) claim of the importance of 'goal confusion'. However, Mortimore's (1993) juxtaposition of learning and administration is consistent with Chubb and Moe's claim about the negative effect on schooling outputs of subservience to bureaucratic needs.

Rows (5) and (6) suggest the importance of school systems for maintaining teacher and student focus on the desired school goals. Standard texts on business strategy (e.g. Johnson and Scholes 1999) argue that organisational effectiveness is best served by clear broad statements of organisational goals supported by incentive and monitoring systems that keep employees tied to this agenda. The references to monitoring and incentives in rows (5) and (6) appear very similar. Orthodox economic analysis focuses on rewards to ownership of human capital in terms of streams of income, but this is an insufficient basis for the analysis of incentives within an organisation. Theories of motivation suggest that sense of social belonging and self-actualisation also provide important incentives for behaviour. Both of these may be satisfied by participation in the process of determining the direction of an organisation. The motivator of self-actualisation may also be served by a sense of personal achievement for a student or a teacher achieving good results. Thus, a school that seeks to induce teachers and students as owners of human capital to use that capital most effectively in the achievement of academic attainment may provide incentives in the form of social participation, influence and recognition, self-esteem and personal achievement. We examine how the market-based reforms have influenced these incentives in Chapters 6 and 7.

Mortimore's list might also be understood in terms of characteristics of organisations that are striving to improve the quality of their information about production processes. Given partial information the frontier of production will only be found by aiming high and feeling one's way towards a frontier of capability that cannot be perceived until it is experienced. Likewise, given partial information, collaboration between professionals may provide a better chance of realising a best attainable objective than relying on the knowledge of one individual. However, it is interesting to note that there is no reference to processes such as teacher learning, teaching style or the grouping of students by ability. The references to 'strong school leadership' in row (7) can be interpreted as a management style that exercises prerogative in establishing aims for the mix of outputs and monitoring the achievement of these aims. There is a tension here between the imposition of strategic aims by senior management and the emergence of the aims from dialogue between staff suggested by row (8). Rows (7) and (8) can also be interpreted in a way that presumes strong management involvement in the development teaching practices. Van de Grift and Houtveen (1999) present evidence suggesting that the practice of educational leadership in Dutch primary schools has developed such that a positive influence on pupil outcomes is now being observed. Both Goldhaber and Brewer (1997) and Murnane and Phillips (1981) find that the percentage of teacher time devoted to group work is negatively related to test scores, but this may result from endogeneity. Teachers may be more likely to rely on whole class teaching with more able children who make more rapid progress in their attainment.

The questions for our purpose in this book are (1) are the differences between schools identified by school effectiveness research open to external influence? And (2) are some schools less effective because they do not know what effective schools know or because they operate in a context that provides insufficient incentives to find out and apply what effective schools know? Two arguments suggest that market forces might provide external incentives for schools to adopt the characteristics described in this section. First, if they are under greater pressure to raise outcomes they have more reason to adopt practices they already believe will raise those outcomes. Second, they face a greater incentive to search out information on how to raise outcomes either through accessing the knowledge of others or through developing new knowledge about schooling through their own innovation and experience. We consider school objectives in Chapter 4 and the incentives created by schooling markets in Chapters 6, 7 and 8.

3.4 Conclusions

Schooling produces multiple private and social outputs, so a full assessment of markets in education must take this range into account. This places a heavy burden on the incentives that encourage schools to aim for an output that is allocatively as well as technically efficient. Market incentives that encourage schools to focus on one output or to ignore externalities will not maximise welfare. Open enrolment, which allows parents to send their children to the school of their choice, could provide suitable incentives in a fully informed world. Parents would choose schools according to the match between the schools' outputs and their own preferences. This is exactly the kind of solution that the market might be expected to generate, encouraging schools to specialise in meeting particular wants. However, in a world that is less well informed, it is not so easy. A government seeking to respond to this difficulty might improve the quantity of information available to parents. The publication of school performance data, as in England, is an example of this kind of policy. However, such a policy has to decide how to measure the different outputs and how to make that information publicly available, without introducing bias in relation to the range of private benefits and also encouraging parents to internalise externalities. We consider these problems in more detail in Chapter 7. These problems are compounded if valuations of alternative outputs and ability to interpret information about schooling outcomes varies systematically according to parents' SES background. We discuss the evidence for these propositions in Chapter 5.

We have also noted in this chapter that it is necessary to judge market reforms in terms of their impact on altering, rather than introducing, parental choice. As we saw in Section 3.2, some degree of choice of institution has long been a feature of post-compulsory education in England as elsewhere, with zonal systems being characterised by 'selection through mortgage'. This observation raises a number of issues that we follow up in later chapters. First, whilst the term 'quasi-market' is useful in classifying a large number of diverse partial extensions of market forces, in practice the choice for policy is far more varied than 'state allocation', 'quasi-market' or 'full market'. Parents and schools can be allowed varying degrees of freedom of choice and this adds to the interest, as well as the complexity in analysing market reforms in education. We follow up this issue in Chapter 4. Second, data generated from zonal allocation systems and choice of post-compulsory institution are products of established rather than emerging contexts. They have an advantage over data collected during a period of contextual change, and the learning behaviour that accompanies it. They, therefore, provide rich sets of data on the effects of choice processes in education. Evidence that competition between schools raises attainment and of the effect of parents' and pupils' expectations and switching costs on post-compulsory choice illustrate the implications that this research may have for a wide range of contexts for schooling choice. Third, these studies remind us that the impact of an education reform that changes the role of market forces is best evaluated in terms of how this reform changes choice processes and schooling outcomes. Perfect markets and pure systems of state allocation are useful theoretical reference points, but they are not practicable policy options. That is, we cannot foresee the circumstances in which either the state or parents are fully informed in the manner required by these policy stances.

The survey of schooling production processes also provides valuable insights for the assessment of the effect of market forces on schooling. Although analysing these processes is fraught with difficulty, current evidence suggests several features of schooling that are particularly important to our later analysis:

1   Academic attainment is powerfully correlated with home background, and parental support and expectations have an important effect on value added.
2   A pupil's attainment is strongly and positively correlated with the ability of their peer group. There is also some evidence to suggest that returns to peer group effects may be diminishing: the effect of an above average ability peer group makes more difference to the attainment of a less able child than to a more able child.
3   The gains to attainment from a smaller class size over the range of variation currently found in OECD countries are, at best, fairly small.
4   Many (most in England and the Netherlands) schools are smaller than the cost-minimisation optimum and few are larger. Small schools and small year groups (e.g. in the 16–19 age groups) are cost inefficient.
5   The quality of a school's management of resources does make a significant difference to average pupil attainment and the key features of effective schools are consistent across countries.

The powerful effect of home background and peer groups on pupils' attainment has important implications for the incentives that schools should face in the education market. If parents are principally attracted by evidence of average absolute attainment or by the ability of the peer group, then schools face an incentive to maximise the average ability of pupils they enrol. The strength of this incentive is apparent in current evidence suggesting that home background and peer effects far outweigh school effects in determining attainment. From points 3 and 4, we note that average costs are more strongly related to school size than average attainment. This has important implications for reliance on changes in enrolment, the key mechanism by which market forces should bear on schools. That is, an unpopular school experiencing a falling roll will also experience rising unit costs and falling cost effectiveness as measured in terms of the cost of a particular level of value added. Nevertheless, point (5) suggests that there is scope for incentives to encourage schools to adopt more effective practices. The overall effect of any change in market forces on schooling will depend on their combined impact on these five features. In the following chapters we seek to identify this impact.

4 Market reforms
Funding and open enrolment

4.1 Introduction

In Chapters 1 and 2 we reviewed theoretical arguments and the policy contexts that have influenced the implementation of market reforms in many OECD countries. We also noted in Chapter 3 that long-standing systems of allocating school places, such as zonal systems, incorporate some kind of choice mechanism and that any system for allocating school places might most usefully be evaluated against a best available alternative as opposed to an idealised market or idealised state provision of education. This leads us to ask what alternative methods of allocating school places might a policy maker choose between? In the next five chapters we seek to answer this question by surveying the range of policies that have been employed. In so doing we focus on the 'market' element within each: the scope for parents to choose between schools, the scope for schools to choose outputs and methods, and the interactions between these choices. In this chapter we focus on funding and enrolment. In Chapter 5 we review the operation of open enrolment in practice, relying principally on data from studies carried out in England and Wales. In Chapter 6 we examine teacher licensing, training and remuneration, and in Chapter 7 we consider issues of governance and monitoring. Accounts of the political processes that have established these policies may be found elsewhere (e.g. Carl 1994; Lauder *et al.* 1999; Karsten 2000).

We recognise that each system of allocating school places is rooted in traditions of practice and culture. If, as Lawton (1996) would have it, education is the process by which culture is transmitted from one generation to the next, then we would expect subcultures to seek to maintain systems for allocating school places that secure this objective. Thus we cannot properly understand the operation of markets in schooling in the Netherlands if we abstract from religious history, or understand the development of Magnet schools in the US without reference to desegregation (Carl 1994). We would also, therefore, expect cultural change, such as secularisation, to impact on the operation of any form of market influence in the allocation of school places. The impact of sociocultural conditions on the operation of market forces is amply illustrated by the contrast between the impact of apparently similar regimes in OECD and developing countries and this is a prime reason for including references to the latter in this chapter. A comprehensive account of the operation of market forces in schooling in developing countries is, however, well outside the scope of this book.

We organise this chapter in ten sections. Section 4.2 itemises the variety in the use of market forces in education and introduces four main categories that we use to analyse and evaluate these differences. The remainder of the chapter investigates the first two categories and we return to the other categories in Chapter 7. Section 4.3 introduces the theme of the balance of funding between central and local government, private sector sponsorship and parents. Section 4.4 briefly reviews the significance of the balance of central and local government funding. We are only concerned here with possible market implications of this choice. In Section 4.5 we examine the distribution of funding between the state and sponsorship from private sector organisations. In OECD countries this has principally involved sponsorship from Christian denominations, but more recently there has been an increase in various forms of business sponsorship as well as a broadening of the base of religious involvement in education. In Sections 4.6 to 4.9 we examine alternative bases for relating funding to parental choice. Section 4.6 focuses on systems where parents choose between paying full fees at private schools and paying no fee for enrolment at a public school. In Section 4.7 we review open enrolment systems in which public schools depend solely on state funding which is allocated on the basis of the number of pupils choosing the school. We pay particular attention to ways in which parental choice may be limited or extended through the design of open-enrolment systems. Section 4.8 examines voucher systems in which parents are able to supplement the amount allocated to them by the state, and in Section 4.9 we examine the implications of relying on 'for-profit' as opposed to 'not-for-profit' private providers of schooling. We present our conclusions to this chapter in Section 4.10.

4. 2 The variety of market forces in schooling provision

The market forces currently operating in national educational systems originate from differing time periods and, to some extent, have different underlying rationales. In addition, the form of quasi-market operating in each place is the product of social and cultural history as well as political intention and ideology. Thus, while market forces play some role in the allocation of schooling in many countries, there is considerable variation in the extent and focus of this role. In each case parents are able to exercise some degree of choice between schools, but in some countries this freedom is constrained by schools' ability to decide the basis on which they accept applicants. In other cases, parental choice is constrained by their ability to supplement a voucher provided by state funding. The extent to which the licensing, training and remuneration of teachers have been reformed to conform to market principles differs between countries and regions. As does the degree of freedom granted to local schools to manage their own affairs and this influences the capacity of schools to respond to parental preferences. There is also variation in the incentives created for schools and parents by quasi-markets. For example, in some cases all pupils attract the same unit of resource from governments to schools, whilst elsewhere some pupils attract higher government support than others. Another difference in incentives arises from whether schools operate on a for-profit or not for-profit basis. These differences are summarised below.

Box 4.1: Market freedoms for parents, teachers and schools

Funding basis for schools

1 Revenue varies with pupil enrolment at a fixed rate per pupil
2 Revenue varies partially with pupil enrolment at a fixed rate per pupil
3 Revenue varies with pupil enrolment, but with variable rates for different types of pupil
4 Revenue varies with pupil enrolment at a market price per pupil
5 Income derived from private sources other than pupil enrolments
6 Enrolments at private schools partially funded by the state
7 Schools able to retain financial surplus for spending in the next financial year
8 Schools able to distribute surplus to owners

Parents: open enrolment

9 Able to choose school, subject to capacity of chosen school (open enrolment)
10 Able to choose school, subject to meeting minimum selection requirements (selection)
11 Able to choose school, subject to willingness to pay (e.g. voucher system)

Teachers: training and pay

12 Able to enter and leave teaching profession with minimal constraints
13 Able to earn salaries consistent with external local labour market conditions
14 Able to receive incentive pay on the basis of performance

Schools: local school management

15 Able to choose basis for enrolment of pupils
16 Able to negotiate resource prices
17 Able to choose supplier of resources

---

18 Able to choose curriculum to be offered
19 Able to choose mix of resources employed
20 Able to choose teaching methods: deployment of resources
21 Able to choose the quantity of resources
22 Power to manage schools vested principally in governing boards or headteachers

Information and monitoring

23 Curriculum-based exit examinations
24 Comparable information on schools available for parents
25 Comparison through value added
26 Inspection Systems

The possibilities outlined above illustrate the limitations of terms such as 'market' or 'quasi-market' to describe schooling systems. The description of the market mechanism found in orthodox economics, described in Chapter 1, would require the presence of items 4, 7–8, 11–21, and 24 in this list. We will use the term 'quasi-market' to require, as a bare minimum, one of items 1–3, one of items 9–11, one of items 15 to 22, and item 24. That is, in a quasi-market parents must have some freedom to choose between schools, the resulting movement of pupils must affect school revenue and schools must have some freedom to deploy the resources they receive. This definition admits as quasi-market systems situations where the revenue per pupil is fixed by the state. The significant aspect of this definition is not that all schools receive the same payment per pupil. This would be found in an orthodox, perfectly competitive market, where all producers are 'price-takers' and the quality of schooling provided is identical. The significance lies in the unresponsiveness of payment per pupil to changes in the total demand for, and supply of, schooling in the local market and the absence of premium payments to schools for quality provided. In this chapter, rather than dwelling further on the precise definition of the term 'quasi-market', we summarise different aspects of the use of market forces in education as encompassed by the first two categories in Box 4.1.

4.3 Sources of school funding

Although the majority of schools in most countries have traditionally been administered and funded by the state (Levy 1987), we may identify three other sources of funding for schools: the local community, sponsorship from religious or business organisations and parents. Each source may finance capital or current expenditure. Privately owned schools may have their current expenditure financed through revenue earned via state contracts and publicly owned schools may subcontract services to private providers. Market forces may be used to partially direct each of these sources of funds, but the combination of sources used has some influence on the character of the market forces involved. The advantage for each potential supplier of capital funding for schools is the opportunity to influence the quantity of resources devoted to schooling and the way in which these resources are deployed. Private suppliers of items of current expenditure (from textbooks to agencies providing supply teachers) are more likely to be motivated by opportunities for profit. Reliance on 'for-profit' capital funding of schools has been less usual and we consider the implications of this in Section 4.9.

In Sections 4.4 and 4.5 we concentrate on the implications of the choice of balance of funding sources. The recent history of education reform has seen many examples where policy has been changed to shift this balance. For example, in England, successive governments have restricted the scope of Local Education Authorities (LEAs) to raise taxes to finance increased spending. Business sponsorship of schools has also been encouraged through the introduction of 'City Technology Colleges' and, more recently, through 'Public–Private Partnerships' (PPPs) in which private capital has financed renovations and extensions of school buildings. Parental funding has been widely encouraged in Eastern Europe as part of the liberalisation process since 1989 (Kersh 1998; Kreitzberg and Priimagi 1998; Švecová 2000). The World Bank has encouraged governments in developing countries to rely on private education to satisfy demand that cannot be met by current levels of state spending on education (James 1991; Jimenez *et al.* 1991). Increasing reliance on private funding and to a lesser extent on community funding can be found in Tanzania (Lassibille *et al.* 2000) and China (Mok and Wat 1998). Samoff (1991: 382) describes this process in Tanzania: 'generally, a community organizing committee recruited from political notables, sought church support, secured an appropriate site, mobilized voluntary labour, raised funds, employed partially trained staff, publicized its existence, and began to admit students'. Mok (1997: 270) reports that 'more than 70 per cent of primary and secondary schools in Guandong (China) have looked for alternative (private) income sources since 1978'. Private spending on schooling may also increase when rising demand for education is not satisfied by public provision, as in Greece (Kanellopoulos and Psacharopoulos 1997). We now examine current practice and implications of shifts in the balance of funding.

4.4 Funding via central government or local community

The balance of funding provided by central government or the local community determines the scope for communities (as opposed to individual parents) to choose the level of resources they wish to see devoted to schooling. This choice may be exercised through the ballot box and, through locational changes, the tax return. Within the United Kingdom voters in Scotland have consistently chosen to support a higher rate of spending per pupil in state schools than voters in England. This funding difference was associated for some time with higher average levels of attainment in Scotland than in England, although this gap has closed, whilst the funding difference has remained (Adnett *et al.* 2000). When taxation is raised on a very local basis there is scope for mobile households to choose where to live according to the level of school funding they wish to support (Tiebout choice as described in Chapter 3). However, the freedom of local municipal areas in England and Wales to set the level of school spending has been severely curtailed through controls on local taxation. The government school inspection service has also identified serious weaknesses in the operation of a number of Local Education Authorities, with the following extract from an inspection report reflecting the tone of such criticism:

> For much of the 1990s, political instability, evidenced in successive administrations and culminating at one stage in the virtual paralysis of the decision-making process, has handicapped practical action on education. Constraints on council finances have meant that although spending on education remains above the government's standard spending assessment, the funding of schools relative to that level has reduced.
>
> (OfSTED 1999, para. 5)

Another report on a LEA called for 'a change in the corporate culture of the LEA with clearer and more appropriate working relationships between (elected) members and officers, more transparent decision-making and a more consultative approach to schools'. It goes on to state that 'the senior officers' capacity for strategic management and leadership is poor' (OfSTED 1998b, paras. 5 and 6). Whilst such harsh judgements are to be found in only a minority of LEA inspection reports, they have been used as a basis for replacing local democratic control of schools by private sector management in a number of instances. In this way we see central government switching the responsibility for capital improvements it is unwilling to fund from taxation to private finance. We examine the role of private finance in not-for-profit schools in Section 4.5 and in for-profit schools in Section 4.9.

4.5 Private sector sponsorship

Religious, primarily Christian, organisations have traditionally played a prominent role in providing capital and overseeing the management of schools in a number of OECD countries. Analysis of the effect of this sponsorship is made complex by the variation in the proportion of schools' revenue accounted for in this way. Seven out of eight private enrolments in the US are religiously affiliated institutions, although sponsorship in these institutions generally accounts for a minority of total revenue. Levy (1987) reports that Catholic schools in the US rely on sponsorship for roughly one-quarter of their revenue. We return to the question of importance of the proportion of funding accounted for by sponsorship later in this section. For many decades France, Belgium and the Netherlands have operated schooling systems in which the state funds public and not-for-profit private schools, with the majority of private schools having a religious basis. In France, the proportion of the school population educated in the state-subsidised private sector is estimated at between 15 per cent (van Zanten 1996) and 18 per cent (Caille 1993). In the Netherlands, two-thirds of schools are private. Roughly 10 per cent of publicly financed schools in England and Wales are Catholic (Morris 1998). In France and the Netherlands, private schools have to demonstrate that they have a distinctive character or philosophy to be eligible for the subsidy (OECD 1994). Whilst the rationale for these schools drew initially from a desire to preserve religious observance, growing secularisation is changing the basis of parental choice between schools. For example, Ritzen *et al.* (1997) claim that the basis of choice in the Netherlands is shifting from religion to class.

Higher levels of attainment for religious schools have been reported in Belgium, the Netherlands, England and the US. Educational attainment of pupils from ethnic minority and lower SES backgrounds has been reported as higher in Catholic schools than in public schools in the US (Hill *et al.* 1990; Figlio and Stone 1997) and Belgium (Brutsaert 1998). Stevans and Sessions (2000) find a small, but significant academic advantage for private Catholic over public schools in the US, but find no performance gain for urban pupils from non-white ethnic groups. Dijkstra and Peschar (1996) identify distinct effects of religious schooling in the Netherlands on academic educational outcomes. They find the effect of Catholic schools stronger than the effect of Protestant schools. Mortimore *et al.* (1988) found a positive effect of Catholic schooling on primary school attainment in London. However, Bondi (1991) finds no evidence of religious affiliation on the attainment of primary school pupils in Scotland.

Amongst the possible explanations for an advantage for religious schools are: (1) a good match between the educational aims and moral values of the home and school; (2) parents opting to send children to a distinctive out-of-neighbourhood school may be more committed to supporting their children's education; (3) these schools may provide more positive peer group effects for pupils' learning; (4) religious schools may be less subject to 'bureaucratic intrusion' from municipal authorities; and (5) the impact of religious affiliation on the culture of these schools may be particularly conducive for learning. With regard to proposition (1), religious schools owe their establishment to a desire by religious communities to nurture children in developing particular moral values and beliefs, and this has traditionally been important in parents' choice of a religious school. An early study of Catholic schooling in the US (Greeley and Rossi 1966) concluded that the Catholic effect was principally due to the contribution made by parents and that the school only had a noticeable effect when the parents had strong Catholic convictions. Morris (1997, 1998) presents data from schools in England to support this argument. Comparing two Catholic schools he finds that the school with the stronger value added emphasises traditional Catholic beliefs and moral standpoints and exhibits a strong cultural homogeneity. In the later paper he observes that where Catholic schools serve a coherent and practising community having a clear and specific Catholic culture, the Catholic teachers working in them, who are likely to be steeped in the same culture, would seem to have an easier task in transmitting a set of values and attitudes than their colleagues in county schools where pupil backgrounds may be more culturally diverse.

(Morris 1998: 100)

Using survey data collected in Australia in the early 1980s, Anderson (1988) finds that 95 per cent of the recruits of Catholic schools have Catholic mothers and that mothers of children at Catholic schools were more than twice as likely as mothers at other schools to attend church at least once a month. He also finds a strong statistical association between attendance at a Catholic school, religious belief, religious observance and social conservatism. However, his data indicate that this is a family and not a school effect. Catholic families that are politically and socially conservative are more likely than other Catholics to choose a Catholic school for their children. In England and Belgium, where Catholic schools are funded by the state, a different picture emerges. Noden *et al.* (1998) note the loyalty of parents from a Catholic background to Catholic schools. In their small sample of interviewees all bar two had applied to Catholic secondary schools. However, they also observe an association between Catholic schooling and processes that may attract a wider range of parents. 'The religious affiliation of the school was also widely taken as an indicator of good discipline and academic quality' (*ibid.*: 227). In Belgium, where Catholic schools are supported by the state, religious and moral development appear to be less important in parents' choice than instructional quality (Billiet 1977).

With regard to proposition (2), parental support for students' learning may be inferred from the higher graduation rates reported by Catholic schools (Evans and Schwab 1995; Neal 1997; Sander 1997). This inference is based on the relationship between home background and students' post-compulsory schooling choices, discussed in Chapter 3. However, the studies cited above do aim to correct for the 'selectivity bias' introduced by propositions (1) and (2). For example, Dijkstra and Peschar control for social background and the strength of parents' religious affiliation. Peer effects (proposition 3) are less clearly controlled for, although Brutsaert (1998) finds no significant correlation between SES mix and the attainment of lower SES children.

Any case for extending the role of religious schools further, as currently proposed by the government in England and Wales, depends on propositions (4) and (5). The case for the bureaucracy argument is weakened by the presence of regional church boards in the administration of church schooling, whether in the private sector (as in Australia or the Netherlands or the USA) or the public sector (as in the UK). However, this judgement may be tempered by Hannaway's (1992) evidence of organisational differences between public and Catholic schools in the USA. She uses data in which teachers and principals report their views on the relative importance of different stakeholders on key schooling decisions. She finds that school boards and area superintendents exert significantly more influence on the curriculum, instruction method and resource allocation in public schools than in Catholic schools. It is not clear why one type of bureaucracy would be better than another. Thus, the case for extending religious schooling would appear to rest on the fifth argument, and current evidence does not allow a conclusive judgement on its validity.

We turn now to attempts to secure business sponsorship, where the UK and the US have followed rather different paths. The City Technology College (CTC) scheme in the England and Wales and the New American Schools Program aimed to use business sponsorship to introduce 'mould-breaking' schools (Carl 1994). The CTC scheme in England failed to match expectations in that relatively small amounts of business sponsorship have been attracted and those schools established under the scheme have not offered radically different forms of schooling. Research summarised by Edwards and Whitty, conducted during the early years, concluded that 'CTCs' main appeal was neither a direct relevance to employment … nor the usually substantial provision for information technology, but parents' beliefs that these new schools were at least partly selective, were better resourced and were more likely to uphold traditional values and discipline' (Edwards and Whitty 1997: 36–7). The New American Schools Program in the USA has attracted far more significant funding, with large contributions from a string of major transnational, US-based companies. It has also pursued a rather different strategy. Sponsors' donations have been used to fund a research and development programme in which school districts and individual schools are invited to participate. Unlike the CTC initiative, the New American Schools program has sought to work with and through existing structures set up to channel state funding into education. One similarity with the CTC initiative is that the level of state involvement is now stronger than initially envisaged.

More recent policy in England has sought to engage private capital in partnership with public sector bodies in capital funding for developments in schooling. In this respect it echoes the approach to private capital in the New American Schools program. Education Action Zones (EAZs) were introduced in England in September 1998. The policy aimed for 10 per cent of English state schools to be within an Education Action Zone by September 2001. Each EAZ includes a small group of urban schools working in partnership with each other, the municipal authority and business sponsors to raise educational standards in disadvantaged areas. 'Among the schools are many where standards have been at a relatively low level and some judged by inspections to have serious weaknesses or be in need of special measures' (OfSTED 2001, para.7). Capital for these zones is provided partly by the state (75 per cent) and partly by sponsorship (25 per cent). The aims of these zones are illustrated by the objectives of one such zone below.

Box 4.2: The objectives of an Education Action Zone

What's Expected

Increase 5+ GCSE A*−C from 33% to 51% by 2003
Increase level 5+ Science in Key Stage 3 from 26.5% to 47.5% by 2003
Raising achievement at the end of each Key Stage, ages 7, 11, 14 and 16
More children achieving the highest levels at the end of each Key Stage
Real improvements in the quality of teaching and learning
More pupils staying on in further and higher education
A reduction in the number of pupils 'not yet settled' at age 16
Improved attendance
Reduced exclusions
Improving the quality of leadership and management in schools
More parents and carers involved in supporting their child's education
More support for parents and carers

Stoke-on-Trent Education Action Zone (DfEE 2001e)

As concern with the intractable nature of educational standards in these areas has continued, new policies have followed rapidly on the heels of EAZs under a general banner of an 'Excellence in Cities' programme. Notable amongst these are plans for 'City Academies'. This policy combines the public–private partnership encouraged by the EAZ programme, but returns the focus to the individual school. 'Businesses, churches and other faith groups, and voluntary bodies interested in sponsoring and managing a City Academy are invited to discuss their ideas with the DfEE. Potential sponsors may be involved in running existing schools, but need have no direct educational experience' (DfEE 2001e).

Sponsors of a City Academy will provide around 20 per cent of the initial and on-going capital costs and the schools will be:

- at the heart of their communities, sharing their facilities with other schools and the wider community;
- registered as independent schools, subject to inspection by OfSTED, but charging no fees;
- endowed with 'state of the art' facilities (whether in new build or refurbished premises), with sponsors making a contribution towards the capital costs;
- owned and run by sponsors, and receive government grants on conditions agreed with the Secretary of State;
- able to admit up to 10 per cent of pupils to each new year 7 cohort on the basis of aptitude for the school's specialism.

The rationale for the state seeking to attract private capital in a partnership model is not immediately obvious. We dismissed the public borrowing limit argument in Chapter 2. As the state can always borrow at a lower rate of interest than a private company, it must pay a premium for relying on privately raised capital. If private capital secures control of the strategic direction of the school, it might be argued that it may use its private sector expertise to introduce clear focus and efficient procedures (although as we have seen in the case of CTCs in England this does not appear to have resulted in distinctive schools). If private capital only secures a minority stake in partnership with existing municipal and school management, the outcomes will be dependent on the interactions between these partners. Ideally, this relationship will create a synergy between complementary expertise. Alternatively, it may increase conflict between competing schooling aims, undermining attempts to improve schools.

4.6 Parents paying for schooling

Basic economic theory predicts that greater reliance on parents paying for schooling will increase the impact of parental income, school fees and parental tastes on the effective demand for schooling. The effect of income and socio-economic background (which may be partly related to tastes, as noted in Chapter 3) have received more attention in published research and we concentrate our attention in this section on these variables. There are considerable difficulties in estimating income elasticity of demand when the government plays the major role in funding schools. Nevertheless, studies suggest that the income elasticity of demand for schooling is considerably greater than one, meaning that the demand for schooling rises proportionately faster than income. This is important for two reasons. First, as income in a country rises, the demand for schooling will rise by a higher proportion. If schooling is supplied only by the state and real spending on education increases in line with real income, then there will be excess unfulfilled demand. Second, at any one point in time, the proportionate difference in demand for schooling from high-income and low-income households will exceed the proportionate difference in their income.

Whilst spending on education varies positively with countries' per capita income, private spending on education also varies inversely with government spending. Private household spending on education varies significantly across countries even within Europe (Table 4.1), forming over 1 per cent of all private spending in countries such as Greece.

In Greece, private spending on education accounted for 4.7 per cent of total spending of households with a non-zero spending on education in 1988. This high level of private spending can be attributed (Kanellopoulos and Psacharopoulos 1997) to previous limited public provision of Higher Education (HE) in Greece and the prohibition of private sector provision for HE. This resulted in high private spending by households in competition for scarce

Table 4.1   Private spending on education in selected European countries

Country	Private spending on education as a percentage of total household expenditure in 1988
Denmark	0.32
Greece	1.58
France	0.45
Ireland	1.22
Luxembourg	0.97
Netherlands	0.41

Source: Kanellopoulos and Psacharopoulos (1997)

university places and foreign language tuition in preparation for students entering HE in another country. Kanellopoulos and Psacharopoulos estimate the private income elasticity of this demand at 3.2.

Parental demand for fee-paying schools is related to their income in OECD and developing countries (Psacharopoulos 1987). In a study of schooling in a city in Pakistan, Alderman *et al.* (1996) find that the probability of a child attending a private school is strongly positively correlated with parental income and negatively correlated with the level of school fees. However, some parents in lower income brackets chose to send their children to fee-paying schools. One interesting aspect of this decision is that class size *and* teacher salaries are significantly lower in the private schools. Assuming that teacher salary affects teacher quality, this implies that these parents believe that class size has more impact on educational attainment than teacher quality. A US study by Williams *et al.* (1983) found that roughly 5 per cent of families earning under $15,000 a year sent their children to private schools, compared to roughly a quarter of parents earning over $50,000. Anderson (1988) found that the probability of attending a private school in Australia rose by 2 per cent for each $1,000 increase in the father's income. However, other factors are also important, notably whether the father attended a private school and is in a high status occupation. Values also play a role. Anderson finds that if the father attaches a high value to financial reward in career choice the child is more likely to attend a private school. Anderson also finds that parents with 'high intellectual interests' (such as a liking for philosophical discussion) are more likely to send their children to a private school.

Using UK data, Noden *et al.* (1998: 225) also observe a variety of factors influencing parents' choice of a private education. In some cases this choice arose from 'a strong (family) tradition of using the private sector'. Some parents also spoke of the choice of private schooling in terms of choosing an appropriate peer group: 'I want to feel safe and know that the people my children are going to school with are the sort of people I would converse with anyway' (*ibid.*: 225). Other parents had chosen private schooling at primary level in order to enhance their child's chances of passing entrance examinations at selective secondary schools. In this study, parents also identified the factors that they believed would influence their child's academic attainment: smaller class sizes, personal attention and peer groups.

The location of schools may also have a strong influence on parents' choice of private schooling. For example, enrolment in a public school in Zimbabwe is not always a realistic option for parents. Private fee-paying community schools in Zimbabwe serve 70 per cent of the population, a majority of whom live in rural areas where distance entails that only one school is available (Ilon 1992). One consequence of this is that parents in rural areas send their children to local schools that are less well resourced than government schools elsewhere in the country and pay higher fees for the privilege.

We turn now to evidence of the outcomes of private compared with public schools. The evidence that private schools achieve higher levels of academic outcomes than state schools is frequently reported in academic studies and reinforced in the public consciousness through publications of academic league tables based on raw scores. However, the important question for efficiency and welfare is whether private schools achieve a higher value-added than state schools. US evidence (McPartland and McDill 1982; Murnane 1986) has suggested that the higher absolute levels of attainment of students at private schools primarily reflect their higher ability on entry to the school. A study of private and public schooling in Australia by Williams and Carpenter (1991) finds a small private secondary school advantage in valued added. They also find that pupils of similar ability are more likely to continue into higher education if they have been taught in a private school. However, although they account separately for parental expectations in their model, they do not take the ability of the peer group into account, relying on pupils' reports of the likely destinations of their peer group. They attribute the greater likelihood that pupils from private schools will continue into higher education to qualities of the school, rather than the selection process for higher education. Van Cuyck and Dronkers (1990) find contrasting results for the Netherlands. They find that, after controlling for student ability and socio-economic background, students from public schools were significantly more likely to continue to a university education than students from private Catholic schools.

Jimenez *et al.* (1991) present results from a study of private and public schools in the Dominican Republic. They categorise schools into three groups: high status private schools that charge high fees and enjoy high status, public schools and lower status private schools that charge low fees and have a reputation below that of public schools. After controlling for socio-economic background and initial attainment they find that both types of private school produce a higher value added than public schools, with the highest value added in the high status private schools. However, this effect is almost entirely accounted for in their data by a combination of teacher education and peer effects.

Psacharopoulos (1987) reports superior effects of private schooling over public schooling in Colombia, but he does not include peer effects in his model. In Tanzania, he finds that private schools marginally outperform public schools in academic subjects, but trail in commercial, technical and agricultural tests. Another study of Tanzanian schools by Lassibille *et al.* (2000) finds that the value added by public schools is significantly higher than that of private schools. Both studies agree that as the public schools have higher costs per unit, the cost effectiveness of private schools is higher (ranging from 1.17 to 1.45 that of public schools). They also find that the expansion of private schools in Tanzania was accompanied by a 'decline in access to secondary schooling among children from disadvantaged backgrounds' (*ibid.*: 2).

Of these studies, those that report an advantage to private schools have not taken account of peer effects. In contrast, studies including peer effects in their model report no advantage to private schools. The implication for the individual parent is that their child will gain an academic advantage from attending a private school and they must then judge whether this gain is worth the fees they will be charged. However, this provides no basis for a policy of encouraging attendance at private schools as, on this interpretation, the result is simply a redistribution of peer effects which increases inequality and may lower overall educational attainment.

Given uncertainties in the interpretation of the data, it is sensible to consider also the process by which it has been suggested private schools may gain an efficiency advantage. Chubb and Moe (1988, 1990) argue that private schools are able to focus on more narrow objectives than public schools. For example, privately owned schools in the US, unlike public schools, are not bound by the requirement of religious neutrality and are subject to less legislation on discrimination. They offer a more restricted curriculum (Salganik and Karweit 1982; Coleman *et al.* 1982). These factors should provide advantages in terms of demand and supply. On the demand side, it may be argued that specialised schools enable parents to choose a school that supports their personal values and concentrates on securing the particular educational outcomes they seek for their child. We have already noted some evidence for this process in the case of religious schools. On the supply side, it is argued that schools with narrow objectives gain production efficiencies from their specialisation (Clark 1984). Difficulties in finding adequate measures of educational outputs other than academic attainment render this hypothesis difficult to test. However, Smet and Nonneman (1998) find evidence that, for schools in Flanders, average costs decline as schools offer a broader range of curricular outcomes across the academic–vocational spectrum.

Moreover, according to Brown (1992), the difference between private and public sector schools is restricted to what he terms 'secondary objectives', suggesting that private schools aim for 'primary' objectives that are as broad as those found in public schools. He defines primary objectives or services as including traditional academic subjects such as mathematics, workplace socialisation through vocational studies, athletic activities, music and art. He defines secondary services as those that cater for the social and spiritual welfare of the child, although he provides no rationale for determining what constitutes a primary and what constitutes secondary service.

4.7 Open enrolment systems

In this section we refer principally to the open enrolment systems that have been introduced in a number of US states (Hess 1992), the UK and New Zealand. In an open enrolment system parents are able to choose a preferred state approved school and each school is funded according to the number of students enrolled. This creates a potential for parents to influence decisions made by schools in so far as funding flows to schools that best satisfy parental demands. This presumes that parents have an opportunity to choose between schools and have sufficient information and ability to interpret information and identify quality differences between those schools. We examine these assumptions in Chapters 5 and 7. For the moment we will assume that these conditions are satisfied and we examine the processes by which an open enrolment system may work and the varieties of open enrolment systems. In particular, we consider (i) the funding provided to the school; (ii) the scope provided to the school to deploy that funding; and (iii) the adjustment mechanism in over- and under-subscribed schools.

There are two important ways in which per-pupil funding to the school may be varied. First, funding devolved to schools may be only partially related to pupil enrolment (Option 2 in Box 4.1). For example, in Stockholm only 50 per cent of school budgets are directly linked to enrolment. One reason for this is that funds for capital expenditures are generally managed at the district level, on the basis that the need for such funds reflects the long-run history of the building stock. The proportion of a school's funds provided on a per-pupil basis will affect the impact of a change in the number of pupils enrolled. An additional pupil enrolled will reduce average income per pupil to the extent that a proportion of income is fixed. The relationship between the fixed element in revenue and the fixed costs of the school (those costs that are unchanged when the number of pupils enrolled changes) thus becomes pivotal to the effect of enrolment changes on school finances. However, in so far as marginal changes in the number of pupils can be absorbed into existing classes there is a countervailing effect whereby the increase in school income is not matched by an increase in school costs.

Second, the state may vary the rate of funding to the school according to the characteristics of pupils enrolled (Option 3 in Box 4.1). By matching per-pupil funding to the cost of schooling different types of pupil, the state can try to avoid schools enrolling only those pupils who are cheapest to teach. For example, in England and Wales, per-pupil funding is calculated according to a complex formula taking into account pupils' special needs and other sources of disadvantage. A summary of the principles underlying this procedure is given by Levačić and Ross (1998). Given the association between social disadvantage and parental income, this enables the state to secure a flow of per-pupil funding to schools in which there is an inverse relationship between parental income and per-pupil funding. Preserving equality of opportunity provides a strong basis for the value judgement underpinning this policy. Disadvantage that accrues from differences in the level of parental support before and during schooling is typically discounted by such systems.

The scope provided for schools to choose the deployment of funds generated by pupil enrolments influences the incentives created by open enrolment. We are interested here in the combination of open enrolment with items 15–21 in Box 4.1. We develop our analysis of these combinations fully in Chapter 5, but we illustrate them here with reference to education reforms first introduced in New Zealand in 1989. Responsibility for resource mix and recruitment of teachers was devolved to boards of trustees responsible for individual schools. Initially, the state retained responsibility for paying teachers' salaries and some administration costs, though budgeting responsibility has since shifted more towards the local school. The New Zealand Curriculum Framework provides general guidelines for schools, but permits more freedom than experienced by schools in England. As responsibilities are devolved to schools more decisions become open to influence by parents' choice of school. A school may judge the wisdom of employing a more expensive teacher or broadening its curriculum partly on the basis of their impact on parental demand. However, the scope for this influence depends on the way in which the system deals with the relationship between parental demand and school capacity.

Open enrolment may be constrained by limits on school expansion and contraction or by policies directly impacting schools' enrolment of particular types of pupil. We concentrate first on problems associated with limitations on the expansion and contraction of schools' capacity. Schools in New Zealand become closed to further enrolment when they indicate that they are in danger of overcrowding, whilst in France parental choice is also restricted if enrolments at another local school become too low. In contrast, when schools in the Netherlands become oversubscribed the state takes responsibility for increasing the school's capacity. When a school becomes oversubscribed places may be allocated according to chance or according to a variety of decision rules: (i) distance of residence from the school; (ii) whether a sibling is already educated at the school; (iii) general academic ability; (iv) aptitude for the school's specialism; or (v) parental commitment. The basis on which over-subscription is resolved is likely to have a substantial influence on the impact of an open enrolment policy.

Initially, the reforms in New Zealand guaranteed a school place for 'in-zone' pupils and provided for a ballot system to determine which 'out-of-zone' applications would be accepted. Subsequent changes allow schools to choose how they allocate places to applicants, with no requirement to offer places to children living in the former zone of the school. In England, LEAs are responsible for making sure that parents have an opportunity to express their preferences in choice of school and are charged with making sure the allocation of places maximises the degree to which these preferences are satisfied. School places must not be allocated on the basis of gender (other than for single-sex schools) or ethnicity, but the admissions authority (the LEA or the school depending on the governance) may determine its own criteria in relation to the points (i)–(v) cited above. These criteria must be published. Schools are allowed to be non-selective with regard to ability, partially selective or wholly selective, with the proviso that only a wholly selective school may choose not to recruit up to its capacity (DFES 2001). We investigate the impact of these policies in Chapter 8.

Open enrolment might also be constrained through quotas. Quotas may specify an exact proportion, a minimum proportion or maximum proportion of enrolments that should be from a target group of pupils, or achieved by a particular enrolment process. A quota might set a maximum proportion of pupils to be enrolled via a selection process, a minimum proportion to be enrolled with special educational needs or an exact proportion to be enrolled from an ethnic group. Quotas of this kind may be justified by a belief that desegregated schooling results in a better set of outcomes from the schooling system. Carl (1994: 314) refers to this as 'open enrolment coupled with an overriding requirement of racial balance'. A scheme in Cambridge, Massachusetts introduced within-district open enrolment with racial-mix quotas to reduce segregation. In three years between 1985 and 1988 the proportion of children in elementary schools passing reading, maths and writing basic skills tests rose from 54 per cent to 87 per cent (Hess 1992: 159). Desegregation of pupils via movement between school districts was also the objective of schemes in St Louis and Milwaukee. In practice, the movement of pupils was one-way: from city to suburban districts.

Quotas might also be introduced to secure a particular distribution of peer effects. Mixed ability schooling will provide a more equitable distribution of academic outcomes given positive peer effects and a higher aggregate level of academic outcomes if peer effects are subject to diminishing returns. In addition, social and ethnic mixing in schooling may result in greater social cohesion if it results in better levels of mutual understanding between social groups. It is interesting to note that open enrolment systems tend to be combined either with formulas that utilise per-pupil funding or quotas to combat potential problems of inequality. In principle, a system could deploy both of these devices.

4.8 Voucher systems

We include within this section all schemes by which the state pays all or part of the school enrolment fee on behalf of the pupil. These schemes may operate when some schools remain fully publicly owned and funded (such as the Assisted Places Scheme (APS) in England) or where enrolments at all schools are accompanied by voucher payments. We briefly review some models of voucher systems and then examine evidence of outcomes in practice. The introduction of a voucher changes the relative price to the parent of private schooling. As the voucher value increases, the relative price of private schooling falls and more parents will choose a private school in preference to their neighbourhood state school. Equilibrium occurs when no parent can get an additional benefit from choosing another school that exceeds the additional cost that they would incur in enabling their child to go to the school. In this situation, schools are under pressure to reduce costs and respond to parental preferences.

Some predictions of the introduction of a voucher system are unambiguous: enrolments at private schools will increase and (barring regulation that prevents market entry) the number of private schools will increase. However, claims for the efficacy of voucher systems (e.g. West 1997) generally ignore several factors that are likely to exert a significant effect in practice: the continued presence of public schools alongside private schools, the presence of peer effects, and the impact of donations from sponsoring organisations. Models of voucher systems which take these factors into account (for example, Hoenack 1997; Rangazas 1997; Epple and Romano 1998) suggest that the theoretical grounds for expecting outcome gains from the introduction of a voucher system are not conclusive. Epple and Romano's model (in which peer effects play a strong role) predicts that 'the entry of private schools and consequent more efficient sorting of students across schools caused by vouchers increases average welfare and achievement only a little ... while having larger distributional effects' (*ibid.*: 35). Rangazas concludes that the effects of a voucher scheme on outcomes is ambiguous, with potential efficiency gains in private schools being balanced by potential efficiency losses in public schools and through private schools accumulating market power. With these predictions and questions in mind we now turn to evidence from the implementation of voucher systems.

Voucher systems so far implemented have varied in a number of respects: (1) the proportion of the enrolment fee paid by the state; (2) how eligibility of pupils to participate in the scheme is determined; and (3) how eligibility of schools to participate in the scheme is determined. If the value of the voucher equals the average cost of schooling in the state sector it can be argued that the scheme redirects government spending, but does not affect its level. If the voucher is less than the average cost of government schooling, the scheme can contribute to a reduction in government spending. However, scope for this is limited by the financial viability of private schools, as evidenced by the increase in subsidy to private schools in New Zealand in the 1970s in order to avoid financial collapse (McGeorge 1995). The scheme may be made open to all pupils or restricted to a certain group. A number of schemes have restricted eligibility to pupils from low-income families. Typically, schools must register with the state to be eligible to be reimbursed for the vouchers they accept. This enables the state to control eligibility and to provide incentives for schools to aim for a balance of outputs and adhere to production practices acceptable to the state. That is, the state could choose to use quota systems to determine eligibility and could use differential vouchers to increase the incentives for schools to enrol certain types of pupil. We first consider schemes (in Chile and Sweden) that have been open to all pupils and then schemes (in England, the US, Colombia, Bangladesh) targeted at particular groups of pupils. We conclude with a brief review of the Dutch scheme that effectively provides a basic voucher for all pupils and a 'premium' voucher for some.

Chile introduced a voucher scheme in 1981 to direct state support for enrolment of pupils at deregulated private and municipally run schools. Vouchers equivalent to average per-pupil spending of the Ministry of Education were made available on equal terms for all parents. Eligible schools had to comply with government regulation concerning the curriculum and the quality of accommodation. During the 1980s this led to a major shift of pupils from municipal to private schools. At the same time, real spending on education (combined public and private) decreased, with education spending as a proportion of GNP declining from 5.3 per cent to 3.7 per cent. As yet, evidence suggests that there has been no overall increase in school enrolment as a result of this reform. However, private schools appear to have outperformed public schools on cost effectiveness (Carnoy 1998) and average attainment (Espinola 1995; Rounds Parry 1996), whilst increasing inequality of outcome in relation to socio-economic background has resulted (Schiefelbein 1991). Private schools have achieved greater cost effectiveness partly through higher average class sizes and their advantage in average attainment is due in part to the socio-economic background of pupils they have attracted. In 1990 the distribution of pupils between private and municipal schools was strongly related to household income (Table 4.2).

Unfortunately Carnoy does not provide figures for the period before 1981, so it is not possible to judge whether the data in Table 4.2 suggests an increase or decrease in stratification. Many over-subscribed schools used selection to determine their intake and Rounds Parry (1996) found that average test scores were higher by almost 6 percentage points in schools selecting their intake, after controlling for average socio-economic background.

Between 1991 and 1996 a voucher scheme operated in Sweden whereby any pupil enrolling at approved private schools attracted a state subsidy equivalent to 85 per cent of the average per pupil cost of state schooling. Although survey evidence suggested that this policy was popular with parents, only 7 per cent of parents applied to send their child to a school outside their neighbourhood. Yet this figure appears high in the context of the low proportion of students educated in private schools, being only 1.1 per cent in 1992/93. The impact of this subsidy is indicated by the 20 per cent increase in enrolments at private schools in the year after the policy was introduced. This increase was not, however, evenly distributed across parents. 'Parents with a university education

Table 4.2   Enrolment in Chile's municipal schools and household income

Household income	Percentage of pupils enrolled in municipal schools in 1990
Lowest 40% of income distribution	72%
40%–80% of income distribution	51%
Top 20% of income distribution	25%

Source: Carnoy (1998)

and living in urban areas were better informed about school choice and more likely to choose another school from the one assigned' (Carnoy 1998: 333–4).

Voucher schemes targeted at low-income groups have been introduced in Milwaukee in the United States, in England, in Bangladesh and Colombia. In the Milwaukee scheme the value of the voucher is set at the average cost of education in government schools. Introduced in 1990, vouchers of up to $2,500 were made available for children from families in the lowest 1 per cent of the income range. By 1995/96 the value of the voucher had risen to $4,375. In practice, the aver-age income of families with children participating in the scheme is half the average income of families with children in state schools. Survey evidence indi-cates that parents who participated in this scheme felt their child's education improved as a result (Carnoy 1998). In an initial review Witte (1992) suggests that this scheme has not significantly improved the performance of students taking part in the scheme after controlling for socio-economic background. In the mid-1990s evidence as to whether the scheme had significantly improved educa-tional outcomes remained unclear (Witte 1996b). Initially, teacher salaries in the participating schools were lower, with the effect that cost effectiveness of these schools was higher than non-participating schools. However as the scheme progressed this salary differential and cost effectiveness advantage disappeared (Carnoy 1998). While these results are not very encouraging, supporters of voucher schemes such as West (1997) have been able to point to evidence that the scheme has not encouraged segregated schools and that students from the very poorest families are well represented on the programme.

A recently elected Conservative government in 1980 introduced the Assisted Places Scheme in England. The scheme was designed to cater for pupils with above-average ability from families with below-average income. It assumed that these children would necessarily gain a better education at a private school. Given the importance of peer group effects in schooling outcomes (discussed in Chapter 3), there were good grounds for this assumption in so far as they related to gains to the individual pupil. However, these need to be set against the nega-tive peer group effects resulting from their departure from state schools. Through this scheme the state paid the full enrolment fee at a private school. By 1995 about 29,800 such places were being funded (West 1997).

The Bangladesh scheme was introduced in 1982 to increase enrolment of girls from low-income families and succeeded in increasing secondary enrol-ment from 27.3 per cent to 47.5 per cent in 5 years (King and Bellew 1993). Colombia introduced a voucher scheme in 1992 to increase the proportion of children from low-income families continuing with secondary education and to relieve overcrowding pressure on government schools. Since 1996 school eligi-bility has been restricted to not-for-profit schools. By 1997 it involved 100,000 children in 2,000 private schools (King *et al.* 1997). In this scheme local munic-ipalities choose whether to join the scheme, making a commitment to fund 20 per cent of the value of vouchers when they agree to do so. The value of the voucher has risen sharply during the operation of the scheme. Between 1994 and 1996 the value of the voucher rose from roughly one-half to three-quarters of the average cost of schooling in a state school. Pupils are only eligible to participate if they have attended a state primary school (King *et al.* 1997). Take-up has been strongest amongst urban municipalities facing pressure on their public schooling provision and able to draw upon an existing private school capacity. The number of vouchers issues in the scheme was cut back sharply between 1994 and 1996 reflecting a change in political mood. The scheme has resulted in the following categories of schools: public schools non-fee paying; private schools with low fees not participating in the voucher scheme; private schools with medium fees participating in the voucher scheme; private schools with high fees not participating in the voucher scheme. King *et al.* (1997) explain this phenomenon by suggesting that parents use vouchers to 'trade-up' to the middle-ranking schools, leaving the low-quality, low-fee private schools to parents who do not have access to vouchers.

In Holland the government is obliged to fund all schools at an equal level (Louis and van Velzen 1991) and private schools are only able to charge fees for extra-curricular activities (OECD 1994). Primary schools get additional teachers if they enrol a higher proportion of children with poorly educated parents (OECD 1994; Ritzen *et al.* 1997). The effect of this weighted system is that the payment the school receives for enrolments from ethnic minority students is 90 per cent higher, and for students from low socio-economic backgrounds 25 per cent higher, than for students from privileged backgrounds. Schools appear to use these resources to reduce class sizes. Per-pupil funding from the state may be supplemented by contributions from parents. Ritzen *et al.* (1997) note that many private schools in the Netherlands demand a financial contribution from parents, although there is a low ceiling on allowable fees and students cannot be excluded on the basis of non-payment (James 1991). As parents from higher socio-economic groups can afford larger contributions, these payments introduce incentives for schools and parents. Schools have an incentive to recruit parents from higher socio-economic backgrounds and all parents face an incentive to send their children to schools with a high proportion of children from high socio-economic backgrounds.

The extent of state funding for private schools varies. In France, the state pays the salaries of teachers in private schools, but other costs have to be met by funds raised by the school or the charitable foundation operating the school. Whilst the state is responsible for teacher recruitment for public schools, private schools are responsible for their own recruitment. These levels of subsidisation are high by international standards (Jimenez *et al.* 1991) and they are associated with a high degree of state regulation, notably over the curriculum. In contrast, subsidies and regulation in Australia private schools are low. The positive relationship between the level of subsidisation and the degree of regulation may be viewed in terms of a principal–agent relationship where the subsidy from the state provides the incentives for entrepreneurs to submit to the regulation (James 1991). One interesting aspect of public funding for private schools in Sweden is that some newly established private schools resulted from community initiatives to retain a local school that the state wished to close for financial reasons.

There are differences between government control of the curriculum in these three countries. In France the curriculum in all schools is governed by centralised rules and national examinations, with private schools having some scope for local curriculum variation. In Holland schools are, in principle, free to develop their own curriculum, but while content and delivery are 'firmly vested in the hands of professional interest' (Louis and van Velzen 1991: 502) differentiation between schools' curricula and teaching methods is small (Glenn 1989). However, government control over the curriculum is influenced in each of these countries through final examinations for secondary schools.

4.9 For-profit versus not-for-profit schools

In Section 4.5 we considered the role of private sector sponsorship of schools. In this case schools are operated on a not-for-profit basis and the interest of the sponsoring body lies in influencing the school's choice of outputs or benefits from being associated with charitable sponsorship. With regard to the former, the web site of one private sector sponsor of a city technology college and an Education Action Zone in England describes their involvement in the former as:

> Through serving on the liaison group with the College, we help to equip students to tackle their future life and career through a series of joint activities such as involving them in designing carrier bags for (company name) and a desk tidy (company name). Our store managers give regular talks in the College, and we conduct mock job interviews to prepare them for the real thing.
>
> (www.dixons-group-plc.co.uk)

This kind of private sector involvement in schools (whatever its merits or otherwise) is quite different from a company that runs a school with an objective of making an operating profit.

The following notice from the Department for Education and Employment illustrates a growing interest in for-profit, privately operated, but publicly funded provision of education in England:

> The public sector is looking to the private sector for expertise, innovation and management of appropriate risks. The private sector is looking for business opportunities, a steady funding stream and a good return on its investment. For the partnership to work each party must recognise the objectives of the other and be prepared to build a good, long- term relationship. As more and more deals are signed, PPPs are moving steadily into the procurement mainstream, with all the benefits that economies of scale and replicability have to offer. As of July 2000 the education and employment sectors had signed 46 deals worth in total nearly £700m.
>
> (DfEE 2001c)

This notice emphasises an intention to attract the 'for-profit' sector as part of a 'Public Private Partnership (PPP). Under such schemes, companies may tender to:

> manage all or part of a university or college's facilities, providing such services as security, catering and maintenance; refurbish and manage facilities, such as catering, for a number of schools; or generate income, for example by improving a university or college's heat and power plant so that excess capacity can be sold to external customers.
>
> (DfEE 2001d)

We now consider some advantages and disadvantages that might be anticipated by relying on for-profit as opposed to not-for-profit schools (where the latter include schools funded by the state, the private sector, or a combination of both). The key difference between these two forms of organisation lies in the incentives. The justification for relying upon for-profit companies to run schools lies in the belief that the prospect of being able to secure a profit provides the owners of a school or managers of a service contract with a stronger incentive to achieve allocative and technical efficiency. It may be argued that a for-profit company will be more rapid in its response to changing parental preferences because the opportunity to achieve higher profits through serving unmet wants will overcome adherence to 'tried and trusted ways of doing things'. Increasing technical efficiency by driving down costs will also increase profits and, therefore, gain to the private owner.

However, there are a number of reasons why these expectations might not be fulfilled and additional countervailing effects that may be considered as outweighing these possible benefits. Orthodox theory lays down a number of conditions to be met before we may expect for-profit firms to generate the benefits noted above. In particular, there must be the potential for competition from other providers and consumers and producers must be well informed and active. We consider the validity of these assumptions in relation to schooling in Chapters 5 and 8. Here, we note the importance of information asymmetries in schooling and the relevance of these to 'for-profit status'. The incentive for 'for-profit' companies to increase allocative efficiency only applies if parents are well informed and switching costs are low. For-profit organisations also have a greater incentive than 'not-for-profit' organisations to be opportunistic, as they are able to retain the rewards from this opportunism. If parents are not in a good position to assess the quantity or quality of what is produced, they have reason to prefer an organisation that operates on a not-for-profit basis to one that operates for profit (Hansmann 1987). Parents choosing a school face high penalties from a poor choice as it is costly to move a child out of a school once the child has formed a supportive peer group (Brown 1992). However, government could deal with this problem if it provides a regulatory and enforcement regime that ensures both minimum quality and the provision of accurate information to parents. We consider this further in Chapter 7.

4.10 Conclusions

We now summarise our observations on the balance between state and other sources of funding and begin by noting that securing influence over schooling aims through providing funds for capital or current expenditure is not a new phenomenon. Private capital has, in many circumstances, been seen as a way of increasing the quantity of school-age education and more recently it has also been solicited to increase schooling quality. Given a high income elasticity of demand for education and a limited capacity, or more accurately willingness, on the part of governments to raise taxation this pattern is not surprising. Though, as we noted in Chapter 2, it does not necessarily follow that it is desirable.

We also draw a distinction between private sources of funding to cover capital and current expenditure. Private capital funding secures influence over strategy that does not follow from private funding of current expenditure. In the light of our discussion of schooling production processes in Chapter 3, private capital raises two questions. First, private capital provided on the basis of not-for-profit sponsorship may seek schooling outcomes that do not maximise parents' private benefits. This situation could be perpetuated in an open enrolment system if parents are ill informed and face substantial additional costs if they were to choose another school. On the basis of survey evidence of parents' satisfaction with sponsored schools, we believe this is currently not a significant problem. The other interpretation of parents' reported satisfaction would be that they are systematically wrong about their schools' relative outcomes. Second, private capital may ignore social benefits from schooling. In practice, it may be more appropriate to regard private capital as influencing the selection of social benefits provided by the school. In so far as religious schools sustain a religious community they provide social benefits to that community. If they promote pro-social behaviours that are valued by those outside this community then the social benefits will be that much greater. However, if in sustaining one religious community schools generate misunderstanding and friction between communities they generate social costs that might potentially outweigh the benefits. Moreover, it is more likely that parents choosing such a school would internalise the social benefits than the social costs.

In this section we have also reviewed evidence suggesting that sponsored schools achieve higher private outcomes. If parents also internalise some social benefits from these schools it is not surprising to find that they tend to be popular in open enrolment systems. However, it is not yet clear whether the advantage in private benefits arises from the parents who choose these schools or the nature of the schooling provided. This latter point draws our attention to the role of sponsorship in the generation and dissemination of knowledge about effective schooling. Recent policy in England and the US has experimented with contrasting approaches to the harnessing of business sponsorship. One approach, adopted by the CTC programme in England, separates business sponsorship from existing public providers with the suggestion that innovation will be a natural consequence of the objectives and methods introduced by the business sponsors. A second approach adopted by the New American Schools program harnesses business sponsorship in research and development which assumes that effective directions for innovation need to be discovered and developed. The implementation stage of the New American Schools Program also operates through existing providers rather than through setting up new schools outside current systems. A third approach may be seen in the Education Action Zone initiative in England, in which researching effective methods has a lower profile than in the New American Schools scheme and collaboration between private sponsorship and public providers is intended to be an aspect of each stage of the initiative. It is, as yet, too early to see clearly whether the second and third approaches are more successful in these objectives than the first.

Our review of open enrolment schemes in this chapter provides the starting point for our analysis in the following chapter. This contains our review of parent and pupil behaviour in schooling quasi-markets.

5 Market reforms

Parental choice in an open enrolment system

5.1 Introduction

In this chapter we build upon Chapter 3 by developing our analysis of parental choice in the context of market reforms. We use the term 'parental choice' to refer to the combined choice of parents and children. We focus in this chapter on parental choice in an open enrolment system, developing our analysis of item 9 in Box 4.1. In such a system parents do not have an opportunity to 'top up' the state allocated per-pupil funding, although they may financially support the school through parent–teacher organisations. We retain the assumption that parental preference follows from their estimation of consumption and investment benefits from schooling compared to the costs of accessing that schooling. However, parents evaluate these benefits within the context of their time preference, their degree of uncertainty about the outcomes of their child's education and their response to that uncertainty. As we noted in Chapters 1 and 3, this uncertainty encourages decision-makers to follow the choices of their peer group and is likely to encourage the use of simple heuristics.

We begin the chapter in Section 5.2 by outlining the way in which a switch from a zonal to an open enrolment system affects the choices available to parents and we divide these into immediate and secondary effects. Secondary effects emerge once schools have begun to respond to the changes initiated by a switch to an open enrolment system. In Section 5.3 we review evidence regarding the locus of choice within the household: how important are the preferences of the parent and the child? The remainder of the chapter provides a review of empirical evidence, drawing largely on UK research. There are some substantial difficulties to be faced in developing a comprehensive picture of parental choice in practice and we begin our analysis of methodological difficulties in Section 5.4. In Section 5.5 we introduce our basis for categorising research findings on parental choice in an open enrolment system. We are interested in policy issues and this dictates our structure which is based on eight key questions posed in this section in Box 5.1. We then complete our discussion of methodological issues in relation to these questions in Section 5.6 through a review of a selection of the survey studies on parental choice in the UK. In Sections 5.7 to 5.14 we review evidence pertaining to each of our key policy questions and in Section 5.15 we present our conclusions.

5.2 The choices provided by quasi-markets in schooling

The introduction of open enrolment in place of a zoning system allows parents to send their children to an out-of neighbourhood school and there are immediate and secondary implications for parents in this change. The immediate effects are seen in the option for parents to live in a neighbourhood that is distant from the child's school whilst bearing the costs that will ensue. Open enrolment may also result in an increase in search behaviour by parents. The secondary effects are seen in the automatic and discretionary responses of schools to the incentives created by open enrolment. Schools' responses in the market place frame the choices subsequently available to parents. We now consider these immediate and secondary effects in more detail.

The main immediate effect of an open enrolment system is that parents can detach their choice of school from their choice of neighbourhood. They may prefer the type of housing or the local amenities in one neighbourhood and a school in another. It may be argued that, with the burden of housing costs removed, parents on lower incomes are more able to express their ideal choice of school. In a zoning system, parents on higher incomes are more likely to consider schooling quality as a factor in their choice of neighbourhood as their higher income allows them to consider a much greater range of neighbourhoods. Thus, on the introduction of open enrolment, these parents will be much more used to thinking in terms of 'active school choice'. In the first years of the introduction of open enrolment this might lead to an observation that parents from higher income groups are more proactive in their exploitation of market opportunities. According to Gorard (1999) this is precisely what is observed in practice. Knowledge of differences between schools is valuable for parents in a zoning system, but this knowledge only has value in so far as schooling quality is important for neighbourhood choice. Parents for whom this will be the case have an incentive to develop their knowledge of different schools through their network of social contacts. The introduction of open enrolment allows them to exploit this knowledge in new ways.

A second immediate implication of the introduction of open enrolment is that choice of school has implications for transport costs. Increasing distance between the home and chosen school incurs costs for the parents in terms of payment for travel and time spent supporting travel arrangements and incurs costs for the child in terms of time spent travelling. Households with higher incomes are more able to bear financial costs and may consider schools more distant from their home. However, households where all adults are in full-time employment and are away from home for many hours due to their employment may also find it difficult to bear the time costs of supporting travelling arrangements for their children.

Any form of school choice, whether operating through a zonal system or through open enrolment, imposes an information gathering cost on parents considering their child's schooling. However, there are several reasons why we might expect search behaviour to be greater in an open enrolment system. First, parents who are only able to afford low-cost housing are now, in principle, able to consider schools in high-cost neighbourhoods that were previously out of their reach. Second, we might expect parents to be more interested in school choice as their children approach critical ages related to school transfer. In a zonal system parents need to gather information on schools before they choose where to live. In a quasi-market, detailed data gathering can be delayed until children reach an age when schooling begins or they need to transfer to another school. Any tendency for the quality of each school to change over time will reinforce the incentive for parents to seek data on school quality at these critical periods. Third, in a zonal system school choice is only one aspect of neighbourhood choice and, assuming that parents have a finite budget for search costs at any particular time, gathering data on schools competes for time in parents' priorities with gathering data on other amenities.

The secondary effects of the introduction of open enrolment on parental choice may be divided into automatic and discretionary responses of schools. We review these responses in more detail in Chapter 8, but we offer a summary here to emphasise the interaction between demand and supply in a quasi-market as in any market. There are two main 'automatic' effects. First, within current capacity constraints, school rolls change in response to the choices of other parents. These changes in roll may be interpreted by parents as indicators of school quality. For example, a small and falling roll may be interpreted by parents as a sign of a school in danger of disruptive closure rather than a sign of a school less likely to suffer from problems of pupil behaviour. Second, the choices of other parents may cause a change in the peer group effects offered by schools. If parents of more able children are more likely to move their children to an out-of-neighbourhood school and they are more likely to choose a school which has a higher than average proportion of more able children, then peer group effects will become less evenly distributed across schools. Parents of more able children are likely to enjoy above average incomes, given the association between parents' socio-economic status and pupils' educational outcomes (as noted in Chapter 3). Hence, they are more able to bear the costs of sending their children to out-of-neighbourhood schools. However, under a zoning system, they are also more likely to have chosen a home in the neighbourhood of a school that has a high proportion of more able pupils. This follows from the association between high income, socio-economic status, house prices and pupils' educational outcomes. Consequently, the second 'automatic' effect will depend on the geographical distribution of house prices, stratified neighbourhoods and schools. The effect of open enrolment on polarisation has been the subject of considerable analysis and debate which we review in Chapter 8.

The secondary effects of open enrolment depend on the freedom for school discretion that is introduced within the quasi-market. Schools may differentiate themselves in order to attract certain parents. They may do so through altering the quantity or quality of the schooling they offer. For example, schools can extend the length of the school day through providing supervision and extra-curricular activities before the formal school curriculum starts in the morning and after it has finished in the afternoon. They may offer specialist subjects or a wider curriculum choice. They may devote more of their resources to raising academic achievement or to social development. They may concentrate upon maximising consumption benefits or investment benefits. The more that schools seek to differentiate themselves the more they may cater for the preferences of a particular group of parents. In so doing they restrict the choice between similar institutions that is offered to parents. That is, there is a potential for a trade-off between allocative and technical efficiency. The more closely a school is aligned to the outcome preferences of a group of parents the less likely these parents are to choose another school and the less pressure there is on the school to be technically efficient in providing these outcomes.

5.3 Who chooses: parent or child?

The locus of choice of school is important if children would make choices different from those of their parents. This is suggested by evidence that children have different priorities from their parents and develop their preferences in a different way. Gorard's (1999) review of research on parental choice suggests that class size and a traditional style are more important to parents whilst extracurricular activities are more important to children. This suggests that children give more weight to consumption benefits and parents give more weight to investment benefits. Children are more likely than parents to rely on anecdotal information (Smedley 1995). Research evidence is unclear on the relative importance of the preferences of parents and children. Some studies (Thomas and Dennison 1991; Walford 1991) have suggested that the child's voice is preeminent, whilst others (e.g. Woods 1992) suggest that the parental view is dominant. Woods found that only a very small minority of decisions on schooling choice were made by children, with 80 per cent of parents reporting that they made the decision alone. Interviews conducted by West et al. (1995) revealed that school choice was mainly the responsibility of the child in only 7 per cent of cases, compared with 46 per cent of cases where the main responsibility was taken by the mother. However, school choice is best seen as a long-term outcome of the parent–child relationship. As we noted in Chapter 3, studies of choice at 16 show that the decision is largely in hands of the child, whose preferences are substantially framed by the views of parents. Conversely, studies of choice of secondary school (e.g. West and Varlaam 1991) have reported that parents have considered the preferences of the child very strongly in their decisions. In middle-class families these processes tend to be weighted in favour of parental influence and in working-class families the weighting is towards parental deference to the preferences of the child (Reay and Lucey 2000). This suggests that the class effect on the weighting of investment and consumption benefits discussed in Chapter 3 is reinforced by the process through which households form schooling choices.

5.4 Methodological issues in researching school choice

There is a substantial body of research evidence on parental choice in schooling quasi-markets. Data have been collected through in-depth interviews and through questionnaire surveys. These data are subject to the standard criticisms of data collection methods: questionnaires restrict the ability to express personal conceptions and preferences and in-depth interviewing generally yields small samples that may be unrepresentative. Questionnaires that present a list of factors that may be important in school choice deny respondents the opportunity to express reasons that are not on the list and constrain the nuances of meaning that respondents may wish to convey. Respondents are also unable to indicate how they regard the factors as related, overlapping or conflicting. In addition, two respondents may attribute quite different meanings to the same phrase in a questionnaire. Gathering information in this way entails a substantial loss of contextual data that might have been reckoned crucial to the allocation of responses to categories of meaning and this loss is particularly significant if decision-making is thought to be, at least in part, a social process. Bowe *et al.* (1994a) also argue that portraying the basis of decision-making in terms of causal factors imposes the appearance of a rational process. That is, although parents may be prepared to indicate the relative importance to their choice of each of a list of factors we cannot infer that they reached their decision through a careful weighting of each of these factors. If parents, like other choosers, rely heavily on simple heuristics it is quite probable that a single incident or piece of information became a dominant influence in their decision-making. However, other methods of data gathering are also subject to significant difficulty. Open questions in questionnaires and interviews rely heavily on imperfect memory. Interviews may over-represent the views of highly literate respondents who are able to describe their process of choice at great length (Gorard 1999). In addition to these general problems of data collection, there are five problems of method in researching parental choice that have attracted particular comment in the literature.

First, the problem of securing a representative sample is particularly acute in researching parental choice (Tooley 1997). This is evident in questionnaires that are returned by a self-selecting sample of parents (e.g. Collins and Snell 1998) and in-depth interviews carried out with a group of parents willing to participate in research (West *et al.* 1998c). Whilst a stratified sample might be used to collect data from households of different socio-economic types or parents who have chosen particular types of school, this cannot solve the problems that arise through self selection into participation in these methods of data collection. It seems unlikely that parents who choose to complete questionnaire surveys or are willing to be interviewed will be representative of all parents. Parents who have devoted more effort to choosing a school are more likely to be interested in answering questions about their choice.

Second, in so far as choice of school is the product of a long process of decision-making, researchers face a problem in deciding when to collect data. Data collected close to the moment when the school is chosen may misrepresent the causes of choice by paying insufficient attention to background factors which develop orientation towards that choice. Data collected well in advance of the final decision may misrepresent factors that only becoming pressing once the point of final decision is near (Gorard 1997b). Data collected about choice of schooling before the point at which the allocation of school places has been confirmed may reveal the process of decision-making, but may be less informative about the constraints that influence the final outcome. Data collected after school places have been allocated may tell us more about constrained outcomes, but are also more at risk from post hoc rationalisation and selective memory (West 1992).

Third, interpretations of parents' responses in surveys or interviews need to distinguish between causes to which parents refer and background causes which they may not articulate. For example, we may anticipate that parents' own schooling, their social class and their income may have some bearing on their choice of school, and this is born out by a number of studies. However, these data are not collected by some studies and this makes it more difficult to compare the results provided by different researchers.

Fourth, parents' answers to questions are likely to be related to their perceptions about the differences that exist between schools. For example, parents facing a choice between several schools that offer a similar curriculum are unlikely to indicate that curriculum is an important basis for their choice. The same parents might answer such questions in a different way if they were faced with a different set of options. In addition, we might expect the pattern of parental choice to change as the social networks which inform parental decisions adjust to market reforms. For example, Echols *et al.* (1990) report that in the first year that reforms were introduced in Scotland, 10,000 parents lodged requests for their children to attend schools outside their neighbourhood. Six years later this figure had risen to 28,000. Coldron and Boulton's (1991) survey of parents suggested that proximity was by far the most important factor in school choice; survey data from Collins and Snell (1998) ranked proximity as only the fourth most cited reason for a more popular school, whilst it remained the most cited reason by parents at a less popular school. Gorard refers to this development of a market culture amongst parents in terms of a distinction between an 'undeveloped' and an 'established' market. 'Over time, the majority of the population is likely to become more aware of their rights under legislation and therefore more "alert" players of the choice game' (Gorard 1998: 255). This dawning awareness is described by Waslander and Thrupp reporting on enrolment changes in schools in New Zealand:

When zoning was abolished in 1991, students from Pakeha (white) families were the quickest to avoid the school ... Maori and Pacific Island

Polynesian families did not abandon the school quite so quickly, a fact that local principals put down to a lack of knowledge about the abolition of zoning.

(Waslander and Thrupp 1995: 13)

Finally, published data are not independent of the intentions of the research from which they are generated. Much early research intended to reveal to schools the factors that were influencing the way in which parents chose between them. Implicitly, and sometimes explicitly (e.g. Smedley 1995), these data were presented in ways designed to help schools decide whether to engage in a particular style of promotion or how best to deploy their resources so as to attract parents. However, whilst decisions about whether to promote the school chiefly through open evenings or brochures are important for the individual school, they are less significant from the point of view of policy. Questions that are central to policy such as the degree to which decisions are driven by consumption or investment demand, the decisiveness of peer group selection and the accuracy of parental knowledge may be addressed only indirectly through the categories in which data is collected and gathered. Moreover, there are many aspects of school choice of keen importance for policy and data may be collected with one aspect of policy to the fore. Research (e.g. Gewirtz *et al.* 1995; Ball *et al.* 1996; Reay and Ball 1997; Reay and Lucey 2000) that has sought to reveal the decision-making processes of parents from different social classes exemplifies this to a certain extent. Consequently there are problems facing any effort to build up a general picture of parental choice on the basis of evidence from different programmes of research. We begin our review of research evidence, then, with a sense of caution about how definitely we are yet able to pronounce on the nature of parental choice in quasi-markets, the judgement of Gorard (1999) notwithstanding.

5.5 Policy questions on parental choice

In Chapters 1 to 4 we have developed an analysis of policy issues which we now use to identify eight questions that research on parental choice might help us to answer. These questions are presented in Box 5.1 below and they provide an a priori structure for our review of research on parental choice in open enrolment systems. Readers interested in a review that derives its categorisation from an analysis of the research itself might consult Gorard (1999). In our review we rely primarily on UK research for two reasons. First, the methodological problems discussed in the previous section and which we illustrate in the following section make the task of comparing research results rather problematic. In restricting our review to the UK we aim to limit the extent to which these problems are compounded by different contexts for parental choice. Second, there is a substantial body of research evidence on parental choice in open enrolment systems in the UK. In fact, the breadth and scope of this research has been sufficient to prompt one commentator (*ibid.*) to conclude that this area of research is 'wrapped up'.

Policy is interested in the promotion of 'better choices' by parents, children and schools and we use the questions in Box 5.1 to organise our discussion of whether 'better choices' have been encouraged. In summary, 'better choices' should lead to higher levels of social welfare through increasing technical and allocative efficiency as discussed in Chapters 1 and 3. Our questions in Box 5.1 seek to identify the aspects of parental choice which will determine whether this actually happens.

Box 5.1: Areas of policy interest in parental choice

1   Are externalities internalised?
2   Is school choice driven by investment or consumption demand?
3   Do parents prioritise peer group characteristics or school effectiveness?
4   Are parents significantly influenced by the level of school resourcing?
5   Do parents have access to the information they need and do they interpret information accurately?
6   How important is school location?
7   Do parents want different outputs from schools?
8   How representative are parents who send their child to an out-of-neighbourhood school?

We now discuss each of these questions in turn, referring to the numbers in Box 5.1 above.

1   As we noted in Chapter 3, parental choice may lead to positive and negative externalities. These choices are, therefore, more likely to lead to an increase in aggregate social welfare if these externalities are internalised. Positive externalities accrue from socialisation and productivity gains that will improve the productivity of future work colleagues. Negative externalities accrue if markets and social structures are unresponsive to changes in pupils' average level of attainment. When choosing a school, each parent influences the distribution of production externalities through the impact that their child will have on the learning of others. If parents ignore positive externalities then, in the short run, enrolments at schools that produce greater positive externalities will be sub-optimal. In the long run, all schools will face no incentives to produce these outcomes. In Chapters 1 and 3 we rejected the suggestion that schooling is a 'zero-sum game' and argued that positional demand from parents is as likely to generate unintended positive externalities as intended negative externalities, apart from the case of peer effects. We are, therefore, less concerned with internalisation of other negative externalities.

2   Policy has also tended to assume that school choice will be conducted on the basis of parents' judgements about what is best for their children's future. That is, investment demand is expected to dominate the decision-

making process. If this is incorrect and parents choose primarily on the basis of which school will provide the most enjoyable schooling for their children then open enrolment will not provide an incentive for school effectiveness. We are therefore interested in what research has to say about the relative importance of consumption and investment demand in parents' decision-making.

3 The outcomes of schooling depend on the child's peer group as well as the effectiveness of the school so we are also interested in the emphasis that parents place on peer group selection. Parental reliance on peer group selection would undermine the incentives of open enrolment for school effectiveness. Where peer group effects are subject to diminishing returns (so that the benefits from working alongside a more able child are greater for a less able than a more able child) parental reliance on peer group selection might lead to a net increase in negative externalities.

4 In Chapter 3 we discussed the absence of strong evidence to support the view that the level of resources significantly affects pupil attainment. Nevertheless, parents may well believe that resources (and notably class size) exert a strong influence on attainment and this could prove to be an important factor in their decisions. A Gallup survey in Denmark suggested that 7 out of 10 parents would be willing to pay higher taxes to enable class size to be reduced to 20 (Times Educational Supplement 2001A). In England, central government has used additional resourcing as an incentive to induce schools to participate in policy initiatives (such as 'grant maintained' or specialist school status). Such actions are unlikely to dissuade parents from believing that resources are an important aspect of school effectiveness.

5 Parents have access to a wide range of information about schools, much of it specifically prompted by policy. The success of the open enrolment strategy depends on parents acquiring necessary information and interpreting that information appropriately. We are, therefore, interested in parents' perceptions of the information they need and whether this perception is shared by schools and government. We are also interested in whether parents do acquire the information they believe they need and whether they interpret that information accurately.

6 We are also interested in the importance of school location in parents' decision-making. The open enrolment policy requires that location should not seriously inhibit parents' choice. That is, transport costs and wariness towards out-of neighbourhood districts should not be sufficient to prevent parents choosing between alternative schools.

7 For quasi-markets to provide incentives for welfare improving school diversity there must be a spread of preferences amongst parents who are willing to move their child to out-of-neighbourhood schools. If all parents seek the same balance of school outputs schools should be homogeneous.

8 If the spread of preferences amongst parents who are willing to move is systematically different from the spread of preferences of other parents then

schools only have an incentive to respond to the preferences of some parents. The preferences of 'non-movers' will be neglected.

5.6 Ambiguity in current research evidence

In Sections 5.7 to 5.14 we analyse research evidence that can shed some light on the questions posed in the previous section. In this section we show how the categories we employ in relation to our policy questions relate to the categories used by researchers in presenting their results. In doing so, we illustrate and extend some of the methodological problems referred to in Section 5.4. We refer principally to UK studies of parental choice. Studies of parental choice have revealed many factors cited as influences upon choice of school and researchers (e.g. Coldron and Boulton 1991; OECD 1994; West *et al.* 1995) have used different classifications to make the analysis of these cited reasons more manageable. These categories have generally been suggested on an a priori basis, with the exception of Gorard's (1997a) principal components analysis of choice criteria. In the light of the questions in Box 5.1 and our analysis of choice in Chapter 3 we find it useful to categorise factors affecting choice in terms of: internalised externalities; parental beliefs about the benefits to their child whilst at school (consumption); parental beliefs about the benefits of schooling for their child's future (investment); the importance of the peer group; the impact of resources; indication of a desire for a 'specialist' school; and the importance of school location in parents' choice of school for their child's education. We summarise the findings of seven pieces of research in Table 5.1.

Some categories used by researchers are easily reallocated using our typology. For example, parents' desires for their child's security and welfare (Coldron and Boulton 1991; Gorard 1997a) and children's interest in extra-curricular activities (Gorard 1997a) are examples of consumption demand, whilst academic attainment (Coldron and Boulton 1991; OECD 1994; Gorard 1997a) and helping children to get jobs (Glover 1992; Echols and Willms 1995) are examples of investment demand. However, some anticipated benefits from schooling are not easily divisible between consumption and investment. For example, when parents report that their decision is based partly on their impression of the school's ethos or organisation this might reflect a judgement that their child will be happy at the school or that their child will make good progress in their learning. Discipline in schools is cited in every study referred to in Table 5.1 yet we cannot firmly tell from this whether parents perceive discipline as a factor primarily affecting their child's happiness at school or as a factor primarily affecting their learning and attainment. This would not be a great concern if we could be sure that 'production processes' in school are such that these outcomes are in joint supply. However, as we observed in Chapter 3, current evidence does not encourage this assumption. Consequently we are left with a situation in which research on parental choice has frequently reported indicators that parents use in their decision-making without revealing a full picture of what

Table 5.1 Allocation of initial categories used in parental choice research

Category used in initial data collection	Researchers	Broad category of allocation in this review
Social education	5	Internalised externalities
Caring pastoral system	1, 2, 3, 4	Consumption
Child's friends there	1, 3, 4, 6	Consumption
Believe the child will be happy	1, 3, 6, 7	Consumption
Clubs and activities	1, 3, 4	Consumption
Sporting record	2, 4	Consumption
Amount of freedom given to kids	3	Consumption
Bullying	3	Consumption
Examination results	1, 2, 3, 4, 5, 6, 7	Investment
Homework policy	2, 3, 7	Investment
Teacher quality	4, 5, 3	Investment
School makes its pupils work harder	2, 3, 6	Investment
Pupils stretched	3, 7	Investment
Better at helping kids to get jobs	2, 3	Investment
School emphasises academic subjects	3	Investment
School assesses pupils regularly	3	Investment
Quality of education	7	Investment
Record of students entering HE	2	Investment
School emphasises practical skills	3	Investment
Best for education	1	Investment
Single sex	5	Peer group
The kind of kids we want ours to mix with	3	Peer group
Good ethnic mix	1	Peer group

Continued:

Table 5.1 Continued:

Facilities	1, 2, 3, 5, 6	Resources
Internal decoration	4, 5	Resources
Good science/technology facilities	4	Resources
Good language facilities	4	Resources
Small class size	7	Resources
Range of subjects	1, 3, 5, 6	Specialisation
Emphasis on special subject	3, 4, 7	Specialisation
Way teaching is organised	2, 3, 5	Specialisation
Treatment of less able pupils	1, 3	Specialisation
Treatment of more able pupils	3	Specialisation
Will receive Christian education	1	Specialisation
Easy to get to	1, 2, 3, 4, 5, 6, 7	Location
Discipline	1, 2, 3, 4, 5, 6, 7	Not attributed
Child's preferences	1, 3, 4, 6, 7	Not attributed
Smart uniform	1, 2, 4, 6	Not attributed
School reputation	1, 4, 5, 7	Not attributed
Atmosphere	5, 7	Not attributed
External appearance	4, 5	Not attributed
Small school	3, 5	Not attributed
Displays in school	2, 4	Not attributed
School–parent relationships	3	Not attributed
School is unpopular	3	Not attributed
School's problem with vandalism, drugs and crime	3	Not attributed
Close relatives attended and were unhappy	3	Not attributed
Truancy problem	3	Not attributed
First impressions	5	Not attributed
Suit child's needs	7	Not attributed

Sources: Bradley (1996); Coldron and Boulton (1991); Echols and Willms (1995); Glover (1992); Hammond and Dennison (1995); West *et al.* (1995, 1998a)

parents believe is indicated and in this respect interview data has a clear superiority over questionnaire data.

This problem is particularly acute in interpreting parents' references to their child's happiness (West *et al.* 1998c) and school atmosphere. A number of researchers, employing different methods, have suggested that 'school atmosphere' is very important to parents. Two-thirds of the middle-class parents interviewed by West (1992: 96) referred to the atmosphere of the school. Ball *et al.* (1996) conclude that, for the middle-class parents they interviewed 'the feel of the school, its ethos and atmosphere, as conveyed by teachers' and students' attitudes and behaviours, the state and nature of the buildings, the location, the headteacher's speech etc., play a major role in the final decision'. The three parents whose views are reported in Box 5.2 might each have indicated in a questionnaire that they rated 'good atmosphere' very highly.

Box 5.2: Extracts from interviews with parents referring to school atmosphere

(1) The feeling … it seemed a happy school as I went around … I felt … comfortable in it, as I was walking around. This is the funny thing, it's quite interesting how people perceive things because … when I talked to some of them, no way would they consider Parsons. You know what I mean, it's just how you interpret the feeling of the school, and I got slightly stressed about this because I thought, well … I certainly didn't like Overbury at all, and that's the one that everyone seems to choose as their second one.

(Parent reported by Ball *et al.* 1996)

(2) As soon as I walked into the place … there was an immediate atmosphere, and I suppose what I recognised actually was something of the old grammar school ethos, which of course I was familiar with myself and I immediately felt a little bit on familiar territory.

(Parent reported in West *et al.* 1992)

(3) There was the most calm atmosphere I saw in any secondary school and that's important I think for (my child) who needs a certain amount of quiet and structure in order to study well.

(Parent reported in West *et al.* 1992)

Parent (1) in Box 5.2 feels comfortable with a 'happy' atmosphere, but worried because other parents prefer another school. Parent (2) feels on familiar ground, and therefore comfortable in an atmosphere they associate with their own schooling, whilst parent (3) is looking for an atmosphere that will be conducive for their child's learning. Each of these parents appear to be looking for a school where their child will 'fit in', but they also seem to be suggesting different emphases in terms of consumption and investment. The position is further complicated by the link between emotions and learning and the degree to which parents take this into account when making their schooling choices as exemplified by these quotes from parents interviewed by Hammond and Dennison: 'If they are happy at school, there must be a better chance of them being successful' and 'if a bairn isn't happy, then a bairn will not learn' (1995: 111). For these and other reasons (for example, our expectation that the nature of parental choice will develop as quasi-markets become more embedded) we are cautious in our interpretation of evidence accumulated over the past decade.

It is also clear from Table 5.1 that existing research provides a confusing picture of the relative importance of different factors in parents' choice and this impression is reinforced by the data in Table 5.2. The data in this figure show the relative importance accorded to each of our categories from the evidence referred to in Table 5.1. The factors reported in each piece of research were ranked according to the number of responses indicating that the factor was very important. The ranking was then calculated as a fraction of the total number of factors cited (so the third ranked factor out of twelve becomes 9/12 or 0.75). The rankings were then averaged across the factors cited in each category. Whilst this is a very crude method of comparison, a similar picture of diverse evidence emerges if we restrict ourselves to comparing the ranking of the most frequently cited factors: discipline, academic results, school facilities and location.

This spread of results may be the consequence of very different samples and the strongest impression created by a review of the research evidence is that parents are not all looking for the same thing. This is confirmed by data provided by Bradley (1996) which suggest that the reasons for parental choice do vary from school to school. However, we also suspect that the differences are due in part to differences in the way in which data have been collected, and this interpretation is consistent with our caution regarding the methodological difficulties in collecting data on parental choice. An indication of the severity of this problem is provided by West *et al.* (1995) who include tables of parents' responses to questions asking them to cite reasons for their first-choice school, reasons they liked their preferred school and factors that parents spontaneously mentioned as important in their choice. The figures in these tables for parents citing 'nearness to home' as a reason (with ranking in the table in brackets) were 19/70 (1/9), 11/70 (10/11) and 26/70 (3/13). These problems suggest that, despite the scale and variety of research that has been conducted into parental choice in open enrolment systems in the UK, only tentative inferences may be drawn from the results. We devote the remainder of the chapter to these inferences.

5.7 Are externalities internalised?

Our earlier discussion identified consumption and investment externalities arising from parental choice. However, whilst (as we discuss in Section 5.9) there is considerable evidence that parents consider the effect of other children on their child's education, studies of parental choice rarely cite data suggesting

Table 5.2 Relative importance of factors in school choice as suggested by parental surveys*

	Externalities	Consumption	Investment	Peer group	Resources	Specialism	Location	Not attributed
Glover (1992)	0.50	0.68	0.56	0.25	0.35	0.31		0.66
Hammond and Dennison (1995)		0.48	0.97		0.51		0.59	0.32
Echols and Willms (1995) reasons for not choosing	0.42	0.74	0.50	0.67	0.21	0.24	0.46	0.49
Echols and Willms (1995) reasons for choosing		0.66	0.50	0.70	0.37	0.40	0.49	0.50
West et al. (1995)		0.55	0.59	0.45	0.50	0.55	0.18	0.82
Bradley (1996)		0.70	0.40		0.70	0.20	0.60	0.55
West et al. (1998a) state school parents		1.00	0.39	0.27			0.09	0.79

Note: *Figures calculated by ranking factors identified as 'very important' and producing a figure for average ranking of items grouped in that category.

that parents consider the effect of their own child on others. This seems a little surprising as it is quite possible to conceive of circumstances in which parents would consider the externalities created by their choice of school. In our own research (reported in Davies *et al.* 2000, 2002) some headteachers referred to the commitment of some parents of above-average-ability pupils to supporting their local school in circumstances where the headteachers believed that these pupils provided positive peer effects for others whilst enjoying weaker peer effects themselves than they would gain in a neighbouring school. Equally, a parent who chooses a school on the basis that it is best equipped to cope with difficulties their child might cause is also internalising an externality. Evidence of positional demand from parents in the sense described in Chapter 3 is rare. Questionnaire surveys have provided little opportunity for this to be expressed. Interview-based research on the effect of social class on parental choice (e.g. Gewirtz *et al.* 1994; Ball *et al.* 1996; Reay and Lucey 2000) amply illustrates parents' desire to secure 'the best' for their children, but quotations from parents do not refer to, or directly imply, a fixed set of schooling outcomes for which pupils are competing. What does emerge strongly is a sense of competition for limited places at 'good' schools and the peer groups these schools provide. We return to this issue in Section 5.9.

Research on parental choice has also yet to suggest that parents take social investment externalities into account in their choice (Table 5.1). That is, the outputs from schooling include socialisation in terms of the social behaviours that pupils will exhibit on leaving school and their readiness to participate as citizens in a democracy. The degree of respect and responsibility which, as adults, pupils will display towards others and their willingness to participate in democratic processes will generate important externalities. The reference to social education by a small number of parents in Glover's (1992) study remains an isolated example of evidence that these externalities are considered by parents. This may be because researchers have failed to prompt parents to express their preferences in these terms, parents attach a low weighting to this goal, or it may be that parents judge that all schools will perform similarly on this count. However, there is little evidence that parents have sought to confirm this assumption and quasi-markets in which the easily available information focuses on academic attainment do not encourage them to do so. It is possible that these externalities are significant in influencing parents' choice of religious schools, but evidence is so far lacking.

There is, therefore, little reason to expect current quasi-markets to provide schools with incentives to develop the quality of their socialisation outcomes, and in so far as these outcomes compete with academic attainment in the deployment of schools' resources there are incentives for schools to ignore socialisation. Given this potential for market failure there is a case for government regulation in support of schooling outcomes that would be under-provided by the market. For this reason, the introduction in England of citizenship education as a compulsory element of schooling and a strengthening of requirements in the delivery of personal and social education seem far from coincidental in the wake of the development of a quasi-market in schooling. It is difficult to see how regulation could improve response to the production externalities referred to earlier. If the production externalities referred to earlier can be quantified, schooling efficiency could be improved by compensating funding to schools such that funding per pupil rises in the cases of negative externalities and falls in the case of positive externalities. However, in so far as these externalities are choice variables for the household this would set up counter-productive incentives.

5.8 Are choices mainly driven by consumption or investment demand?

Table 5.2 provides no clear answer to the question of whether consumption or investment factors are more important for parents as a whole. Early questionnaire surveys in England and Scotland encouraged the view that consumption factors were more important. For example, researching parental choice in Scotland, Petch (1986) concluded the child's happiness and the school's discipline were the most important factors in school choice. Coldron and Boulton (1991) used several classifications including 'security' and 'academic/educational' to group parents' answers to an open question on the reasons for their choice of school. They included references to the child's happiness and 'caring teachers' in the 'security' category and 'will bring the best out of the child' and 'good examination results' in their 'academic/educational' category. Roughly a third of the reasons cited by their sample of 222 parents were consumption factors, with roughly half that percentage being accounted for by investment factors.

Subsequent evidence is mixed. Support for the pre-eminence of consumption may be inferred from a number of studies finding that parents' over-riding concern is with the discipline in the school and the prospects for their child's happiness (e.g. West *et al.* 1995; Bradley 1996; Gorard 1998; West *et al.* 1998c). A number of mothers interviewed by Reay (1996) referred to their judgement of the prevalence of racism in schools as being central to their decision-making. However, other studies (e.g. Hammond and Dennison 1995; Echols and Willms 1995; Collins and Snell 1998) find a stronger emphasis on investment in their data, with the result that no clear-cut priority emerges. As noted above, part of this difference may be due to the method of data collection. Collins and Snell, for instance, seem to allow insufficient opportunity for parents to express a preference for consumption factors. Moreover, it may be that the relative importance of consumption and investment depends on whether parents have chiefly seen their choice as an avoidance of some schools or as a positive endorsement of the school they have chosen. However, this inference is not supported by data provided by Echols and Willms (1995), who separately investigated reasons for rejecting the local school and reasons for choosing an alternative school. As they comment, their data show that 'the reasons parents chose a particular school were similar to their reasons for rejecting the local school.' (*ibid.*: 151). We now turn to the question of whether consumption is relatively more important for some parents than for others.

Investment appears to be relatively more important to middle-class parents than to working-class parents. Echols and Willms (1995) found that parents who chose an out-of-neighbourhood school were more likely to be high SES status and more likely to be interested in academic quality. Coldron and Boulton note that the response 'best for education' (an investment factor) was 'given by a much higher proportion of those in the professional and semi-professional categories (of employment)' (1991: 173). They also note that 'parents who did not expect their child to perform well in academic terms … main hope was that their child's experience at secondary school would be a happy one' (*ibid.*: 174). Thus, although their intention is to show that consumption factors are more important than investment factors in schooling choice, Coldron and Boulton's data also suggest that parents who believe their child is of above average academic ability will be more concerned than other parents with investment factors. This finding is consistent with data from other studies. Woods (1992) reports that investment was cited as an important choice factor more frequently by parents who chose schools that achieved high academic results, whilst location was more important to parents who chose lower achieving schools. Reay (1996) uses a phrase from Bell (1994: 587) to depict her observation from interviews with parents that 'the middle classes were much more likely to have their eye on some distant horizon'. Ball *et al.* (1996: 107) found that middle-class parents they interviewed were more likely than other parents to take examination results seriously, whilst for some working-class parents 'their child's happiness is of great importance to them, but happiness is a matter of social adjustment, friendship and engagement with the "local" rather than the achievement of long-term goals or the realization of specific talents'. There is also evidence (Fox 1985; West 1992) that parents who choose to pay for their children to attend a private school are motivated strongly by a sense of investment in their child's future.

However, Noden *et al.* (1998) found no significant difference between the aspirations of working-class and middle-class parents for their children, as indicated by desire to see their child continue to higher education and desired occupational status. They also found only small, non-significant differences between the number of schools visited by parents whilst arriving at their choice or the distance between home and school. Moreover, they found that whilst middle-class children who were unsuccessful with their first-choice application still found a place in a school with an examination performance higher than the average for middle-class children, a working-class child who failed to secure a place in their first-choice school ended up in a school with an examination performance lower than the average for working-class children.

The tendency for middle-class parents to place a higher priority than working-class parents on investment in schooling is consistent with evidence we noted in this chapter that time preference is related to social class. This relationship may be interpreted in several ways: (i) working-class parents may be more likely to regard their child rather than the school as chiefly responsible for the level of educational attainment; (ii) working-class parents' expectations of the investment benefits of schooling to their children may be skewed downwards due to weak investment returns to modest levels of attainment, reliance on social norms in choice-making or lower levels of accurate information; or (iii) lower levels of income may constrain ability to incur costs associated with sending children to out-of-neighbourhood schools. We now consider each of these possible explanations.

A number of studies have suggested that working-class parents tend to attribute academic progress to the attitude and capability of the child rather than to the effectiveness of the school. This can be seen in the words of parents quoted by Reay and Ball:

> He got into the wrong company or whatever, and he started skipping school and things like that, he didn't turn out to be very good and he didn't even do his GCSE ... so it's not necessarily about whether the school is good or the results is very good because it depends on the children.
>
> (Reay and Ball 1997)

> The second one is doing better than the older one, she's quite bright, the second one ... but it's not the school, it's the child. It's not down to ... you can't blame the school.
>
> (*ibid.*: 92)

Wells (1993) reports results from in-depth interviews with 71 parents and students in St Louis, USA. She found that one-third of interviewees chose the local school on the basis of location, racial composition of the student-body, family tradition and fear of the unknown. Her analysis of these interviews suggested that these parents believed that it would be more difficult for their children to learn at the local school, but that the responsibility for learning lay primarily with the child.

If parental expectations are formed on the basis of what they regard as normal for their social group, then their schooling preferences will be constrained by the expectations of others. Reay (1996) describes the process of decision-making of a group of working-class mothers and notes their reference to the impact of social groups and primary school expectations on the formation of what is considered to be normal behaviour. Ball *et al.* (1996) stress the role of access to and perception of information concerning school choice. On the basis of 26 semi-structured interviews selected from a total of 137 interviews conducted in a three-year study they categorise parents into three groups: privileged/skilled choosers, semi-skilled choosers and disconnected parents. Privileged/skilled choosers value the idea of choosing a school and are equipped to make to seek and interpret data relevant to that choice.

Inadequate information is a potential source of inefficiency for all parent choice, but this is compounded if some parents are better informed than others.

Ball *et al.* (1997) present evidence of parental choice in England that suggests that middle-class parents are better informed than working-class parents when it comes to school choice. They interpret the different reputations enjoyed by schools amongst different groups of parents as indicating a greater ability amongst middle-class parents to interpret the available evidence. In contrast, Lauder *et al.* (1999) found that when New Zealand parents were asked to name the school they would choose if 'money and distance were no object' there was no significant difference between the preferences of social groups.

If income has been a significant factor we would expect to find that parents' ideal aspirations would not differ greatly according to class, but that when final choices are made we would observe a significant difference according to parents' SES status. This view is consistent with the data provided by Noden *et al.* (1998) in England and Lauder *et al.* in New Zealand. Lauder *et al.* (1999) report on the relationship between social class and school choice in two New Zealand cities. They divided the schools into three categories of 'high circuit', 'middle circuit' and 'low circuit' according to the analysis of Ball *et al.* (1997). However, when the time came for parents to pursue an application for schools there was a marked difference between social classes. Sixty-five per cent of high SES parents applied for 'high circuit schools' compared with 23 per cent of low SES parents. Conversely, 35 per cent of low SES parents applied for low circuit schools compared with 6 per cent of high SES parents. They also found that whilst 88 per cent of applications to high circuit schools from high SES families were successful, only 72 per cent of applications from low SES families were successful. They do not report attainment or residence information for these applications.

In the face of this mix of evidence a few tentative conclusions are possible. First, consumption factors, particularly relating to discipline and the child's security, are important in the school choice of many parents and for some parents these considerations are more important than investment. Open enrolment should therefore add to incentives for schools to provide disciplined and secure environments. We might, however, also expect teachers to be happier teaching in well-disciplined schools so it is not clear why replacing teacher by market control should change the incentives operating upon teachers in relation to discipline. There is a new incentive for teachers and school managers to communicate to parents clear signals that their school is 'well-disciplined' and we should expect them to exploit whatever opportunities exist for this purpose, regardless of whether these opportunities significantly affect the level of discipline in the school.

Second, the level of importance attached by parents to consumption as well as investment creates problems for policy, as these outcomes are, as observed in Chapter 3, at least partially in competitive supply. Schools face a difficult choice in whether to increase the resources they devote to improving investment outcomes at the expense of reducing consumption outcomes. The use of setting or mixed ability teaching illustrates this point. If schools believe that setting improves academic attainment but mixed ability teaching improves behaviour and self-esteem, they face a clear choice between consumption and investment outcomes (except in so far as self-esteem contributes to subsequent achievement). Open enrolment encourages school managers to respond to this dilemma on the basis of their judgement of the spread of parental preference. Our review of research evidence suggests that this judgement is highly problematic. Policy makers have to judge what weighting should be attached to pupils' happiness at school and what weight should be attached to investment outcomes. There is little evidence in policy documents that pupils' happiness is entering the implicit social welfare function driving the introduction of quasi-markets in education. We would therefore expect open enrolment to create incentives for schools to vary their emphasis between consumption and investment in a way that differs from policy makers' intentions.

Third, although open to dispute, the balance of evidence suggests that middle-class parents place more emphasis than working-class parents on investment in educational outcomes. If parental choices are equally influential, regardless of social class, we would expect schools to vary their emphasis on consumption and investment according to whether they are primarily seeking to attract working-class or middle-class children. The corollary of this is that we would expect working-class children to be happier at school and middle-class children to gain higher levels of attainment relative to their initial ability. The alienation of working-class children from schooling has been long documented (e.g. Willis 1977). The point here is, if open enrolment is not encouraging schools to reduce this level of alienation, then why not?

5.9 Do parents prioritise peer group characteristics or school effectiveness?

Parents require detailed and complex information about school quality if they are to make informed choices as required by orthodox theory. Even supposing they are only interested in academic attainment, they need to know the value the school will add to their own child's attainment. This may be divided into two key elements: the value-added attributable to the school and the value-added attributable to the peer group. As James (1991) points out the value-added attributable to the school is very difficult for the parent to observe. However, it is more feasible for parents to observe the peer group, not least through observing the decisions of other parents. Parents have reason to be interested in the peer group whether they place more emphasis on consumption or investment in their choice of school. They may judge the likelihood that their child will be happy in a school or the likelihood that they will make good progress in their learning on the basis of the background of the children they observe attending the school.

Interview and survey data provide evidence of parental interest in peer group characteristics, but this comes through much more strongly in interview data than questionnaire results. This may reflect the reluctance of parents to express feelings about the peer group in a questionnaire. Although it is feasible that parents might overemphasise the peer group in interviews, it is difficult to see what would motivate this. Drawing upon Bourdieu, Ball and colleagues (e.g. Ball *et al.* 1996; Reay and Ball 1997) interpret their interview data as indicating parents' search for

> a match between family habitus and school habitus ... One father put this succinctly in terms of what he referred to as the 'package' offered by any school: 'that's what you were looking for, the package, which tended to be the other people that were going there.
>
> (Ball *et al.* 1996: 98)

Some questionnaire surveys of parental choice have not reported any interest by parents in the peer group. Of the studies cited in Tables 5.1 and 5.2, about half reported interest in the peer group, with a study by Echols and Willms (1995) reporting by far the highest level of importance. Bradley (1996) included a 'social mix acceptable to parents' as one unit of analysis in a study of the schooling choices of parents at four secondary schools. Less than 20 per cent of parents identified this criterion as among their top five most important factors in school choice. Gorard (1998) observes that peer group characteristics are relatively unimportant for most parents in Wales and this may result from the relative homogeneity of societies within local schooling markets in Wales, with the consequence that there is not much scope for variation in the peer group. If peer groups are important when parents observe significant differences between children, what characteristics are they particularly interested in?

References to the impact of the peer group on the child's safety and happiness can be found in the interviews with parents cited by Ball *et al.* (1996), and implicitly in parents' responses in surveys citing the importance of the child's friends also attending the school (e.g. Echols and Willms 1995). West (1992: 98) quotes one parent referring to 'the social aspect was that it was seen to be a very safe middle-class kind of school'. However, references to the effect of the peer group on work ethic and educational outcomes are more frequent. For example, a parent quoted by Ball *et al.* (1996: 98) explains 'they're not very motivated, they're not very bright, and he tends to work at the level of the children he's working with'. Many of the parental voices reported by West (1992: 214) refer to the peer group provided by the school, for example: 'In a private school it isn't the norm not to work'. Noden *et al.* (1998) find that middle-class parents are significantly more likely to send their child to a school that is high-ranking in terms of league tables of examination results and that this class difference is accounted for by the greater likelihood of middle-class parents applying to selective schools. A majority of the middle-class parents interviewed by Ball *et al.* (1996) also expressed a preference for setting by ability within the school. However, a concern with ability was not exclusive to parents of more able children. Reay and Ball quote one parent as saying

> I think also the more we thought about it ... we decided that maybe it wasn't such a good idea to send him there after all. He'd be out of his depth

... and also with Blenheim (school) the kind of kids that he's going to be mixing with there is not a particularly good cross section of society.

(Reay and Ball 1997: 94)

However, there are other important aspects of peer group selection. Ball *et al.* (1996) provide examples of parents citing ethnic mix as a factor in their choice of school. For some middle-class parents in their sample an ethnic mix was a positive, but not a crucial positive feature in a school. However, other parents who were seeking a school with a peer group in which their own ethnic background was highly represented expressed their views more strongly. Parents of girls are significantly more likely than parents of boys to make a single-sex school their first choice (Noden *et al.* 1998) largely on the basis that the behaviour of boys threatens girls' education. Finally, as discussed in Chapter 4, religion is still an important factor for a declining proportion of parents. Whilst the importance of religion is declining in many countries (e.g. Ritzen *et al.* 1997), the choice of a peer group that will reinforce parental values is very important to some parents, as evidenced in the emergence of new schools catering for Muslim and evangelical Christian parents in England.

These data do not conclusively reveal whether parents prioritise peer groups or school effectiveness. However, they do suggest that, as with school specialisation, parents are more likely to stress the composition of the peer group when they perceive great differences between pupils that are important to them. All parents have an interest in sending their child to a school which provides a peer group with which they will 'fit in'. A minority of parents also seek a peer group that will support parental values, and parents who stress investment are more inclined to consider the impact of the peer group on educational attainment. The evidence reported in Chapter 3 supports parental interest in these peer effects.

5.10 Are parents significantly influenced by the level of school resourcing?

In a quasi-market schools can enhance their resourcing in a number of ways. First, we noted in Chapter 3 that there are significant economies of scale suggesting, for instance, that as schools increase in size, say from 600 to 1100, the cost per child of providing the schooling will fall, leaving the school able to devote more resources to improving the quality of accommodation if that is desired. Second, if parents can be persuaded to supplement the school's revenue, then the income of parents is likely to affect the level of this supplement. Third, in so far as this is permitted by the quasi-market regulations, schools can seek to increase their revenue through renting their facilities and attracting business sponsorship. Finally, they can seek additional funds from government through participation in policy initiatives. The latter has been particularly important for schools in England as schools have been able to secure substantial additional funds through participation in successive initiatives (e.g. grant-maintained status, specialist college status). Whilst the quality of facilities never appears as a dominant factor in parents' decision-making, it is cited in surveys by a substantial minority as an important factor in their choice (Tables 5.1 and 5.2). In Bradley's (1996) survey the quality of the school's accommodation and equipment was cited as important more frequently than examination results. The school's spending on physical resources may also contribute to parents' impressions of a 'school's atmosphere'. This is cited frequently by parents in surveys and interviews, but we have not allocated it to a particular category as we cannot be sure what parents mean by 'atmosphere'. As we shall see in Chapter 8, some schools, at least, believe that their purchases of soft furnishings as well as computer equipment have been important in attracting parents to the school.

Overall, current research suggests that the quality of a school's resources does matter to parents, but that this is a rarely a dominant factor in their choice of school. Variations in funding per pupil are, therefore, likely to lead to marginal changes in enrolment but not more. This is a slight worry from a policy point of view because it encourages unstable dynamics in a competitive market. That is, given economies of scale and parent interest in the quality of resourcing, any changes in enrolment have cumulative effects.

5.11 Do parents have access to the information they need and do they interpret information accurately?

There are three aspects to the quality of information problem faced by parents: (1) their knowledge of the potential of their child; (2) their knowledge of the capability of each school to help that potential to be fulfilled; and (3) their knowledge of the balance of outputs that will be achieved by each school and the way in which these outputs will be valued (not least in the labour market). Ball *et al.* (1996) suggest that their interview data show that middle-class parents have a better understanding than working-class parents of the educational potential of their children. They illustrate this through quotations showing middle-class parents identifying particular needs of their children, in some cases distinguishing between siblings.

The quality of information possessed by parents is less strongly reported by researchers than other aspects of choice. Research has more frequently focused on sources of information rather than the accuracy or adequacy of this information. Sources of information used by parents include: reputation amongst other parents, school open days, school prospectuses and league tables. Research conducted in the first half of the 1990s (e.g. Smedley; 1995; West *et al.* 1995; Bradley 1996) suggested that information which schools chose to provide (through visits, open days and brochures) was more important to parents than comparative information they were required to provide and reported in league tables. In fact, Hammond and Dennison (1995) did not include league tables or examination results as a source of information at all. Examination results were seen by parents as one indicator amongst others (Echols and Willms 1993; Ball *et al.* 1996). More recently West and Pennell (2000) found that just under half of 107 parents they interviewed found the league table data difficult to understand. Ball *et al.* (1996) present interview data suggesting that examination result data were treated with caution by middle-class parents who were more interested in 'value-added' and by working-class parents who found them 'confusing'. However, in both instances there is some indication that league tables only became significant to parents when there was a substantial difference between schools' examination results. However, interviews conducted by West *et al.* (1995) suggested that parents were interested in examination results. When asked what kind of information they were looking for half spontaneously mentioned academic results or subjects offered, with this proportion rising to nearly 90 per cent after prompting. Moreover, as the culture of the quasi-market has become more established, league tables seem to have gained a more important place in parents' decision-making (Thomas and McLelland 1997; Woods *et al.* 1998). We develop our analysis of the use of league tables in Chapter 7.

Ball *et al.* (1996: 102) present interview data that suggests that more educated parents, typically middle-class, are more able than working-class parents to interpret the information provided by schools. They divide the latter into two categories: 'semi-skilled' and unskilled' choosers. Semi-skilled choosers 'have strong inclination but limited capacity to engage in the market ... their biographies and family histories have not provided them with experiences or inside knowledge of the school system and the social contacts and cultural skills to pursue their inclination to choice effectively'. Whilst skilled middle-class choosers rely on their understanding of schooling to interpret signals provided by each school, semi-skilled working-class choosers rely more on the judgements of others. This hypothesis is supported by evidence from other researchers (Echols and Willms 1995; Noden *et al.* 1998; West and Pennell 2000). Echols and Willms found that higher status SES parents were more likely to rate visits to schools and secondary school teachers as very important sources of information. West and Pennell found that the level of the mother's academic qualification was strongly related to the probability of understanding league table data.

The variety of factors considered by parents and the complex processes in which some engage in arriving at their final decision suggest that the answer to our third question may be that parents engage in complex rather than simple heuristics in choosing a school for their child. However, Ball *et al.* (1996: 94) note a tendency even by 'skilled/privileged choosers' to use 'seemingly arbitrary factors to reduce (simplify) the pool of schools from which the final choice is made'. Reporting on a study of school choice in Holland, Ritzen *et al.* (1997: 333) conclude that 'because parents have little information about the quality of schools they tend to base their evaluations on visible, superficial, characteristics'.

5.12 How important is school location?

The effect of distance on school choice impacts on families through the hard realities of transport costs and domestic arrangements and also through parents' confidence in their familiarity with the world beyond their local area.

According to Gorard (1999) convenience or transport costs are not rated by parents as significant factors in school choice. Whilst this finding emerges from his own survey results in Wales (Gorard 1998), it is not typical of other studies (see Tables 5.1 and 5.2). For example, Noden *et al.* (1998: 233) believe that transport costs were significant for a proportion of their sample of parents. They quote one parent who explains her decision not to choose one out-of-neighbourhood school, 'it was a question of money ... it would be at least an extra £10 a week'. Distance may be very important for some working-class parents for other reasons. According to Reay and Lucey (2000: 86): 'The working-classes feel most at home in their local comprehensive. Locality is important and is integrally linked to feelings of security, belonging and connection; places and spaces in which to feel relatively safe and comfortable.' Ball *et al.* (1996: 106) use the term 'the disconnected' to classify one group of parents they interviewed who only consider schools 'in close physical proximity to their home and part of their social community'. This would lead us to expect that results of surveys of factors affecting parental choice would vary across schools according to the proportion of parents from each social class. Although Bradley (1996) does not report data on the socio-economic background of parents, it is interesting to note that in his very small sample parents' citation of 'ease of access' as an important factor in school choice varies sharply and negatively with their citation of 'greater emphasis on academic subjects'.

The balance of evidence so far, therefore, suggests that school location is an important factor for some parents, and that these parents are more likely to have a working-class SES status. In addition, willingness to consider out-of-neighbourhood schools is positively related to the importance attached to investment in educational outcomes. This suggests that pressure on schools from parental choice will come largely from middle-class rather than working-class parents. This is likely to affect the degree to which schools serving different localities feel under such pressure and also means that the preferences of parents who are more willing to consider out-of-neighbourhood schools will not be fully representative of the preferences of all parents. We consider this issue more in Section 5.14.

5.13 Do parents want different schools?

The comparison in Tables 5.1 and 5.2 suggests that specialised features of schools' curricula are less important to parents than most other factors cited. There is also more reference to the 'range of subjects' than concentration on a particular subject. We noted in Chapter 3 that risk aversion provides an incentive for parents to seek a curriculum that keeps options open for the future, and the data summarised in Tables 5.1 and 5.2 may be interpreted as supporting this conjecture. However, without more exact information about parents' meaning in using or responding to the phrase 'range of subjects', this interpretation remains one amongst several. In addition, as we noted earlier in this chapter, current research data were collected at a time when there was relatively little difference between school curricula and parents may well have judged specialisation to be unimportant for this reason.

There are, though, a number of indications that parents are not all looking for the same qualities in a school. This is suggested by studies such as Bradley (1996) that compare the preferences cited by parents who have sent their children to different schools and the preceding sections have identified several factors that seem to differentiate the preferences of one parent from another: priority to consumption or investment; importance attached to the peer group as opposed to school effectiveness; peer group characteristics sought; and importance attached to the level and use of school resources. These are not the sources of diversity usually highlighted by advocates of the values of market forces and it is important to consider their significance.

If parents seek a peer group that matches family characteristics, open enrolment will encourage polarisation between schools according to social class, ethnic background and religion. However, given the polarisation created by zoning systems, it is not clear whether this will be increased or reduced by the introduction of open enrolment. As noted earlier, in any given location, this will depend substantially upon the degree of social mix in the catchment areas established in a zoning system. Where these were engineered to provide a socially and religiously mixed pupil intake, open enrolment may be expected to increase polarisation. However, in cases where the zoning system resulted in school catchment areas that were sharply distinct according to social, ethnic and religious background, we may expect open enrolment to decrease polarisation. We discuss these issues in more detail in Chapter 8.

5.14 How representative are parents who send their child to an out-of-neighbourhood school?

If parents are not homogeneous in their schooling preferences, it is important to know whether all preferences are expressed with equal force. As Woods (1996: 325) explains, 'One of the unexamined presuppositions amongst much of the argument in favour of more competitive environments is that all parents are equal in the education market place'. Open enrolment in a quasi-market without vouchers accords the same value to every child. If the spread of preferences amongst parents who actively consider an out-of neighbourhood school is the same as amongst those who do not, then the active choosers will effectively protect the inert choosers by de facto expressing their preferences. Under these circumstances, it would not matter if there were few 'active choosers' as schools have an incentive to respond to the marginal parent. However, if these parents are unrepresentative, then schools will be encouraged to bias their production and outcomes in favour of some parents at the expense of others.

Willms and Echols (1992) found that parents in Scotland who choose an out of neighbourhood school are more likely to be highly educated and in occupations with a higher SES status. This result was repeated in their later study (Echols and Willms 1995) in which they identified significant differences in the average social-class status of parents who only considered their local school, parents who considered another school but chose their local school, parents who only considered and chose one alternative school, and parents who considered several schools and opted for an out-of-neighbourhood school. A similar conclusion emerges from the work of Ball and colleagues (Gewirtz, *et al.* 1995; Ball *et al.* 1996, 1997; Reay 1996; Reay and Ball 1997). The balance of evidence suggests that these parents will be more interested than other parents in academic investment outcomes and this is likely to influence schools' response in the market. Given this, open enrolment will encourage all schools to provide academic courses and discourage them from providing more vocational courses (Davies and Adnett 1999).

5.15 Conclusions

Given the methodological problems encountered by the research described in this chapter, we offer tentative conclusions. Not least amongst these problems are those created by the evolution of market behaviour as parents and schools interact in response to market reforms. Whilst it appears that most parents may adjust within a few years to the opportunities initially created by open enrolment (Gorard 1999), their response to consequent changes in school behaviour may take longer to judge. In particular, if schools become more differentiated in terms of peer groups and curriculum, we might expect parents to cite these factors as becoming increasingly important in their choice.

However, current evidence does enable us to identify a number of problems with open enrolment systems. First, there is little evidence to suggest that parents internalise positive externalities from schooling. Given that schooling processes (as described in Chapter 3) mean that outcomes are at least partly in competitive supply, open enrolment is likely to discourage schools from devoting resources to socialisation. Second, consumption outcomes are important to many parents and pre-eminent to some. This is not a problem for governments if the intention is to ensure that schooling provides the outcomes that parents most value. However, it does become problematic if the intention is to use parents to provide schools with the incentives to adhere to government objectives. Governments typically prioritise investment in terms of productivity gains. It is, therefore, convenient from this point of view that the preferences of parents who move their children to out-of-neighbourhood schools seem skewed towards this objective. Government policy in England, where published comparative information on schools focuses on academic attainment, seems designed to encourage this outcome, an issue we return to in Chapter 7. The unrepresentative nature of the parents who opt for out-of-neighbourhood schools results from a combination of two factors: (i) middle-class parents, who are more likely to choose an out-of-neighbourhood school give greater priority to investment outcomes; (ii) schools have an incentive to prefer to enrol a high achieving pupil who is more likely to be middle-class than a low achieving pupil who is more likely to be working-class. A further implication follows if the curriculum best suited to productivity gains for middle-class pupils is different from the curriculum best suited to productivity gains for working-class pupils. In England, this difference has been the basis for an 'academic–vocational divide'. Vocationally orientated courses which do not attract middle-class parents will not be encouraged by open enrolment if working-class parents are under represented amongst the parents who choose out-of-neighbourhood schools. This outcome is observed in our own research (Davies *et al.* 2000).

Third, in so far as schools identify and seek to serve the preferences of particular groups of parents, a trade-off is created between technical and allocative efficiency. Schools that have secured a niche in a local market improve allocative efficiency through providing a combination of outputs most wanted by a particular group of parents. However, in doing so, they limit their exposure to competition from similar providers, which is typically seen as the spur to technical efficiency. Fourth, interview evidence indicates that choice of school is strongly influenced by the search for an 'appropriate' peer group. Two aspects to this search are the identification of a peer group with whom the child will 'fit in', on the basis of shared social networks and values, and the selection of a peer group that will enhance the child's attainment. For middle-class parents these two aspects of peer group search tend to be mutually supporting and they are informed by the priority given to investment outcomes. The role of peer group selection in school choice is problematic for policy because it provides an incentive for schools to target a particular peer group rather than school improvement.

Finally, parents face significant information problems in choosing schools. One aspect of these information problems tends to reinforce peer group selection. That is, parents are likely to be better informed about peer group characteristics (through their social networks) than about school effects on attainment. This will tend to bias upwards the importance of peer groups in their school selection. Understanding of school effects is dependent on parents' 'cultural capital' which allows them to interpret accessible information about schools. As we noted in Chapter 3, this advantages middle-class parents and makes it more likely that they will consider an out-of neighbourhood school to be a worthwhile investment. However, all parents face a problem in so far as physical school resources (such as equipment and furnishing) are more visible than the skills, experience and effectiveness of teachers. From the evidence reviewed in Chapter 3 we conclude that the differences within OECD countries in the physical resources enjoyed by different schools has little impact on investment outcomes (although it may still significantly affect pupils' happiness at school). Evidence reviewed in this chapter suggests that physical resources influence the choice of some parents and this may be viewed as encouraging inefficiency if consumption benefits are discounted.

These problems do not, however, demonstrate that open enrolment systems are inferior to other systems of allocating school places. These problems may be outweighed by other benefits. Any judgement of the appropriateness of open enrolment as a policy rests on a comparison between this system and other alternative possibilities and we return to this question in Chapter 8.

6 Market reforms

Licensing, training and remuneration of teachers

6.1 Introduction

Market-based reforms of state schooling system typically view teachers as a key intermediary in the process of raising educational standards. Greater competitiveness in the school system should directly increase teacher effort through reduced job security and increased monitoring by managers and parents (Rapp 2000). In addition, schools that face greater competition will favour teachers who increase the ability of the school to recruit and retain pupils. In turn, this suggests that schools, within the constraints of any national pay system, will provide greater rewards to attract and retain the most talented teachers and be less willing to retain the least talented. A common claim is that the national pay system itself needs to be redesigned to provide teachers with greater financial incentives to adopt the objectives of their principals and prioritise improving the academic attainment levels of their pupils. Critics of present pay policies in England and Wales also argue that a single salary spine inevitably leads to recruitment problems in those subject areas where outside earnings are high, such as science and computing, or in those schools with the most challenging pupils.

In the light of these issues, Reynolds (1999) draws attention to an important characteristic of the contemporary educational discourse in Britain. In contrast to that in the US, Australia and the Netherlands, the emphasis has been upon the school effects rather than teaching *and* schooling. Reynolds provides two main explanations for this neglect which are relevant to our discussion in this chapter. First, he identifies a particularly British view that teaching is an 'art', not a science, and that personal factors and qualities rather than training and resources determine the quality of teacher inputs. Second, he suggests there has been an unwillingness to confront the issue of inter-teacher variations in effectiveness, with research being concentrated at the school, rather than the classroom level. Given that British school effectiveness research suggests that the range of variation within schools normally dwarfs the range of variation between schools (Fitz-Gibbon 1996), more attention to 'teacher variation' is warranted.

The credentials required to enter teaching differ across developed economies, though attempts by teacher unions to increase accreditation requirements appear universal. Typically, these attempt to establish parity of their profession with that of doctors and lawyers. At the same time, with over two-thirds of state schools' expenditure being on teacher salaries, governments have been redesigning payment systems to strengthen incentives for teachers in order to raise educational standards. These developments have led to debates concerning occupational licensing and training of teachers and the optimal degree of incentive pay. A shared issue concerns the appropriate mix of intrinsic motivation and market-based rewards. The inability of decision-makers to formulate policies that address this mix reflects uncertainty about the desired degree of teacher independence, the importance of co-operation and teamwork within schools and, ultimately, the form of professionalism desired for teachers in state schools.

As Dixit (2000) points out, these uncertainties have their origins in certain key characteristics of state schooling. First, as outlined in Chapter 3, there are multiple goals, with the different objectives competing for the finite resources available to schools and teachers. Not all of these desired outputs are measurable. Even amongst those that are, the value-added attributable to schools and teachers is difficult to isolate from that reflecting innate ability and environmental influences. Second, the state schooling system has several distinct groups of stakeholders who act, or could act, as the principals in the agency relation with teachers. These groups (government, parents and children, taxpayers, potential employers, teachers and society as a whole) have diverse preferences and attach different weights to individual goals of state schooling. Third, many teachers enter their profession for idealistic reasons, directly gaining satisfaction from improvements in schooling outcomes in accordance with their own valuation of these multiple goals. Finally, for much of the population the local state school has monopoly power. Taken together they indicate that the typical state school is a multi-task, multi-principal, near-monopoly organisation with imprecise and poorly observable goals.

In this chapter we address those aspects of market-based reforms which are directly or indirectly concerned with the occupational licensing, initial training and remuneration of teachers, analysing points 12–14 in Box 4.1. The following section introduces some international comparisons in student–staff ratios, the age and gender composition of teachers and their salary structures. In Section 3 we discuss debates concerning certification and licensing which determine the training necessary to practise as teachers. Occupational licensing by the state has often been seen by economists as a restriction on competition. Such artificial restrictions in an occupational labour prevent those without the approved qualification from entering, thereby reducing supply and raising relative pay. Justification for certification or licensing has to be found in the market failure that would result from unrestricted entry. In Section 4 we examine the reforms made to initial teacher training and methods of recruitment. The bulk of the rest of this chapter, Section 5, considers teachers' pay. Initially we examine the nature of payment systems and the previous dominance of a common pay spine for classroom teachers, with individual salary being largely dependent upon entry qualifications and years of service. We examine the limited evidence on the impact of increased market forces on teachers' pay and the sensitivity of turnover to their relative pay. The remainder of this section examines the rationale for the introduction and extension of incentive pay for classroom teachers. Section 6 summarises the main findings of this chapter.

6.2 Teachers: some international comparisons

Although schools are making more use of computers and other educational technology over time, teachers remain the most important resource in student instruction. Hence, the ratio of students to teachers is often used as an important indicator of the overall resourcing of education. Student/teaching ratios in primary and secondary education vary widely between countries. For example, whilst the OECD average in primary schools in the mid-1990s was 18.3 students per teacher, Ireland's ratio was over twice that of Italy. The range for secondary schools is slightly narrower with an OECD average of just over 15 (OECD 1998). There is some evidence of a trade-off between student/teaching ratios and teacher salaries. Countries with low student teacher ratios, such as Austria, Italy and Sweden, often have relatively low starting salaries for teachers.

Relative teacher salaries differ markedly between OECD countries, but in most countries it appears that their earnings after 15 years of experience are lower than the average for university graduates. In the 1990s teachers' salaries in most countries failed to keep pace with the growth in GDP per capita (OECD 1998). The demography of teachers is becoming a concern in many developed countries. The post-war baby boom and increasing tertiary participation rates have created a large concentration of teachers in the age range 40–50 in countries where the school-age population is expected to grow (*ibid.*). Across OECD countries in 1996, women accounted for 95 per cent of pre-primary, 75 per cent of primary, 57 per cent of lower secondary and 50 per cent of upper secondary schoolteachers. In the majority of countries this gender gap is widening over time. Again there are large national differences; for example the proportion of male lower secondary education teachers in the Netherlands (67 per cent) is more than twice that in Italy (28 per cent).

Lakdawalla (2001) suggests that changes over time in student–teacher ratios and the quality of teachers may reflect the impact of technological change. Recent technology has improved the productivity of the specialised knowledge of skilled workers outside of teaching but not that of the general knowledge of schoolteachers. This change raises the price of schoolteachers but not their productivity. Employers respond by lowering the relative skill required of schoolteachers and raising teacher quantity. Comparing the 1900 and 1950 US birth cohorts, he found that the relative schooling of teachers had declined by three years and their human capital may have fallen by 30 per cent relative to college graduates in general. At the same time the pupil–teacher ratio has more than halved over the last fifty years in many developed countries.

6.3 Occupational licensing

Competitive market analysis views the certification and licensing of teachers as an undesirable restriction on competition. This in turn has led to public choice critiques of teachers and their unions distorting educational resources and outcomes (Hoxby 1996a) and calls to deregulate entry into the teaching profession (Ballou and Soler 1998). The public interest argument for licensing a profession rests upon the notion of imperfect information and the need for consumer protection. Most parties accept the need for the screening of entrants into teaching to restrict entry of paedophiles, etc. The real debate concerns the desired mix and level of certification and licensing, that is the level at which barriers to entering the profession should be set (Kleiner 2000).

The initial economic analysis of licensing concentrated upon adverse selection problems (Leland 1979). Assuming imperfect reputation mechanisms, parents and students are unable to access cheaply quality information on individual teachers. In this case, licensing can ensure a minimum quality standard. Shapiro (1986), in contrast, adopts a moral hazard approach and analyses licensing as a control on the level of training required by a professional. If higher occupational-specific human capital investments by teachers improve the quality of their teaching, then licensing can raise the overall quality of teaching. However, licensing not only incurs administration costs, it also raises the costs of providing a low quality service. Thus, whether teaching should be licensed, and if so at what level, depends upon the comparison of these benefits and costs. In general, the higher quality of teaching required and the weaker the reputation mechanism, the higher should be the licensing standard (Shapiro 1986). Certification – that is, providing information about a professional's training level – can be superior to licensing if training levels are closely connected to quality. However, it can also lead to over-investment in occupational training.

The continuation of recruitment problems in both the US and Europe has led to a polarisation of views as to the required policy response. Some commentators argue for the need to raise the relative pay and status of teaching and to subsidise entrants' training costs. Others advocate the lowering of entry requirements to rectify the recruitment problems. Entry requirements may be lowered either through reducing the level of prior qualification and experience required or by reducing initial training that either attracts very low pay or no pay at all. High entry requirements restrict supply with prior experience and qualifications increasing the homogeneity of supply, and initial training accompanied by low pay discouraging entrants for whom this creates a very high opportunity cost. In addition, to the extent that teaching is an 'experience good' – it is hard to judge whether one is suited to this career without trying it – then high barriers and increasing the costs of entry will significantly reduce supply (Ballou and Podgursky 1997b). Low barriers reduce the costs of entering and increase heterogeneity, perhaps further encouraged through alternative certification programmes for mature entrants. However, to the extent that this weakens compliance with prevailing professional norms and ethics and lowers teaching effectiveness, more post-entry training, monitoring and incentives may have to be provided.

Behind this policy debate lies an empirical one: the importance of teacher quality to pupil educational value-added. The very homogeneity of entrants to teaching contributes to the difficulty in identifying a 'teacher effect', since we need to examine the link between the variation in pupil attainment and variation in teacher quality. Hanushek's (1997b) survey of US evidence found no firmly established link between student attainment and the more obvious measures of teacher quality (e.g. age, experience and qualifications). Studies generally find no statistically significant relationship between teacher education and student performance, though there have been both positive and negative effects found for mathematics. Vignoles *et al.* (2000) conclude that the weight of the evidence indicates that teacher experience and salaries do matter, but that these effects are small. Loeb and Page (2000) challenge these conclusions with a more refined analysis of the relationship between teacher salaries and student outcomes. They make additional adjustments for non-pecuniary aspects of teaching and alternative occupational opportunities. They estimate that in the US, raising the relative wage of teachers by 10 per cent would reduce the high school dropout rates by 3 to 4 per cent. Notwithstanding these contributions, the overall weakness of empirical studies and their inconsistent results regarding teacher effects have blighted debates concerning teacher training.

6.4 Teacher training and recruitment

In this section we deal briefly with two main questions, First we consider how the technical and productive efficiency of training for teachers can be improved. Second, we examine the implications of who bears the cost of this training. With regard to the first question, a major concern of government in England and Wales has been with the choice of the outcomes of training. Amongst alternative outcomes from training we may list: (i) teachers more highly skilled in raising schooling benefits for pupils; (ii) teachers more able to engage innovation and the expansion of knowledge about 'good teaching'; (iii) a teaching force more able to engage in critical debate about desirable objectives and structures in schooling; and (iv) the development of communities of 'scholars' committed to the interests of those communities. The first of these outcomes begs the question of the definition of 'schooling benefits' as discussed in Chapter 3. The second outcome implies that the development of new knowledge will not be the exclusive preserve of either the state or Higher Education. The third outcome suggests that professional empowerment for teachers is desirable and that they will be involved in strategy formation. The fourth outcome has been historically associated with the development of curriculum subjects, not least those that are now taken for granted as essential elements of the school curriculum. Traditionally the balance of outcomes was determined by training institutions in Higher Education, and recent reforms in England and

Wales have been directed at securing government control of this responsibility. In particular, there has been concern amongst policy makers, especially in England and Wales, about the variability in the quality of teaching effectiveness (discussed in Reynolds and Farrell 1996) and the strong influence of college-based teacher educators on that initial training (discussed in Whitty *et al.* 1998). The government's strategy for reforming in England and Wales focused first on initial teacher education laying down requirements for course structure, school experience and more controversially, the competencies that trainees must exhibit to be granted Qualified Teacher Status. A Teacher Training Agency (TTA) was established by the government as a key part of a strategy to secure strong influence over the outcomes of training. This has been strengthened by the publication of inspection data on initial teacher training courses. Supplemented by other performance data, these have been used in the national press to produce 'league tables' of providers. The effect of these league tables on patterns of recruitment and provider performance has yet to be analysed. In the US, the National Commission on Teaching and America's Future (1996) called for the mandatory accreditation of all teacher-training programmes. The intention was to increase coursework and other pre-service training for aspiring teachers. By requiring a one-year internship, it suggested extending the overall entry training to five years. Their recommendations generated a debate about the strength of the underlying evidence of the effectiveness of such additional training (Ballou and Podgursky 2000; Darling-Hammond 2000). In England, the Teacher Training Agency also assumed responsibility for continuing professional development, although strategic responsibility has subsequently passed back to the Department for Education and Skills. This responsibility has been used to identify those training needs that will attract priority funding and inspection of courses has also been focused on checking whether government priorities are being met.

These policy reforms have been aimed principally at improving allocative efficiency as perceived by the government. The implication of these policies is that, of the four outcomes listed earlier in this section, outcome (i) is by far the most important. Moreover, within that outcome the emphasis has been clearly on measurable academic attainment, with this being reinforced by separate initiatives on raising standards of literacy, numeracy, and information and communications technology skills. These policy developments assume that the government is more likely than Higher Education institutions (HE) to judge training needs in a way that will improve allocative efficiency. HE does have an incentive to emphasise those outcomes that are most closely associated with its own development rather than those most closely associated with school. Nevertheless, it might also be argued that these outcomes, notably those associated with (iii) and (iv), are significant to the long-term capability of the education community in general and the teaching force in particular. It is arguable that governments will tend to over-emphasise short-term benefits in the area of training.

Recent reforms in England and Wales have also addressed the question of who should bear the cost of teachers' training. This training might develop professional attitudes and skills that lead to positive externalities in the form of increased co-operation with others, greater ability to support the professional development of others and willingness to participate in voluntary activities in support of the school. If so, then externalities would justify some government subsidisation of training. In England and Wales, the full cost of initial training has been met by the government and this continued even after the government shifted the burden of fees for undergraduate education on to students. In the face of teacher recruitment shortages, bursaries were subsequently introduced to encourage an increase in supply. In principle, the burden of training costs cannot be separated from the level of teacher pay, which we consider in the next section. However, initial indications of the effect of these bursaries, suggest that relatively small sums at this stage (compared to lifetime earnings) may be weighted heavily by prospective trainees.

6.5 Systems of teachers' pay

A common contextual feature of the markets for teachers in the UK and US is persistent recruitment difficulties. In the US over the next decade it is calculated that around 2.2 million teachers have to be recruited. In the UK, where half of teachers are due to retire in the next decade, the recruitment problem has been associated with the apparent low morale of classroom teachers. Specifically, those leaving teaching cite work overload, low status, poor morale and poor pay (Spear *et al.* 2000). Indeed teachers' pay premium over average non-manual earnings has fallen by three-quarters over the last twenty-five years. Low morale is also a reflection of the increased demands which educational reforms as a whole have placed on teachers. According to a recent survey, 88 per cent of respondents claimed that they were unable to work any harder (Marsden 2000). Some evidence for the US suggests that it is the most able teachers who are more likely to exit the profession early (Hoxby 2001). In both countries these problems of recruitment, morale and turnover have been attributed to a lack of financial incentives for good classroom teachers. It has stimulated policy makers' interest in performance incentives and skills-based pay.

Until recently, the pay system for classroom teachers in England and Wales was based on annual increments in the early career years. Beyond a common 9-point pay spine, additional responsibility points were available, for example, for heads of subjects. A School Teachers' Review Body was established to review salaries annually within this framework. In 1998 the vast majority of teachers had already secured the maximum number of points on the common scale with most of these being paid for some additional responsibilities. Although the previous system introduced extra points for excellent performance in 1993, less than 1 per cent of teachers had ever benefited from such payments. While this scheme had the merits of relative simplicity and transparency, the government's 1998 Green Paper claimed that it failed to discriminate adequately between high and low performers. Similarly, in the US, teacher pay in most school districts is based upon a single salary schedule, where an individual teacher's salary is determined by two factors: years of experience and the number of education credits and degrees. One consequence, it has been suggested, is that experienced teachers use their seniority to move towards less demanding classes and schools, leaving the most challenging pupils to be taught by the youngest and least experienced teachers (Ballou and Podgursky 2001). Recently there has been a movement in the US, similar to that in England and Wales, towards rewarding teachers for their knowledge and skills and the overall school performance. Nationally, four sets of teacher standards and assessments have been developed, one of which – the National Board for Professional Teaching Standards – provides a certification process similar to that for doctors in the US (Odden 2001). Several US states offer to pay the accreditation fees or pay higher salaries to Board-certified teachers.

The British Government's 1998 Green Paper (DfEE 1998) developed the argument for an expansion of the use of incentive pay for classroom teachers (Cutler and Waine 1999, 2000, outline the background). The Green Paper provided the basis for the scheme introduced in England and Wales during 2000/1. It was argued that the previous system of teachers' pay had created recruitment, retention and motivation problems. The diagnosis was that 'good teacher performance is not sufficiently recognised'. A new pay structure was proposed which would appeal both to prospective new entrants with high earnings potential outside of teaching, and to poorly motivated existing teachers. A system of annual appraisals (performance reviews) has now been introduced, a key function of which is to produce individual targets for teachers; these must cover pupils' academic progress. Those teachers meeting their targets are eligible for accelerated progression up their pay scales. In addition, performance-related promotion has been introduced for classroom teachers at the top of the scale, together with school-based group bonuses covering about 30 per cent of English schools.

Justification for the expansion of performance-related pay (PRP) was based upon evidence of its widespread use in other occupations. The UK Workplace Industrial Relations Survey indicates that well over half of British establishments operate some incentive pay scheme, though they are less widespread in the public sector (Burgess and Metcalf 1999). This current infatuation of human resource specialists with 'new pay', and PRP in particular, has been interpreted as reflecting a concern to match rewards and strategic objectives better within organisations (Poole and Jenkins 1998). Concurrently, the economics of personnel (Lazear 1999) has begun to provide an economic analysis of intra-organisational pay systems based upon the consequences of incomplete employment contracts (introduced in Chapter 1). In certain employment situations, it has been argued that PRP can generate efficient incentives for employees and offset agency problems. However, PRP may generate dysfunctional behaviour where employees switch their efforts towards behaviour that is directly rewarded, to the detriment of both other aspects of their work and beneficial co-operation with colleagues. The desirability of introducing or extending PRP, therefore, depends not only on the details of any particular scheme and the measurability of desired outcomes, but also upon the particular workplace environment associated with teaching. Within this framework, career concerns, particularly internal promotions and tenure-related wages, may cause teachers to internalise such efficiency considerations even in the absence of explicit incentive contracts.

Performance-related pay for heads and deputies in England and Wales was introduced in 1991. In this scheme, governing bodies were instructed to pay special attention to four criteria including performance. Since 1995, the latter criterion was required to be guided by four essential performance indicators: improvements in the school's examination results; improvement in school attendance; sound financial management, and progress on meeting any action plans resulting from OfSTED inspections (see Chapter 7). The pay scheme for classroom teachers eventually implemented in 2000/1, following a delay caused by successful legal action by the teaching unions, is not a straightforward PRP scheme. The new performance management system requires that teachers be appraised against clear objectives and outcomes. Teachers in the early years continue to have an incremental scale, with accelerated progression possible up to a threshold. Teachers with the required qualifications and experience can apply to cross the threshold and gain an approximate 10 per cent pay increase. The criteria for progression through the threshold were eventually divided into eight standards under five areas of competence: subject knowledge, teaching and assessment, pupil progress, wider professional effectiveness and 'professional characteristics'. Beyond the threshold, further high performance can be rewarded with additional points following an annual Performance Review. In the first of the annual assessments, from July 2000, applications were processed from around 80 per cent of the 250,000 teachers eligible for progression through the threshold. For school heads, the additional workload of implementing the new system has been heavy. One estimate is that the average secondary head spends over 100 hours annually on the appraisal system (Select Committee on Education and Employment 1999). Finally, in March 2001 the first recipients of the School Achievement Award were announced. About three-quarters of the 6,800 awards were for improvement in Key Stage tests or GCSE/GNVQ results and the others on ranking of absolute results with schools grouped on the basis of pupils eligible for free school meals. The awards are expected to result in one-off payments to teachers and other staff of around £300 to £400 in those schools receiving them.

Before we analyse the arguments for extending incentive pay for teachers there are two empirical issues in which we are initially interested. First, how sensitive is teacher turnover and retention to relative pay? In modelling teacher turnover, particularly given the current uneven distribution of childcare responsibilities in households and because a majority of teachers are women, it is important to distinguish between permanent and temporary exits from the profession. Dolton and van der Klaauw (1999) conclude that there is a clear link between relative teacher pay and quits to an alternative career or for family reasons. Overall, the tenure profile of teachers is sensitive to the structure of wages, suggesting that policy makers need to design career salary structures carefully if they are to attain the desired mix of experience and qualifications in the profession.

The second related empirical issue concerns the impact of competition on teacher recruitment and rewards. Conventional economic theory suggests that employers can exploit teachers with high moving costs when local labour markets are not competitive. Hoxby (2001) uses data from traditional forms of school choice in the US. She finds that schools which face tougher competition have a higher demand for teachers who have: attended higher-ranked universities; specialised in a subject area; put in more effort, and show more independence. They are more likely to hire teachers with such traits and pay them more than schools who face less competition. Interestingly, they also appear to have less demand for certification and master's degrees. Indeed, they pay teachers who hold such qualifications less than similarly qualified teachers earn in schools that are less choice-driven. She concludes that greater school choice has the potential to create a professional environment in which more motivated and skilled teachers earn higher pay for such qualities. Merrifield (1999) and Vedder and Hall (2000) provide further support for this hypothesis. Merrifield finds that teachers were paid less in those Texan school districts with less competition. Vedder and Hall conclude that increased private school competition raised the salaries of public school teachers in Ohio's school districts. Some further insights can be gained from comparisons between private and state schools in the US. Ballou and Podgursky (2001) found that although private schools paid salaries that were about 60 per cent of local state school salaries, they were more concerned with valuing aptitude in making hiring decisions. They also found that salaries in private schools reflected aptitude and scarce skills more than was the case in state schools.

These arguments are in striking contrast with those who see the market-based reforms followed in Australia, Britain and New Zealand as destroying teacher professionalism. Specifically, the expansion of incentive pay is seen as a further stage in the rise of the 'managerial' culture and the consequential post-Fordist 'technical proletarianisation of teachers' (Robertson 1996). Critics point to the problems and costs of applying incentive pay within schools and the likely loss of co-operation and teamworking (Richardson 1999). In summary, incentive pay is taken to threaten the continuation of a 'collegiate ethos' within the teaching profession. Investigating this proposition is the concern of the rest of this chapter, Adnett (forthcoming) contains a more detailed analysis.

6.5.1 The economics of incentive pay: an introduction

Until recently the conventional economic analysis of the employment relationship treated employee-effort as fixed. In a competitive market, workers in any job were paid their transfer earnings. Hence, individual organisations could not influence wage rates and the implications of incomplete employment contracts were neglected. With such 'open' employment relationships, analysis often concentrated upon employee and employer search behaviour and, since more productive workers earned higher wages, organisations often lacked incentives to influence worker productivity. The emergence of efficiency wage models and more generally, personnel economics (the use of labour economics techniques to understand the internal workings of an organisation) have radically altered the way mainstream economists view an organisation's payment systems. This movement of economic analysis away from a concern with auction markets replicates the emphasis in the sociological literature on the analysis of 'closed' employment relationships. As yet there has been little cross-fertilisation between these approaches.

Consider the case of responsible jobs where the value of job outcomes is highly sensitive to both the decisions and efforts of workers. Employment contracts for such workers may cover a number of tasks and/or time periods, but are crucially incomplete in that they cannot fully specify terms and conditions to solve the agency problem resulting from the different objectives of workers and their organisations. Organisations here have incentives to design payment systems that reward employees for increased productivity, thereby avoiding or reducing reliance upon alienating direct command and expensive monitoring of worker effort. A fundamental assumption of these approaches is that workers respond to contracts that reward performance. Though the rational choice approach can encompass rewards based upon status, praise or social solidarity, personnel economics has so far concentrated almost exclusively upon monetary rewards. There are three main ways of creating financial incentives. First, pay workers more than they would earn elsewhere: the efficiency wage case. Second, pay could be more directly related to employees' output, either instantaneously or over the working life: the piece rate and deferred payment cases. Finally, where output is multi-faceted and/or incompletely or inconsistently measured, incentives may target inputs to the production process. This is the case of merit-based pay and competitive promotions (tournaments) based on performance evaluation. In this chapter we are concerned with the two latter forms of incentives, and we seek to assess the relevance of personnel economics' analysis of optimal payment systems for teacher remuneration.

As a reading of the surveys by Gibbons (1998), Prendergast (1999) and Dixit (2000) shows, personnel economics has enabled a more penetrating economic analysis of employment contracts and payment systems. Incentive payments, since they are in addition to basic pay, alter at the margin the relative price of employees supplying more effort. Hence, substitution effects dominate and employees will reduce their level of shirking, switching additional efforts into those activities rewarded. As Milgrom and Roberts (1992) explain, the key question concerns the choice of incentive and monitoring intensity. In general, strong incentives should be applied when: a worker's performance is accurately measured; where they have the discretion to respond to incentives; and where outcomes are sensitive to worker effort levels. The Informativeness Principle holds that all performance measures that increase the accuracy with which worker effort levels are measured should be factored into the pay formula. However, in the case of multi-tasking and where certain desired outcomes cannot be measured, incentive contracts are likely to produce dysfunctional behaviour where workers neglect tasks that are not rewarded (the equal compensation principle). It follows that in these complex jobs, explicit incentive contracts are inefficient and will thus tend to be replaced by implicit ones (e.g. merit pay and promotion based upon subjective measures of performance) requiring a more holistic assessment of performance.

If the rankings and targets produced by subjective assessments are to be viewed as legitimate by those being assessed, then they are likely to be expensive for organisations to produce. As Prendergast (1999) explains, legitimacy is threatened by systematic errors which are frequently observed when assessors rank employees. Leniency bias reflects a tendency for assessors to be reluctant to award the lowest rankings to poorly performing employees. Whilst such behaviour may be rational in that it internalises the costs of demotivating the bottom ranked employees, it distorts the overall distribution of rankings. Similarly, centrality bias reflects a further distortion, the tendency for grades awarded to truncate the range of actual performance. In small and stable work groups favouritism appears to be a significant problem, with assessors deliberately distorting targets and outcomes to redistribute merit payments. Finally, subjective assessment encourages employees to switch their efforts into rent-seeking, influencing activities, which curry favour with their assessor. Collectively, these problems have prevented universal adoption of performance-related pay, and encouraged many organisations to de-couple appraisal from pay. Alternatively, some organisations and professions have sought to seek agreement for the explicit setting of performance standards and the use of external assessors.

Prior to the emergence of personnel economics, the emphasis upon a narrow rational-choice perspective prevented economic analysis from providing insights helpful to the design of efficient incentive systems for organisations. Instead, human resource specialists relied upon the insights into worker motivation provided by social and organisational psychologists. Psychological research suggests the importance of reference dependence in influencing behaviour (Rabin (1998) provides a survey of this area). Individuals appear to be sensitive to how pay compares with a reference level based upon past or expected outcomes, rather than just with alternative and marginal rewards as in conventional economic analysis. Loss aversion seems to be common across a wide range of behaviour, with employees being more sensitive to shortfalls below that reference level than to gains in excess. Similarly, socio-psychological research (Sørensen 1994) rejects the simple self-interest theory of preferences, finding that group comparisons and notions of fairness also influence behaviour.

This analysis of incentive pay for teachers will eventually need to incorporate all of these insights and it is important to recognise the limitations of existing economic analysis. As Gibbons (1998) points out:

one simple possibility is that economic models that ignore social psychology are incomplete (but perhaps still useful) descriptions of incentives in organisations. A more troubling possibility is that management practices based on economic models may dampen (or even destroy) non-economic realities such as intrinsic motivation and social relations.

(Gibbons 1998: 130)

Fehr and Gätcher's (2000) survey cites cases where explicit performance incentives appear to have 'crowded out' worker effort motivated by fairness or reciprocity. In order to examine this possibility for the case of teachers, we need to develop an economic analysis incorporating the idiosyncrasies of both professional labour markets and non-profit organisations.

6.5.2 The economics of professional and non-profit organisations' labour markets

As we established in Chapter 1, teaching is a complex activity, involving a wide variety of other inputs, multiple objectives and multi-tasking. Given this complexity and inherent uncertainties, even with the imposition of a National Curriculum and increased compulsory testing of pupils, teachers still exercise a large degree of discretion in the classroom. In other words, teachers' contracts are particularly incomplete. A common characteristic of professional labour markets is an explicit or implicit code of ethical behaviour based upon shared values.

Matthews (1991) sought to examine the economic rationale for these characteristics of traditional professional labour markets. His analysis, which we now extend to the teaching profession, was based upon the presence of asymmetric information and externalities. Asymmetric information prevents the specification of complete employment contracts and makes monitoring, whether by parents, pupils, headteachers, governors or OfSTED, expensive and imperfect. Protection against professionals exploiting both their discretion in the workplace and their superior knowledge may instead be provided by self-interested reputation considerations and internalised morality. Assisting professional workers in acquiring and keeping the trust of their clients is the adoption and enforcement of a code of ethics that prohibits such exploitation.

Externalities also arise, since in most state systems of schooling, teachers provide public goods, such as records of achievements of pupils and objective references for both pupils and colleagues, which provide low-cost screens for colleges, employers, financial markets and other decision-makers. In addition, the quasi-judicial role required in preparing pupils for, and contributing to, the assessment of their achievements may conflict with the provision of a service to parents and pupils. Professional ethics also cover acceptable behaviour in the face of this conflict and, as such, do not merely reflect the revealed preferences of either the client or those of the state.

In the teaching profession, one further characteristic, often neglected by economists, needs to be discussed: teamwork. The overall effectiveness of schools depends in part on the ability of the teachers to work together to produce local public goods. Reviews of British and North American research (Sammons *et al.* 1995, and Reynolds *et al.* 1996) indicate that effective schools tend to have teachers who share a unity of purpose and collectively exhibit consistency of practice and a high degree of collegiality and collaboration. This type of school culture appears to be particularly important in achieving targets such as reducing absenteeism, combating racism and drug abuse. Here, mutually reinforcing key messages and enforcing agreed policies, together with the sharing of information, resources and expertise seem to be critical in determining success.

Given that the presence of asymmetric information and externalities creates moral hazard problems for professionals, a key issue concerns the relative policing efficiency of monitoring and *caveat emptor* compared with regulated competition and professional self-regulation. The latter effectively prohibits certain specific practices, which create an opportunity or temptation to cheat, such as for teachers in the areas of information sharing, assessment and sexual relationships with pupils. While greater competition and increased use of PRP increase the financial incentives for professionals to cheat, traditional professionalism relies upon a shared professional objective function and intrinsic motivation (Matthews (1991) terms this a 'maximand-morality') to prevent inertia and a lack of effort. Rather than the bottom-line motivation of competitive markets, concern with peer esteem and a service ideal are assumed to drive behaviour. In the case of teachers, the latter can be related to the 'public service motivation' analysed by Francois (2000). Unlike the case of regulated competition, here the appropriate maximand-moralities can produce a stable code of conduct. The 'poor' teachers do not drive out the 'good' or distort recruitment in ways that threaten existing shared perceptions of 'duty'. Self-selection and peer pressure forces are generated which sustain those norms. That is, recruiting into the teaching profession only those that share its existing dominant philosophy may be an efficient response to the idiosyncrasies of teaching, ensuring that trust is not abused, and that teamwork and public goods production are sustained.

The model of the survival of altruistic behaviour developed by Eshel *et al.* (1998) can be used to explain the dynamic stability of this 'vocation' model of professional labour markets. Complying with the professional code of ethics imposes costs on teachers that can be viewed as an investment in the provision of a local public good for their colleagues. Where such behaviour dominates in an individual school, other altruists on the staff primarily enjoy the benefits of such altruistic behaviour. Where new teachers have to learn what modes of professional behaviour to follow, then imitation of the observed successful dominant altruistic behaviour of their new colleagues can preserve the survival of such behaviour over time. Eshel *et al.* show that such behaviour can survive even in the presence of decision-makers who are unwilling to contribute to the public good ('egotists') or even gain utility from imposing costs on their colleagues ('hooligans').

The economic study of non-profit institutions has recently utilised similar arguments to generate some complementary insights. In order to gain trust, nonprofits have to gain consumer confidence that they will not exploit their informational advantages. Extending the analysis of Handy (1995) to the case of schools, a school's board of governors offers their own reputations as collateral against such exploitation. However, governors are not involved in the day-to-day management of schools and, in order to safeguard their reputations, they must be able to trust the head and teachers to do their jobs honestly and conscientiously. Because of the need for external and internal trust, and the absence of low-cost indicators of teacher performance, agency problems are likely to be severe. Internal trust problems are reduced if only committed individuals are appointed as teachers. Again extending Handy and Katz's (1998) analysis to the case of schools, governors and heads can attract committed individuals by offering them pay and working conditions that promote self-selection amongst potential employees. Compared with the for-profit sectors of the economy, compensation packages here are likely to involve lower money wages but a larger component of fringe benefits, such as a high degree of discretion, classroom facilities and learning aids. Here adverse selection issues dominate moral hazard issues and the effect of this self-selection process is to reduce the need for both monitoring teachers and paying them efficiency wages. Implicit in this analysis is the assumption that governors, heads and teachers share a common educational philosophy and view of the desired educational outcomes. The matching process, especially the selection interviews, is therefore likely to concentrate upon exploring these views rather than on pecuniary contractual issues.

We now need to bring together these approaches and consider their relevance for the analysis of PRP for teachers. One likely objection to the analysis above concerns the extent to which teaching is a self-regulating profession. Notwithstanding the aspirations of the teaching unions and the new General Teaching Council, teaching in England and Wales does not yet possess the credible regulatory mechanisms found in other countries such as Scotland or in other professions such as law and medicine. In their absence, the question arises as to the extent of shared professional standards and a collegiate ethos. Recent surveys of classroom teachers and heads (Marsden 2000) suggest a strong commitment to their schools, especially as indicated by their strong belief in, and acceptance of, their organisation's goals and objectives. This commitment compares favourably with that found elsewhere in the public (Marsden and French 1998) and private sectors (Workplace Employee Relations Survey 1998). More specifically related to our vocation model of teaching is Talbert and McLaughlin's (1996) finding that while teachers' professionalism (considered in terms of generic criteria for professional work and authority) is highly variable, it is highly sensitive to the strength and character of the local teacher community. Those teachers who participate in strong professional communities were found to have higher levels of professionalism as measured by the technical culture, service ethic and professional commitment. Such results are interpreted as reflecting the dangers of teacher isolation and importance of colleagues in promoting critical reflection and determining work norms and sanctions when managerial or internalised standards for practice are weak or inconsistent (Hargreaves and Dawe 1990). In summary, educational research suggests that where the 'collegiate ethos' is strong standards of professionalism are higher.

Overall, in designing a payment system for teachers the appropriate mix has to be determined of financial incentives, monitoring threats and regulatory constraints, and reliance on the conscientiousness of teachers resulting from their shared professional ethics and morality. Increased use of incentive payments may not only produce dysfunctional behaviour, but also threaten the sustainability of the professional ethic itself. Frey (1993) argues that where a psychological bond exists between principals and agents, increased monitoring can be counter-productive since the perception of a lack of trust causes less effort to be supplied. Similarly, Francois (2000) concludes that even where incentive contracts are feasible, the presence of public service motivation may cause them to be counter-productive. Crucially, however, this argument assumes that governments can credibly commit to output targets and that there is no goal divergence between employees and government.

The high level of commitment found amongst teachers (Spear *et al.* 2000) suggests that incentive pay is not necessary to stimulate additional effort. Indeed teachers currently appear to work relatively long hours (Marsden 2000). Performance pay instead may be designed to alter the allocation of discretionary hours, about a third of teachers' total term-time hours, between alternative activities. Indeed, where government distrusts the discretionary powers of individual teachers this may be their primary reason for extending PRP. If the objective functions of the state and the profession conflict, say, concerning the desired mix of promoting curiosity, creative thinking and fulfilling a pastoral role compared with developing narrow basic skills tested in standardised exams, then fundamental differences in preferred curriculum, teaching methods and organisational structures may emerge. In this case the extension of incentive pay fulfils a similar role to other schooling reforms in the UK (Broadbent and Laughlin 1997; Whitty *et al.* 1998): motivating teachers to adopt the government's objective function.

6.5.3 Performance-related pay (PRP) and teachers: the limited evidence

There has been a tendency to view PRP for teachers as a new policy. However, PRP reforms of teachers' pay have occurred periodically over the last century and a half. In their survey, Murnane and Cohen (1986: 2) conclude that: 'the history of merit pay suggests that while interest in paying teachers according to merit endures, attempts to use merit pay do not'. For example, nearly 140 years ago the British government, under pressure to curb public spending and concerned with educational standards, introduced a PRP system. Elementary school teachers were rewarded partly on the basis of their pupil's attendance levels and examination results in reading, writing and arithmetic (Cutler and Waine 1999). The consequences were a narrower curriculum, increased tension between inspectors and teachers, concentration upon pupils on the margin of passing examinations and, ultimately, the growth of trade unionism amongst British teachers (Coltham 1972). Murnane (1996: 252) reviews more recent and relevant evidence from US experience. He concludes that: 'merit pay based upon supervisor's performance evaluations simply does not work. ... There is no example of a troubled district that has successfully used merit pay to improve its performance'.

As part of an assessment of the operation of performance-related pay in the public services, Marsden and French (1998) investigated the operation of the scheme for heads and deputies mentioned earlier. Their survey of members of the two professional associations suggests that about 30 per cent of heads and deputies receive awards annually, though 44 per cent had not received any award between 1991 and 1994. They found that the more merit pay awarded the more favourable the response of heads and deputies. However, the over-whelming reaction of those covered was negative. 'They do not agree with the principle; its impact on target setting has been small, and that on personal motivation small or irrelevant; and it is believed to damage morale in schools and weaken team working' (*ibid.*: 121). In part this negative reaction appears to reflect unclear and inconsistently applied criteria for awarding performance pay. There was some evidence, as found more strongly in their other public sector case studies, that PRP increases work effectiveness by improved goal-setting. More negatively, whilst reliability concerns (accurately measuring the criteria for evaluation) can be addressed by careful compilation of performance indica-tors and extensive (and expensive) monitoring, there remains a more fundamental problem: validity. Many heads and deputies believe that the performance indicators adopted are measuring the wrong outputs. Marsden and French interpret their respondents as disagreeing with government and/or their governing bodies over the goals of education. Heads and deputies may be rejecting as inappropriate in schooling markets, the proposition that principals have the right to set the nature of their agents' output.

Confirmation of the unpopularity of PRP amongst the profession is provided by an analysis of the response forms to the 1998 Green Paper (Storey 2000), general surveys of teachers' attitudes (Spear *et al.* 2000), and by a survey of teachers conducted as the new scheme was being implemented (Marsden 2000). The latter study found that two-thirds of respondents rejected the principle of performance pay, with over half doing so strongly. Over half rejected the prin-ciple that their pay should take account of pupil progress, with nearly three-quarters rejecting the proposition that linking pay to the Performance Review would result in a fairer allocation of pay. Less than a tenth of respon-dents felt that the DfEE or LEA broadly shared the same interests as themselves when it came to the implementation of performance management.

6.5.4 Extending PRP for teachers: an assessment

The analysis above provides some insights into why incentive pay is much less common than implied by the analysis of single product organisations with single-task workers. In this section we now directly consider the issue of the optimal incentive intensity for classroom teachers. We concentrate upon the UK and individual performance pay and performance-related promotion, since the new School Performance Award scheme currently provides only a small, non-consolidated financial incentive. In the following discussion we ignore the issues of time consistency and opportunistic changes to working conditions and practices. That is, we assume the changes are credible, with future governments adopting identical objective functions, and that teachers interpret them as permanent changes to their terms and conditions of employment. This would appear to be an appropriate assumption, given the broad continuity of educational policy across recent governments. We also ignore the administration costs to schools and LEAs of introducing and maintaining the performance management framework, though, as noted above, these seem to be huge.

Richardson (1999) argues that individual performance related pay is more likely to be successful in schools where teachers accept its principle and legitimacy, goals set are clear, achievable but challenging, and teachers accept the assessments of their performance. In addition, financial rewards in the profession have to be consistently related to performance. Currently, as we have noted above, the evidence (Marsden 2000; Storey 2000) suggests that teachers in general neither accept the legitimacy of the new system of performance management nor trust national and local government to fairly implement it. By far the most contentious area of the performance management framework was the inclusion and measurement of pupil progress. Studies have identified cream skimming and other dysfunctional effects of 'payment by pupil-results'. American experience suggests that using student assessments in incentive systems distorts the allocation of teachers between classes and reduces co-operation with colleagues (Koretz 1996). Moreover, teachers concentrate their efforts on the marginal pupils, that is those students who are close to reaching their set target – for example, five GCSE passes at grades A–C – and neglect those clearly above or below this level of attainment.

The analysis by Holmstrom and Milgrom (1991) of the multitask principal-agent problem can provide an explanation for these outcomes. They consider an occupation like teaching, with an incomplete set of performance indicators and where measurement errors differ across individual indicators. They argue that the complexity of potential responses to incentives requires that payment systems be formulated in conjunction with other determinants of employee behaviour such as promotion criteria, job design, workplace norms and intrinsic motivation.

In general, the desirability of paying an incentive for, say, pupil's performance, decreases with the difficulty of measuring performance in other activities (e.g. pastoral care) which are valued objectives of the principal and which make competitive demands upon teacher's time. Indeed, Bernheim and Whinston (1998) show that once some aspects of performance are unverifiable, it is often optimal to leave verifiable aspects unspecified in the employment contract, even when they are observable to both parties. Incentive pay deliberately alters the structure of opportunity costs which teachers face in allocating their discretionary time and effort. It is difficult to find – if one exists – the set of algorithms which enables heads to reward individual teachers on the basis of pupil results and rely upon monitoring, professional ethics and subjective performance assessments to ensure the desired supply of effort to non-specified and imperfectly rewarded tasks.

One solution is to increase the intensity of incentives but require that teaching be segmented into single tasks (Hannaway 1992). Here, individual teachers are rewarded on the basis of a single output – say, the increase in academic attainment of their class – with other teachers in the school being rewarded on the basis of other desired outcomes such as the development of social skills. The feasibility of such a scheme depends crucially on the ability to segment educational outcomes in this way and the extent to which alternative outcomes are jointly or competitively produced. More generally, in setting targets and assessing performance different teaching activities should only be grouped together when they are complements (Dixit 2000).

The key issue is thus whether an increase in incentive intensity produces positive net benefits to schooling outputs. If a large weight is attached to improving measured pupil attainment in applying the performance management framework then the expansion of incentive pay will raise this performance. However, targeting one aspect of individual performance for teachers working at maximum effort will be detrimental to aspects weighted less heavily. The overall desirability of increased incentives, therefore, depends upon whether the actual weights attached to different educational outputs reflect society's preferences and upon the overall impact on professional standards. In general, when co-operation and collegiality amongst teachers is crucial or where heads are mistrusted, school-based rather than individual wage incentives should dominate. However, finding the right balance of incentives and intrinsic motivation cannot be a process of iteration. Our analysis of the stability of professional norms and ethics suggests that increasing individual incentive pay may change the sustainable equilibrium. A permanent weakening of professional self-regulation can follow an increase in individual incentives. Hence, the importance of establishing the legitimacy of the 'threshold' as the manifestation of the profession's standards.

Career considerations have been normally modelled in personnel economics as being internal to a firm; however, they have yet to be fully analysed for occupations, such as teaching, where a high proportion of skills are transferable and external promotion therefore is common. Rewarding a teacher provides a signal of their quality to other schools and the consequences for the mobility of 'career classroom teachers' may be significant, as appointing outsiders becomes less risky. If, as seems likely, accelerated increments are effectively to be eventually funded from a school's normal budget, then well-funded schools can bid high-performing teachers from those less well endowed. This is likely to lead to a further strengthening of hierarchies in local schooling markets, see Chapter 8, as well as distorting the inter-school relationship between performance and pay.

One further concern relates to the role of headteachers in the award of incentive payments. Our analysis has so far concentrated upon contractual relationships and, given the presence of information asymmetries and incomplete measurement of a teacher's outputs, most schemes require heads to contribute to performance assessments. Such analyses ignore the role of heads as leaders – that is, their role in encouraging and motivating fellow professionals. As Hermalin (1998) argues, the economic rationale for, in our case, teachers to 'voluntarily follow' is that they believe heads have better information about what they should do than they have. They must further believe that the head will not mislead them. In terms of our earlier argument, this could occur if only heads possess the knowledge about the returns to the collective efforts of teachers in generating public goods. Hermalin argues that, to achieve the leadership role, headteachers must convince teachers that their own goals and objectives are consistent with those of their colleagues. Where teachers view incentive payments as inconsistent with their professional norms, it follows that the involvement of heads in the allocation of those payments undermines their leadership role in the school.

6.6 Conclusions: proletarianisation or changing professional norms?

The discussion in this chapter centres around two very different interpretations of the teaching profession. From one viewpoint, teacher professionalism, reinforced by licensing, is seen as the ultimate safeguard for the retention of multiple objectives for state schooling. Policy-making, government and market failures are likely in their different ways to lead to the adoption of narrow targets. In particular, they may promote an undue emphasis on raising academic attainment of pupils, and consequentially a strengthening of social divisions within schooling and society as a whole. From the other perspective, teacher professionalism is seen as a barrier that distorts educational outcomes to those favoured by teachers. 'Collegiate ethos' is here viewed as a force for conserving inefficient and outmoded practices and thwarting the legitimate call for greater accountability.

The increased devolution of financial decisions to local schools weakens bureaucratic and political interference in school management and potentially empowers teachers. In practice, while this may be true for headteachers and school principals and governors, the strengthening of school choice, curriculum constraints, pupil-testing and pay incentives seem overall to have controlled classroom teachers' work more tightly. Whitty *et al.* (1998) conclude that across most countries the shift towards school-based management does not seem to have raised teacher empowerment, though the intensity of their work has increased. Classroom teachers appear to play only a marginal role in school financial decision-making (Levačić 1995). Without pre-empting our discussion in the following chapter, market-based reforms are generally viewed as an attempt to change professional norms and ethics, while strengthening rival stakeholders' power and managerial values.

The analysis above and previous experience suggests that the extension of incentive payments will alter the behaviour of teachers. The behavioural changes may be as dramatic as those caused by earlier attempts in the UK to make teachers' employment contracts more complete by specifying contractual hours of working. Our review of theory and evidence suggests that it will be surprising if increased incentive payments are not associated with an improvement in whatever objective measures of teacher's performance are promoted in the scheme. However, the revised contracts caused teachers to switch efforts from extra-curricular activities, such as organising school sporting and cultural activities, to those consistent with their contractual requirement. We should anticipate that increased incentive pay would also produce examples of unanticipated dysfunctional behaviour.

7 Governance, monitoring and performance indicators

7.1 Introduction

As we noted in Chapter 1, the common underlying assumption of much neo-liberal and 'Third Way' analysis is that government failures cause significant inefficiencies in the public provision of goods and services. Extending or imitating market forces has become a shared policy response, aimed at generating a new performance culture in the (smaller) public sector. While market-testing and privatisation have been the preferred responses of the neoliberals, education policy makers of all persuasion have been willing to encourage public sector management to adopt what might regarded as 'private sector practices' for strategic development. Sometimes referred to as 'restructuring' (e.g. Lawton 1992), this may or may not be accompanied by market reforms. In the case of schooling, this begs two questions which determine appropriate approaches to formulating strategy in schooling. First, which should be regarded as the 'prime business unit', the school or the complete public school system? Second, to what extent are the implications of alternative schooling processes for current and future social welfare known or knowable?

If the complete public school system is regarded as the prime business unit and the implications of alternative schooling processes are known, then 'rational planning' provides an appropriate template for strategy in public schooling. In this case, the state assumes responsibility for forming strategy which schools are charged with implementing. Schools are given flexibility in their purchase and deployment of resources so as to exploit local circumstances and monitoring focuses on checking that schools are keeping to the mandated strategy and exploiting their flexibility in an effective manner. This division of responsibility follows from the managerialist critique of information flows in large organisations. The literature on business strategy that has developed on this issue (see Spender 2001) identifies two kinds of problem. First, if the external environment of an organisation (preferences of customers and the behaviour of suppliers and competitors) is volatile or spatially specialised, a centralised bureaucracy slows an organisation's response to change and restricts freedom to exploit potential cost savings and revenue increases through response to local circumstances. Systems for controlling and monitoring processes in large organisations require standard rigid procedures that resist innovation. Second, communication through long chains of command is prone to substantial reinterpretation. Hence the prescription that the centre of an organisation should restrict its communication to broad goals and its monitoring to broad, rather than detailed, outcomes (Peters and Waterman 1982). Policies to introduce specialist schools (discussed further in Chapter 8) may be seen in this light. The introduction of a specialist schools programme presumes that the state has correctly identified broad parental preferences that have not been satisfied by the production choices of local schools.

If we keep the assumption that the implications of school processes are known, but view the school as the 'business unit', then it is the school that may be expected to adopt rational planning, and monitoring by the state takes a different form. Designating the school as the business unit presumes that schools operate within some form of market that provides incentives for technical and allocative efficiency. In these circumstances, the state must ensure that parents and pupils have good quality information about alternative providers and reduce barriers restricting the choice of alternative schools. This facilitates 'competition by comparison' and may be associated with slogans such as 'standards not structures'. The role of monitoring is then to check that schools are not exploiting market power and to make sure that minimum acceptable standards are maintained. We may relate this monitoring role to the application of principal–agent theory discussed in Chapter 1. The perspective that the whole school system is the business unit implies that the principal is the state acting on behalf of all stakeholders. The perspective that the school is the business unit implies that the parent is the principal and, without regulation, schools will only have an incentive to respond to their preferences. The interests of other stakeholders might be upheld by a regulatory and monitoring system applied by the state. Typically, this has been observed in a tightening of state control over the curriculum as in New Zealand's 'tight-loose-tight' policy (Fiske and Ladd 2000) and the National Curriculum in England and Wales. Other features of this tightening of control have been the introduction of Curriculum Based Exit Examinations and, in England, the introduction of detailed guidance on the teaching of literacy and numeracy.

As school heads and principals become more accountable to parents and national governments for schooling outcomes, it would appear to follow that they need greater empowerment to take decisions without undue regulatory constraint. As President Bush remarked in launching his first policy initiative, 'if local schools do not have the freedom to change, they cannot be held accountable for failing to change' (*Wall Street Journal*, 25 January 2001). This explains the move in many countries towards locally managed schools and school-based management. In some countries, France and the US for example, reforms have attempted to decentralise both governance and regulation. In others, such as the UK, regulations have become more centralised. Moreover, even though both France and the US sought to increase accountability and efficiency, the former concentrated upon devolving power to local government whilst the US emphasised increasing national educational standards (Menéndez Weidman 2001).

If the effects of schooling processes on social welfare are not fully known then rational planning becomes an inadequate approach to strategy and the problem becomes one of identifying more efficient (in allocative as well as technical terms) practices and securing their adoption by schools throughout a public system. With regard to the identification of more efficient practice, the main question is whether this is best undertaken by the state or the school. In so far as research and development requires large resources, there is a case for the state unless schools can collaborate in sufficient numbers to pool their resources. In so far as developments are spurred by responses to local circumstances, the identification of new practices is best undertaken by the school. The mechanism for dissemination of better practices is again dependent on whether the system or the school is viewed as the business unit. If the school system is the business unit then the state takes responsibility for the dissemination of 'better practice' and a key role of monitoring becomes checking whether schools are adopting practices believed by the state to be better. If the school is the business unit, then the spread of valuable information is dependent on that information becoming available. In so far as competitive advantage is the motivation for schools taking the risks involved in developing new practices, they face an incentive to withhold that information from competitor schools.

A policy committed to just one of these perceptions about the nature of the 'business unit' in schooling and the degree to which 'best practice' is known ought not to face too many contradictions in its application. However, at several times in this book, we have observed tensions between policies aimed at increasing the influence of market forces and policies intended to improve strategic management in the schooling system. In this chapter we examine some of these tensions more closely.

Initially, in Section 7.2.1, we examine how reforms have altered the prevailing system of governance structures in education. We concentrate upon three aspects: locally managed schools, competition between different governance systems within the state schooling system and attempts to promote partnerships and co-operation within local schooling markets. We examine the rationale for, and consequences of, devolving budgets and certain other functions to schools. Next, in Section 7.2.2, the theory of institutional competition is utilised to assess whether the market can be relied upon to discriminate efficiently between rival governance structures in schooling markets. The final part of this section (7.2.3) identifies some contradictions resulting from 'Third Way' concerns to encourage co-operation and increase the speed of diffusion of best practice in schooling markets. Section 7.3 addresses the invasion of performance monitoring into state schooling systems. We explore the rationale for that invasion, identifying the advantages and disadvantages of the introduction of performance indicators and the interaction with school inspection. This is followed by a consideration of two related aspects of the New Public Management: benchmarking and the championing of evidence-based policy making. This discussion then leads to an examination of the role of national curriculum-based examinations and whether schooling markets are compatible with the co-existence of high status academic and vocational pathways. The final substantive sub-section of the chapter considers the key issues related to the construction and publication of school performance tables. In developing our discussion we seek to analyse the implications of options 15–22 in Box 4.1.

7.2 Changing the governance structure

7.2.1 Subsidiarity: local school management

Despite differences in economic, social and political contexts, a common tendency of schooling reforms in many OECD countries has been a concern to decentralise managerial decision-making to schools whilst centralising control over the specification and monitoring of educational standards (Levačić 1995; Fiske and Ladd 2000). Local school management has emerged in some developing countries in very different circumstances. For example, in El Salvador locally managed schools developed during the 1980s civil war and included a strong emphasis on elected parents serving on a school governing committee. Since 1991 this structure for schooling, which was initiated in a time of emergency, has been pursued as a prototype for the extension of schooling in rural areas (Jimenez and Sawada 1999). The representation of stakeholders on governing bodies of locally managed schools tends to reflect the circumstances in which this form of governance develops. Bearing in mind the desirability of maintaining an influence on public schools of stakeholders other than parents and teachers, the El Salvador case provides a useful counterpoint to the OECD examples upon which we now concentrate.

In the US, the term school-based or site-based management has come to represent a shift of governance structures, redistributing decision-making authority to local stakeholders and reflecting a strategy for improvement based upon bottom-up change (Murphy 1997). The arguments for extending school-based management proved to be persuasive in the US notwithstanding a lack of supporting empirical evidence (Summers and Johnson 1996). The most radical changes have occurred in the UK, where the local management of schools (LMS) was a key part of the 1988 Education Reform Act. This Act required LEAs to delegate to individual schools a formula-based budget to cover most of their running costs with governing bodies also becoming responsible for appointing, disciplining and dismissing staff. The current target is that up to 85 per cent of school budgets should be devolved. The 1998 School Standards and Framework Act introduced 'Fair Funding'. This extended the range of expenditures over which schools assumed budgetary responsibility and enabled them to enter into contracts with any providers of the previously centralised services. Typically, it also included increased performance monitoring and benchmarking to create additional pressures on LEAs to increase delegation. Absent from the system in England and Wales was any extension of teacher empowerment and, as Levačić (1995) shows, in practice these reforms have in effect empowered headteachers.

The objectives of decentralisation of management in Australia, New Zealand and the UK was to increase the efficiency of resource use and raise school effectiveness through resulting increases in the quality of teaching and learning. A third objective, shared by some US reforms, was to increase accountability of schools to their local community. Devolving decision-making powers to individual schools enables them to respond to local competitive pressures. In the New Zealand reforms, whilst initially a much stronger role was to be played in school decision-making by local communities, reforms quickly revealed tensions between schools responding to the perceived needs of local communities and complying with overall national government strategy (Lauder *et al.* 1999). In addition, subsidiarity arguments rest upon the presence of diseconomies of scale and improvements in the quality of decision-making at the local level (Summers and Johnson 1996). The latter follows since education production is complex, non-routine and not easily monitored at a distance. Decision-making at the national and local government level can lead to inflexible, uniform provision and prevents local managers from exploiting their informational advantages by reallocating expenditure. In support, Levačić (1995) reports savings in heating, repairs, catering and equipment purchasing as a consequence of LMS in England and Wales. On the other hand, local financial control may be of limited benefit given that staffing costs account for over two-thirds of a school's expenditure, and, as discussed in the previous chapter, salary structures are determined nationally. In practice, much senior school management time is devoted to financial management tasks that produce only marginal changes in the pattern of expenditure. This may be a particularly important argument against LMS in small schools. Economies of scale in the provision of services to schools, such as those provided by accountants and educational psychologists, provides a further counter-argument. In addition, with only half of schools in England and Wales operating at physical capacity, the government's ability to match local supply and demand has deteriorated and nearly one-fifth of parents fail to place their children in their first preference school (Audit Commission 1996).

Equity as well as efficiency considerations need to be included in the assessment of the desirability of decentralising school decision-making. In order to address these equity considerations we need to consider both procedural and distributional equity. Procedural equity requires that consistent rules be applied across all decision-making. Hence, in the UK the requirement that LEA's adopt formula-funding based upon objective rather than historical data (Levačić 1995). Distributional equity refers to the impact upon the distribution of income and wealth. Horizontal equity here requires that every child should be treated similarly in the same circumstance, while vertical equity requires that children with different needs should be treated in ways that compensate for these differences. Both of these principles have influenced LMS in the UK. The requirement that every pupil in the same year should have the same allocation of money across an LEA's schools reflects horizontal equity considerations. Vertical equity considerations have led to LEAs allocating additional funds to schools on the basis of the special needs of their pupils and supplementary payments for small schools and those on split sites. The additional funds provided to GM schools by central government, or by those LEAs trying to prevent GM defections, are inconsistent with horizontal equity. While LMS allows schools to adjust their pattern of expenditure to reflect the individual learning needs of their students, it also allows schools to reallocate funds which would previously have been required to be spent on the socially and educationally disadvantaged.

Local school management is not sufficient by itself to ensure that the reallocation of resources results in improved schooling outcomes. Hanushek (1996b) argues that decentralised decision-making needs to be combined with school-based incentives linked to improved student performance. By itself, school-based management could worsen principal–agent problems as heads and teachers gain greater freedom to pursue their own objectives. He also raises the issue of the need for additional training and the changes needed in the required attributes of school managers. Altogether, Hanushek argues that school-based management is not an end in itself. Even when accompanied by appropriate incentives, the positive effects are likely to be longer-term.

Broadbent and Laughlin (1997), while providing a similar description of the consequences of LMS to that of Hanushek, differ in the conclusions reached as to its ultimate objectives. Taken together, their views describe a process of rational planning with which we started this chapter. They argue that under the guise of a delegation of responsibility, such reforms seek ultimately to restrict the autonomy of distrusted professionals and establish stronger centralisation. They also point to the introduction of a National Curriculum, the Parent's Charter, school league tables and four-yearly OfSTED reviews in England and Wales as together shifting towards a private sector approach to management. Outputs now become quantified, accountabilities are related to those outputs, and responsibilities are individualised to enable market controls to be implemented. Broadbent and Laughlin see these reforms as together creating an indirect contracting process with schools competing to improve league table position and parents assuming the role of customers. Those teachers who reject the market approach become alienated and are less likely to apply for senior posts, thereby consolidating the new value system.

Both the study by Levačić (1995) and a survey of headteachers (DfEE 2001a) found that LMS in England and Wales had proved popular with headteachers. The latter survey found majority support amongst secondary headteachers for further delegation of funding and responsibilities from their LEA. However, when offered a list from which to identify what those delegated functions should be, only responsibility for the production of special educational needs statements gained sizeable support. This latter choice may have been motivated by the chronic excess demand for LEA funding in this area, rather than reflecting a concern with improving the overall quality of decision-making. Levačić reports that most schools have been able to manage their finances effectively, though the financial uncertainty induced by a formula-funding system anchored on pupil numbers has lead to apparently socially dysfunctional responses. For example, most schools faced with this uncertainty have accumulated reserves and relied more on temporary staff contracts. Schools have been able to switch expenditure away from operating services and towards improving their physical environment and direct support for teaching and learning, particularly teaching support staff. However, LMS has resulted in headteachers assuming responsibility for financial management, with deputy heads in most primary schools taking over responsibility for curriculum management. At the secondary school level, management structures have become more diverse with a general increase in the dispersion of management roles amongst senior staff. Levačić reports that governing bodies have largely remained passive in the process of financial decision-making. In conclusion, LMS seems to have resulted in increased cost-efficiency and significant organisational changes, though the evidence on overall school effectiveness is of necessity much more tentative.

One dimension missing from the decentralisation debate in the UK has been decentralisation of government. As we discussed in Chapter 3, Tiebout's (1956) vision of efficient regulatory competition was based on local governments competing to attract residents on the basis of differing tax and public goods combinations. In the UK, central government has become unwilling to delegate additional taxation and spending powers to local governments and, most recently, institutional competition has been substituted for regulatory competition.

7.2.2 Institutional competition: competing state school sectors

The 1988 Education Reform Act also effectively created two competing state school sectors in England and Wales: schools remaining within local government control and those opting out of LEA control after a parental ballot and approval by the Secretary of State. The latter grant-maintained schools (GM) were funded directly from central government and were able to select a portion of their pupil intake on the basis of ability or aptitude. By the time of their reclassification in the 1998 School Standards and Framework Act there were around 1,200 GM schools, predominantly in England, covering around 17 per cent of secondary and 3 per cent of primary schools in England and Wales. GM schools attracted premium funding during a transition period and more generous capital allocations than LEA schools (Levačić and Hardman 1999).

The economic rationale for promoting different systems of corporate governance is based upon the theory of institutional competition. This suggests that encouraging competition between different systems not only produces the benefits generated by competition by comparison, but also promotes survival of the fittest. This process has been used to justify the emergence of charter schools in the US over the last decade (Finn *et al.* 2000). It also fits well with the pragmatism of 'Third Way' approaches to educational decision-making with their emphasis on standards rather than structures (Anderson 2001). Advocates of the process argue that if competition between the sectors is free and fair, then, given school choice is in place, the system of corporate governance which best matches parental preferences will succeed over time in raising their market share. Hence, the market dictates which form of school governance should survive in the long-run. Assuming a diversity of parental tastes and multiple providers in a local market, then equilibrium may be consistent with the survival of multiple systems of governance. In addition to assumptions about the consequences of market failures, especially externalities, and equity discussed previously, the model of institutional competition requires further strong assumptions to be made. Crucially, this model implies a strong degree of homogeneity within the competing sectors, significant differences between the sectors in practice as well as in theory, and that local factors unrelated to school governance do not distort market judgements over time. The latter condition requires that governments are able (and willing) to isolate the school governance effect from other factors changing market shares. We shall question the appropriateness of each of these additional assumptions in the following discussion. Finally, it assumes that the costs of promoting diversity are more than offset over time by the dynamic efficiency gains resulting from that diversity.

Early assessments of GM schools suggested that they had generally failed to increase the diversity of provision in local schooling markets (Fitz *et al.* 1993). GM schools competed largely on the basis of traditional conceptions of educational quality. Rather than bringing about greater parental or community involvement, headteacher power appeared to have been enhanced (Gewirtz *et al.* 1995). Benn and Chitty (1996) found that while most GM schools identified themselves as comprehensive schools, they were significantly more likely to have sixth forms, high proportions of middle-class students and low proportions of working-class, poor and ethnic minority students. These findings should not be too surprising given that the reality was that existing voluntary schools were simply renamed and that LMS within the LEA sector meant that the two sectors differed only slightly in their degree of autonomy (Walford 2000). Hence, the real interest of the policy experiment concerns, in practice, the impact of their extra resources on parental preferences (discussed in Chapter 5) and educational attainment levels in the GM sector.

We have noted earlier that one consistent finding of school effectiveness research in the UK is the dominance of pupils' prior attainment and social background in explaining the variance in examination results between schools. Since GM schools have on average more socially advantaged students than LEA schools, and this segregation appears to have increased (see Chapters 5 and 8), then comparisons of performance becomes complex. Levačić and Hardman (1999) analyse the sources of the higher 'raw' scores in national examinations of GM schools. They conclude that once adjustment is made for the level of social disadvantage, then performances in GCSE and A level are not significantly different. In addition, they find that when LEA schools possessed similar examination and levels of social disadvantage amongst their students as GM schools, they proved to be equally successful in attracting pupils. Given the additional funding provided to the GM sector, this suggests that this element of the promotion of sectoral competition had provided poor value for money.

British Conservative governments at the end of the twentieth century introduced two further elements of sectoral competition into England and Wales. As
discussed in Chapter 4, City Technology Colleges (CTCs) were introduced in
1986, though by 2000 still only one-half of 1 per cent of secondary age pupils
attended such schools. These were initially intended to act as an alternative to
academic secondary schools, offering a more entrepreneurial and computer-
based curriculum. Like GM schools, they were self-governing and free of LEA
control. Once again, in practice, the distinctiveness of this sector was blunted
by the constraints imposed by the National Curriculum, the failure of significant financial support to materialise from the private sector and the tendency
for CTCs again to compete by appealing to traditional educational values
(Whitty *et al.* 1993). A further small-scale attempt to extend sectoral competition within the state schooling sector followed from changes made in the 1993
Education Act. These enabled groups of sponsors to propose that an entirely
new school, or their existing private school, be established as a grant-maintained school. Sponsors had to pay at least 15 per cent of the costs of providing
a school site and/or school buildings. In return, the sponsors could ensure that
the original character of the school, religious or otherwise, was maintained and
that the religious beliefs and practices of teachers could influence appointments.
In practice, only fifteen schools in England and Wales became GM under these
regulations (Walford 2000). In part, this paucity of successful applications
reflects the strong presence of religious schools amongst the voluntary sector.
Within England about one-third of all primary schools and one-fifth of
secondary schools are already religious schools. As we discussed earlier, the
successor to this programme was the City Academy programme, launched in
April 2000, which enabled sponsors from both the private and voluntary sectors
to establish new schools. Once again running costs are fully met by the state,
though a year later only six such schools were in the pipeline.

The 1998 School Standards and Framework Act, the first of a new Labour
Government, created three new categories of schools: community, foundation
and voluntary. The first of these effectively contained the previous LEA
schools, whilst the second included the previously aided and controlled schools
or those GM schools which previously had that status. The third new category,
'foundation', covered the remaining GM schools, which retained governor
responsibility for the employment of staff and ownership of buildings. Anderson
(2001: 59) concludes that 'despite changes in admission and funding arrangements, the demise of GM schools was largely in name only'. Similarly, Ball
(1999: 196) argues that notwithstanding the new Labour government's championing of the 'Third Way', in practice 'the basic organising principles of
educational provision have been taken over from the Conservatives untouched
and unquestioned'. Perhaps a more important shift in education policy in
England and Wales was a new emphasis upon benefits of co-operation between
schools and the need to increase the speed of diffusion of best practice. The
following section addresses these developments.

7.2.3 The economics of co-operation and collaboration: Beacons and Action Zones

The new Labour government's first White Paper on education, 'Excellence in Schools', suggested a shift from the previous government's preoccupation with competitive market structures towards encouraging partnership and co-operation amongst schooling providers. As we have seen already in this chapter and in Chapter 4, though a number of initiatives have sought to apply this new philosophy, the movement away from market forces has not been uniform. By early 2001, 73 Education Action Zones (EAZs) and 182 Beacon secondary schools had been established. EAZs are intended to promote innovation and the raising of standards in local areas of particularly intense social exclusion. Typically, such zones involve two or three secondary schools and their feeder primary schools, in total they cover around 6 per cent of the total school population. Selection is through a bidding process. All of the successful bidders in the first round had private sector involvement (Riley *et al.* 1998), though the amount contributed from this source in the first couple of years was far below that forecast. Initial assessments of similar schemes point to the problem of sustaining partnerships built upon diverse interests and within an overall framework of competitive schooling markets and structural and organisational change (Easen 2000).

Beacon schools, introduced in 1999, and specialist schools gain additional funding to assume the task of developing and spreading best practice. Rather than specialist schools using their distinctive expertise to gain local competitive advantage, they are now being encouraged to use it as resource for local people and neighbouring schools (Edwards *et al.* 1999). The Labour government is committed to increasing the numbers of specialist secondary schools to 1,500 by 2006, eight times the number existing in 1997. In addition to technology, languages, sport and the arts, new specialisms are to be introduced in engineering, science, and business and enterprise. A new category of advanced specialist school is to be developed to provide a 'leading edge'. It will be open to those high-performing schools with five years in the specialist schools programme. These would attract further premium funding to enable initiatives such as the development of distance learning and specialist curriculum materials. We discuss this programme further in Chapter 8. The number of Beacon schools are also to be increased from the 1,000 designated by September 2001. These play a more general developmental role in local markets. In future some schools will be designated as Beacons that prove to be adept at teaching 'new economy' skills such as the use of ICT and promoting creativity. Schools which exhibit excellence in working with their community will also be eligible for Beacon status.

Several other schemes in England and Wales have recently been introduced to address under-performance across geographical locations. The Excellence in Cities (EiC) scheme was launched in 1999 and now covers a third of all secondary age pupils in 1,000 schools. Since September 2001, its approach has been extended to smaller areas of deprivation through Excellence Clusters. The programmes provide additional resources to provide focused programmes for the more able and learning mentors to target obstacles to learning external to the school, to establish Learning Support Units to tackle disruption and exclusions, and to increase the number of Beacon and specialist schools in city areas. A fundamental principle underlying these schemes is that 'schools achieve more when they work together to raise standards' (DfEE 2001a: 45). Special funding is also available for school co-operation in those areas where selective secondary schooling persists. In addition to these area-focused schemes, the Labour government introduced a programme targeting over 500 low-performing secondary schools. These receive additional funding in return for adopting a Raising Achievement Plan, backed up with monitoring and advice from OfSTED.

Although the schemes are still in their infancy, the government claims in its 2001 Green Paper that schools in EiC areas have achieved faster improvements in educational attainments than schools elsewhere. This claim relates to both the proportion of pupils achieving five or more A*–C grade GCSEs and those getting at least one GCSE. Improvements are claimed to have been fastest in the most deprived schools. For educational researchers, the key concern is whether such improvements can be validated. If so, then it is necessary to iden-tify whether the sources of the improvement lie with the nature of the individual initiatives, such as the more co-operative schooling environment, or merely the increased funding available.

The 'Third Way' emphasis upon partnerships and co-operation as a means of tackling social exclusion and raising educational attainment appears to be at odds with market-based reforms. The latter see co-operation as a way of subverting market pressures that would otherwise stimulate increased efficiency and diversity. Perversely, it appears that it is the very failure of the more compet-itive schooling environment to promote diverse secondary schooling which lies behind the latest British government proposals to provide financial induce-ments for schools to become specialist providers of a specific curriculum in their local market. The 2001 Green Paper publicises plans to further extend the number of specialist schools, together with a rapid expansion of the number of Beacon schools. Notwithstanding this commitment to extend inter-school co-operation and increase the speed of dissemination of good practice, expansion of successful schools is also identified as a key means of addressing failure (DfEE 2001a). Around four-fifths of those schools designated as failing by OfSTED are turned round successfully. Of the remainder, four out of five are closed, around 120 in the first four years of the 1997 Labour government, with neighbouring schools expanded to take the pupils. The remaining schools, about 25 since 1997, were placed in a 'fresh start' scheme. This latter scheme involved a school re-opening under a new name, new headteacher and new staff.

Many of the most recent policies in England and Wales seek to enable lower-ranked schools in local markets to compete more successfully by specialisation. Specialisation without selection seeks to reduce 'cream-skimming' by reducing the ability of the market leader to pick and choose. Such a strategy has merits, but it requires a careful distribution of specialist labels within those markets. Moreover, it is continually being undermined by an annual system of reporting school performance that in practice validates the traditional academic epitomised by the local market leader. The origins and consequences of the growth of performance monitoring and target-setting in state schooling systems are the next topic to be discussed in this chapter.

7.3 Performance monitoring: theory and practice

In 1996 and 1997 there was a series of government policy initiatives in England and Wales designed to persuade schools to set targets for pupils, and LEAs to set targets for schools (discussed in Flecknoe 2001). Target-setting suddenly became a key facilitator for school improvement. The increased tendency to publish performance indicators in the public sector as a whole has been motivated by several factors. Most fundamental appears to have been a greater desire to increase accountability in order to address principal–agent problems (Smith 1995; Pollitt and Bouckaert 2000). This requires the availability of performance indicators (PIs) which identify the contributions of agents, and that government acts on the basis of that information provided. A theme of this book has been that schooling has multiple goals and a variety of stakeholders who may not share a common valuation of the different outputs. The choice of which measures of performance to monitor and publicise is thus immediately a controversial one. Providing an operational definition of efficiency and effectiveness requires both outputs and inputs to schooling to be quantified, and the issue of equity to be addressed. In practice, as discussed in the previous chapter, the increased monitoring of schools is also driven by governments' desire to regain control of the educational process, in the sense of changing cultures and the priorities of educational decision-makers.

PIs have increasingly been used to influence directly budget allocations in the public sector, becoming integrated with other aspects of management (Pollitt and Bouckaert 2000). In the UK, the 1998 Comprehensive Spending Review directly linked extra investment in public sector services with raising standards. Additional funding is allocated against 'specific, measurable, achievable, relevant and timed' (SMART) targets. For example, the public service agreement signed by the Department for Education and Employment with the Treasury in 2000, requires that by 2004, 80 per cent of 14 year olds should achieve level 5 in maths, 75 per cent the same level in English and similarly 70 per cent in science. It is intended that this contractual process be extended to local government. In 2001, the Treasury negotiated with local governments twenty pilot agreements. These specified additional expenditure set against specific targets. Surrey, for example, is to be allowed to increase expenditure by over £20 million if it meets thirteen targets, including reducing absences from school and improving GCSE results.

Smith's (1995) review of early UK experience in the public sector identifies five further principal benefits of setting performance indicators in addition to greater accountability. We now discuss these potential benefits in the context of state schools. First, PIs may clarify the objectives of the organisation. While this may be desirable and non-problematic in an organisation with a single output and single principal, it becomes a more contentious issue in more complex organisations and activities. Indeed, in education, the discussion of the previous chapter suggests that this may, in practice, be a process by which the priorities of one group of stakeholders, say, teaching professionals, are replaced by those of another group, say, central government.

Second, this process may assist the development of agreed measures of activity and outcomes. These measures should have the following properties identified by Meyer (1977). Outcome validity concerns whether the indicator is measuring the key educational outputs as valued by society. For example, an indicator that only measured the level of attainment achieved by the most able pupils may have little relation to the overall benefits to society of schooling provision. Non-corruptibility concerns the accuracy of the chosen performance indicator. Thus, measurements of absenteeism amongst pupils may be susceptible to manipulation by schools adjusting pupil monitoring and their notification of illness procedures. Finally, the indicator must represent a valid measure of a school's own performance – that is, it must measure accurately the school's own contribution to the overall outcome. For example, unadjusted pupil exam performance, given diverse student intakes, are poorly correlated with the actual contributions of schools to those results. It is to address this particular problem that value-added indicators have been developed, though, since these measures generally take no account of the different resource inputs, they provide no indication of value for money.

Output measurement is only useful if it can be related to the process of production within schools, since only then can the sources of differences within and between schools be analysed. Hence, a third benefit of introducing PIs may be that a greater understanding of the production process may be gained, and a fourth that of facilitating comparison of the performance of different schools. Both of these again require that the contributions of schools to educational value-added can be separated from factors, such as the characteristics of pupil intake, outside of the schools control. The fifth benefit identified by Smith is that performance indicators facilitate the setting of targets and priorities within individual schools. Clearly, credible and widely used performance indicators dictate the agenda for prioritising improvement within schools.

While there have been benefits gained as a result of the extension of performance monitoring and the introduction of performance indicators in the public sector, there have also been some costs. The opportunity costs of more testing is a narrower school curriculum, as preparing, completing and providing feedback on assessments displaces other learning activities. There are also significant direct costs of collecting, analysing and auditing information, but of more concern are the likely dysfunctional responses generated by the adoption of performance indicators (Smith 1993). Adopted PIs will inevitably fail to incorporate some of the multiple schooling outputs and inaccurately measure others, especially since some of these are not easily captured through quantitative indicators. The resulting incompleteness of the PIs encourages tunnel vision where heads ignore aspects of a school's performance not covered by PIs. Where PIs are developed within schools, and given the interdependencies between different schooling outputs discussed previously, then other forms of sub-optimisation may arise. Individual subject teams may concentrate upon achieving their own local targets, reducing co-operation with colleagues elsewhere in the school to the detriment of school-wide outcomes. In addition, most PI schemes concentrate attention on immediate outcomes and lead to the neglect of long-term objectives. In education such myopia problems may be severe as, say, staff are allocated on the basis of short-term considerations rather than longer-term career and school performance needs. Finally, inaccurate measurement encourages schools to enhance measured performance rather than actual performance and creative reporting occurs in areas like pupil absenteeism where some discretion at school level exists.

These problems associated with introducing and operating performance monitoring in the public sector have led to a number of strategies being developed to minimise dysfunctional responses (Smith 1995). Most have advocated staff involvement, flexibility in the use of PIs and caution in making simple comparisons between alternative providers, strategies that notably have not been employed in the UK schooling sector. Instead, PIs were centrally chosen and the system of school inspection changed to emphasise effectiveness and efficiency considerations. Both reforms appeared to have been implemented to challenge existing professional norms effectively. We delay our detailed discussion of the introduction of school performance tables in order to first consider school inspection.

7.3.1 School inspection

In the UK, the Office for Standards in Education (OfSTED), which is independent from the DfES but headed by an appointee of the Secretary of State, has a remit to raise the standards of attainment and the overall quality of schooling through periodic independent inspection, informed independent advice and public reporting. The inspection visits reach an overall assessment of a school's performance based upon pupils' standards and attendance, quality of schooling provided, the school's climate and culture, and its management and overall efficiency and value for money. The 1992 Education (Schools) Act that established OfSTED semi-privatised these inspections, which are now carried out by teams of inspectors who tender for specific contracts. To report on the quality of education provided by the school is one of the four general reporting duties required of the registered inspectors. The other three concern standards, finance and the spiritual, moral, social and cultural development of the pupils. This legislation specified that each school should be inspected every four years (later modified to every six years, though more frequently for 'weaker' schools) with consultations with parents being part of the inspection process. OfSTED

(1998a) states that for secondary schools 'the purpose of inspection is to identify strengths and weaknesses so that schools may improve the quality of education they provide and raise the educational standards achieved by their pupils'. Reports are in the public domain, and OfSTED's annual report lists both excellent and 'failing' schools. The latter are provided with set requirements for improvement. The overall process of inspection is described in Grubb (1999).

Riley and Rowles (1997) surveyed the impact of the new OfSTED system and how LEAs had adjusted to their reduced inspection role. They conclude that the new quality framework has been successful in requiring schools to focus more on their quality needs. It appears to have been particularly helpful in stimulating improvements in those schools most resistant to change. Doubts remain about the differing quality of the inspection teams, the discouragement of risk and innovation, and the overall quantity of work for teachers and school managers associated with the inspections (Winkley 1999). A survey of headteachers (Fitz-Gibbon and Stephenson-Forster 1999) indicated that OfSTED had failed to win their confidence. The survey provides estimates of the costs of an inspection to a school. The median response was 40 staff days preparing documentation, 10 days of head's time on documents, and 5 staff days on extra meetings of staff. Kogan and Maden (1999) estimated that in the late 1990s the full cost of an OfSTED visit was around £26,000 for a median-sized primary school and £65,000 for a secondary school. One major disadvantage of the new system has been that the use of sub-contractors has destroyed the continuous relationship between teachers and inspectors. This has contributed to a reduction in the availability of external advice and expertise to teachers (Finkelstein and Grubb 2001).

There is little direct evidence of the impact of OfSTED inspections on the quality of schooling outcomes. Cullingford and Daniels (1999) attempt to examine the impact of inspection on the performance of a school's pupils in GCSE exams. They find that while the proportion of pupils gaining high grades (five or more A*–C grades) has been increasing, the schools which had been inspected achieved a slower rate of increase. Inspections during March and April seemed to be particularly disruptive as measured by pupil performance in GCSE examinations. There are obvious sample selection problems with such studies since we do not know the criteria OfSTED adopts to choose which schools to inspect first or their time of visiting during the year.

A key concern of government's intent on raising aggregate levels of student attainments is to ensure that incentives are created for all schools to improve their performance. A common strategy is to develop independent benchmarks to increase the comparability of school performances given the diversity of their intakes. We now consider the attractions of benchmarking before addressing the UK's experience of publishing school performance tables.

7.3.2 Benchmarking and evidence-based policy making

Benchmarking is a tool for raising efficiency where the performance of one organisation is measured against a standard, either absolute or relative to the performance of other organisations (Cowper and Samuels 1997). Such an analysis of performance, practices and processes, both between and within organisations, has the target of generating self-improvement (Jackson and Lund 2000). The presumption being that any deviation of performance from the benchmark should be investigated and lead to both targeted changes in behaviour and continuing monitoring. Benchmarking of results thus tends to lead to the benchmarking of processes; Francis *et al.* (1999) provide a survey of recent UK experience in developing benchmarking practices in the public and private sectors. As Schmid *et al.* (1999) explain, the ultimate aim of benchmarking is to establish a controlled learning process supported by monitoring and scientific analysis. The appropriateness of such methods rests upon issues concerned with comparability and transferability.

In the UK recently, the extension of benchmarking has been linked to a 'Third Way' championing of evidence-based policy making. Increasingly policies are initially piloted with the results used to refine their full implementation. Practice often appears to diverge from the original intentions, with policymakers responding to the results from formative studies rather than awaiting the results from more precise measurement. One example of such haste was the rapid expansion of the Excellence in Cities programme in England. It seems clear that the time-horizon of policy makers is shorter than that of those evaluating the new policies. Identifying best practice and encouraging policy transfer within such a policy-making process becomes even more problematic than our previous arguments may have suggested.

Overall, we agree with the strategy favoured by Tronti (1998), who concludes as follows:

> in order to obtain meaningful and desirable results, convergence must not be based only on the blind imitation of the best performers ... benchmarking implies a complex scientific, social and political process, whose success requires the accomplishment of many interrelated tasks. Among these are: understanding the reasons behind performance gaps, learning from better performers, evaluating the operative implications of institutional changes and adopting them through policy-making (while keeping social consensus), maintaining (or creating) a strong link between research and policy-making, through increased monitoring and evaluation analysis.
>
> (Tronti 1998: 511)

The issue remains as to what outcomes to benchmark. The existence of national curriculum-based examinations in many countries enables simple performance tables to be constructed for state schools. We look at their development and use in the following sections.

7.3.3 National curriculum-based examinations

In many countries, national or regional exit exams certify and signal the educational achievements of secondary school students to universities and employers. Since the nature and content of these exams influence both teaching and learning, educational reforms typically involve changes in the examination systems. US debates on educational reform have recently focused on the attractions of policies that make standards more homogeneous across schools. Elsewhere a key issue has been whether, in a market-driven system, a credible vocational qualification stream can co-exist when academic national curriculum-based examinations previously dominated. We examine both of these issues in this sub-section.

In the US, Costrell (1994) and Bishop (1997) have developed the case for Curriculum-based External Exit Exams (CBEEEs) based on world class content standards. It has been claimed that CBEEEs will improve teaching and learning and refine the signals provided to the labour market of relative academic achievement of entrants. The absence of mandatory CBEEEs has been argued to contribute to a large variation in school quality. Somanathan (1998) develops this argument to show that where informational asymmetries prevent employers observing the quality of school attended by an applicant, greater school diversity can lead to inefficient human capital decisions. Somanathan advocates CBEEEs to correct this inefficiency, since they improve information flows and reduce the distortions favouring college entry. However, as Adnett *et al.* (2001) show, CBEEEs in quasi-markets, where published school performance tables influence the pattern of demand for schooling, may distort market behaviour. In particular, they may prevent the market from generating rewards to successful schools with a low proportion of able students, or providing incentives for improvement for less successful schools with a high proportion of able students. The consequence being that the diversity of schooling outcomes may increase in a local market, an argument we develop in more detail in the following chapter.

Bishop (1998) develops these arguments further: if CBEEEs lead to employers attaching greater weights to academic achievements in hiring, then rewards become greater for successful studying and learning. Economic models of student behaviour suggest that in such circumstances a further consequence is a rise in student effort. Bishop provides empirical support for these hypotheses, using international, particularly Canadian, data. However, it may be difficult to design and/or sustain CBEEEs that provide both an appropriate signal to employers and those recruiting into higher education. Indeed, a concern in the UK has been that CBEEEs, in combination with market-based reforms, have strengthened a tendency towards academic schooling drift to the detriment of vocational relevance.

In attempting to respond to this tendency, as well as the altering of the pattern of employment discussed in Chapter 2, the British government introduced National Vocational Qualifications (NVQs) in the late 1980s. These are competency-based qualifications aimed at increasing attainment levels in core skills. They articulated six core skills (communications, problem-solving, numeracy, IT, teamworking and self-improvement) and created a series of occupation-specific assessments to test these core skills. General National

Vocational Qualifications (GNVQs), covering broad vocational areas, followed from 1991. These attempted to simplify the maze of qualifications previously available outside of the traditional academic curriculum. Though arguments based on parity of esteem required that GNVQs also become an alternative pathway into higher education, in practice, rather than promoting institutional competition between these different systems of qualifications, the government aided the consolidation of these new qualifications within the existing providers of schooling and training (Raggett and Williams 1999).

GNVQs were designed to prepare students for broad sectors of employment and to bridge the parity of esteem between academic and vocational qualifications. The low esteem of vocational qualifications reflected social class differences in the profile of those following the two pathways, and elements of informational and institutional failure (Davies and Adnett 1999). Despite the substantial growth of GNVQ enrolments in the 1990s, Edwards *et al.* (1997) found that when compared with A-levels, they still attracted a low proportion of high-achieving students. Davies and Adnett (1999) argue that quasi-market reforms had contributed to this failure to establish parity of esteem for high-quality vocational schooling. In particular, the choice of which examination results to highlight in school performance tables have consolidated local school hierarchies based upon pupil attainments in traditional academic CBEEEs. We now explain the reasons for this conclusion in the following section.

7.3.4 School performance tables

Historically, schools have concentrated performance monitoring on individual students. Typically, the assessments used in this monitoring are based on both absolute standards, whether the student achieves specified learning objectives, and relative standards based upon peer and national performance. As we have seen, market-based reforms to the state schooling system have consistently tried to open up this monitoring process and extend it to encompass both teacher and overall school performance. In general, it would be inefficient for stakeholders in the schooling process to attempt to satisfy independently their own information needs. In theory, government provision of open and transparent cross-sector PIs can therefore be cost-effective. In practice, the diverse interests of stakeholders and the problems of measuring the multiple schooling outcomes make the choice of PIs a highly sensitive issue. The pragmatic decision made by many governments has been to concentrate upon examination results, presumably assuming that they must bear some relationship to the outcomes valued most by parents.

Given the problems of specifying and measuring the objectives of schools, Hanushek (1994), amongst others, has argued for the setting of minimum national performance standards for schools. In the US, even in the absence of national CBEEEs, a growing number of states are using annual school-level test scores as part of their school accountability systems. In the UK, the incoming Labour government set five-year targets in 1997 for the whole of the primary age group in English and mathematics. More recently, in its 2001 Green Paper, the British government set the state schooling system very specific targets; surprisingly, given their diminished role, these were set at LEA level. They included increasing the percentage of pupils obtaining five or more GCSEs at grades A*–C by 4 percentage points between 2002 and 2004, while ensuring that at least 38 per cent of pupils achieve this standard in every LEA. At the supra-national level, the European Union has recently developed sixteen indicators on the quality of education to assist national evaluations of schooling systems (European Commission 2000). These cover four broad areas: attainment levels; educational success and transition; monitoring of school education; and educational resources and structures. The Lisbon European Council meeting in March 2000 set the target that the EU should become 'the most competitive and dynamic knowledge-based economy in the world'. In seeking to achieve that goal, the Education Council has established a set of targets – for example, by 2010 reducing by half the proportion of 18 to 24 year olds with only lower-secondary level education who are not in further education and training.

The rationale for extending school choice, discussed in Chapters 1 and 3, assumes that decision-makers can cheaply access information on the relative performance of local schools. We now consider how such information has come to be provided in England and Wales through the publication of school performance tables. In 1980, secondary schools in England and Wales were required to publish their exam results. From 1992 the government published exam results and other PIs such as attendance rates. Also in 1992 the Local Government Act required the Audit Commission, a non-departmental public body, to produce annual comparative indicators of local authority performance in England and Wales. Sweden introduced a similar system in the same year (OECD 1997). Within education in England and Wales, published PIs for LEAs include the percentage of 3 and 4 year olds with a state school place, expenditure by pupil, and the percentage of draft special educational needs statements prepared within six months. The latter can be classified as 'results benchmarking' and, as such, by adopting a large number of diverse indicators, merely identifies issues rather than setting particular targets or narrowing the range of outputs over which public attention is focused. In contrast, the annual school examination performance tables compiled by the DfEE for secondary schools initially consisted largely of measures of the proportion of pupils obtaining good passes in national curriculum-based exams at ages 16 and 18 and the incidence of unauthorised pupil absences. The Labour government did seek to shift the focus from the proportion of high-achievers by introducing an indicator of average point score per 15 year old in 1997. This government was also committed to introducing a 'value-added' indicator based upon the improvement of pupils between Key Stage 3 tests at age 14 and GCSE performance. In the face of opposition from some headteachers, who argued that this would penalise schools with good Key Stage 3 results, a more general indicator of school progress was introduced in 1998.

West and Pennell (2000) show how even the quality press has tended to concentrate upon unadjusted exam performance in reporting this data. As a consequence of this selective publication, Northern Ireland and Wales decided to discontinue publishing school performance tables in 2001. Instead, they now require individual schools to publish details of their own performance. As we noted in Chapter 5, school league table performance has become an important influence in parental decision-making, a finding consistent with US evidence that consumer choice is highly sensitive to relative test scores (for example, Murray and Wallace 1997). Woods *et al.* (1998) found that there was a rising trend in the proportion of parents who cited league tables as influencing their choice of school. Additionally, West *et al.* (1998b) find some evidence that schools have been 'cream-skimming' to improve their league table position. They cite a 'comprehensive' school that had adopted its own banding procedure in order to obtain an academically balanced intake. In 1997, 77 per cent of its pupils obtained five or more high grade GCSEs compared to a national average of just 45 per cent. In general, Gewirtz *et al.* (1995) and Woods *et al.* (1998) found that schools were placing increased emphasis upon academic and exam performance and targeting for recruitment middle-class and more able pupils. The predominance of PIs based upon the proportion of their pupils achieving five good passes has led to further dysfunctional responses by schools. A widening gap between the highest and lowest attaining pupils has been attributed to schools concentrating resources on borderline candidates (West and Pennell 2000). The same authors also review the evidence suggesting a link between the publication of league tables and the trebling of permanent exclusions in the early 1990s. In turn, this outcome stimulated the DfEE in 1999 to set local targets to reduce the number of school exclusions by a third by 2002. Here, the dysfunctional effects from target-setting generated a new set of targets that again produced dysfunctional effects. These latter ultimately led to legal action against the refusal of teachers to teach re-admitted pupils.

Many authors have pointed out that the emphasis upon 'raw' exam performance makes it impossible for parents to distinguish between schools which 'do well (or poorly) *in spite of* their circumstances from those which do well (or poorly) *because of* their circumstances' (Gibson and Asthana 1998a: 278). Goldstein and Thomas (1996) and Goldstein and Spiegelhalter (1996) are amongst many who argue that average unadjusted examination results obscure information and are inferior to value-added measures of pupil attainment. However, the publication by the DfEE of a pilot exercise on value-added indicators for secondary schools generated some fundamental debates about the suitability of existing data and the methodology employed (Prais 2001). The National Curriculum for England and Wales assumes that more able students will progress at a faster absolute rate than less able students. For example, between the ages of 11 and 14, more able students are expected to have a 'value-added' increase in attainment of two levels whilst the less able are expected to have an increase of only one level. This view of progression relies upon the more able students possessing a greater ability to learn, implying that it is easier for teachers to add value to the attainment of the more able students. Thus, even when value-added is apparently measured by the performance indicator, comparisons between schools are problematic since more able students are cheaper to teach.

We noted above the dangers of poorly designed and poorly implemented performance indicator systems. Unsurprisingly, much of this section has mirrored our discussion in the previous chapter of the problems of implementing performance pay for teachers. PIs that lack comparability, transferability and therefore general acceptance by those subject to them are unlikely to generate effective incentives for all schools to improve performance. Given that we are dealing with multi-product institutions with heterogeneous inputs, dysfunctional responses to the introduction of simple performance indicators are likely to be common, as we have seen. Where measured performance affects funding directly or indirectly through recruitment, then any particular choice of indicators and weights will cause schools to switch behaviour to boost performance, as evidenced above. Dependent upon the extent to which the differing outputs are in competitive supply, then the resulting 'improved' performance is to the detriment of unmeasured outputs. Hence, the potential attractions of developing value-added measures. The fundamental objective of value-added performance indicators is to isolate statistically the contribution of a school from all the other determinants of student achievement. However, as Meyer (1997) points out, some policy makers dislike such PIs because they may lower performance expectations in those schools that serve disproportionately disadvantaged students.

We have argued that the school performance tables as currently publicised in England and Wales distort information flows and provide inadequate incentives for both high-ranking and low-ranking schools to even improve exam performance. Their sole virtue is that they provide a simple numerical measure of quality, understandable by most parents and students. Implicit in the critique above is the proposition that the recalibration of league tables in terms of value-added will provide improved signals to parents and pupils about the quality of alternative local schools. However, as we explained in Chapters 3 and 5, a parent who derives utility exclusively from their child's attainment will want a signal as to how each school will add to their own child's attainment. Though the absolute average level of attainment incorporates both school quality, peer group and intake ability effects, value-added indicators still bundle together school quality and peer group effects. Now consider where parents are unsure whether relative school performance is stable across the whole ability range, or where there are other consumption and investment benefits associated with mixing with high ability students and their families. In these situations parents choosing between schools may prefer to rely on absolute average attainment levels for the additional information provided on intake ability, regardless of the consequences for aggregate educational attainment in the local market. Choice as to which indicator(s) the government should publicise thus remains problematic. Governments cannot assume that school choice will automatically promote the 'survival of the fittest' or the raising of aggregate educational attainment.

7.4 Conclusions

We have addressed a wide range of issues in this chapter. A common theme that has emerged is how school choice reforms have been supplemented, if not modified, by policy changes to governance, inspection and target-setting. Clearly, governments have come to believe that increasing consumer choice is insufficient by itself to generate the increases in quality and diversity desired of the state schooling system. It may also reflect an assessment that gains from reducing x-inefficiency may be more easily realised than those from increasing allocative efficiency.

One way of categorising this development is as a response to the perceived dysfunctional effects of school choice reforms. In particular, their tendency to reinforce local schooling hierarchies and increase the diversity of schooling outcomes. An alternative interpretation is that policy initiatives may not share common assumptions about the nature of the 'business unit' and the level of current knowledge, with the effect that contradictions develop in the application of education reform. That is, individual initiatives may produce large and unforeseen dysfunctional effects when combined with other elements of the reforms. Thus in England and Wales, the emphasis on competition by comparison has clearly been reinforced, albeit over a very narrow range of outputs, by the publication of school performance tables. However, succeeding reforms have encouraged both institutional competition and market segmentation. The current emphasis upon specialist schools effectively creates 'niche' monopolists in local markets, reducing the level of competition based upon overall schooling standards, while, at the same time, equally high-profile initiatives seek to encourage co-operative behaviour amongst local schools. This latter behaviour is normally viewed as being inconsistent with, and seemingly destructive of, the 'market-discipline' philosophy. We return to this debate in Chapter 9 after our overall review of the impact of market-based reforms on school behaviour in the following chapter.

8 Schools in the market place

8.1 Introduction

In this chapter we examine the behaviour of schools in local markets and the impact of this behaviour on educational outcomes. We concentrate here on the behaviour of public schools in the open enrolment system introduced in England. The chapter is organised in three main sections which consider the effect of schooling markets on productive efficiency, the distribution of educational benefits from education across individuals and the diversity of outcomes provided by the school system. Policies to increase the role of market forces in schooling have been based on a belief that competition between schools will improve the schooling system according to each of these criteria. Critics of these policies believe the opposite. To review these debates we organise each section into two parts. The first part reviews predictions of alternative theories and the second part considers evidence pertinent to these predictions. We conclude the chapter with a section devoted to an evaluation of the theories.

8.2 Productive efficiency

8.2.1 Theories of the relationship between competition and productive efficiency

Two aspects of quasi-markets might be expected to increase productive efficiency in schools: incentives are provided by competition from other schools and scope to respond to these incentives is provided by self-management (Chapter 7). Before examining these predictions in more detail we must clarify the meaning of 'productive efficiency' and 'competition' in a schooling context. First we summarise the meaning of productive efficiency as discussed in Chapter 3. In that chapter we categorised the outputs of schooling as: productivity gains, socialisation benefits, personal fulfilment benefits and consumption gains. Each of these is made up of a private benefit and a net externality. In evaluating the production of a school we must therefore distinguish between the production of total private benefits (which will be the benefits relevant to self-interested parents and pupils) and total social production (which we expect to be somewhat higher). In addition, as most of these categories are not traded and they are partly in competitive supply, we have to employ a strong value judgement in applying weights to each output before we can speak of 'total' private or social school output. Whilst it is convenient to use public examination results as a measure of schooling output, it is important to remember that this is ultimately a proxy for pupil attainment that involves a value judgement giving a strong weight to productivity gains and a very low weight to consumption benefits and personal fulfilment. Value judgements, even of this magnitude, are apt to become taken for granted if not frequently and explicitly restated. Most analysis of the productive efficiency of schools adopts this particular value position and this is reflected in the following discussion. We return to a broader view of school productivity at the end of this section.

Using examination results as a composite measure of all schooling outputs, productivity is given by value-added per unit of input. However, we cannot conclude that the productive efficiency of a school has increased simply on the basis of improvements in the absolute or value-added levels of pupil attainment. We also need to know how much it has cost the school to secure that improvement. Costless improvement has strong political appeal for governments seeking to restrict their expenditure, but it is a rare reform that is able to deliver this happy outcome. Resources are generally consumed in the process of change, not least through financial inducements to schools to participate in policy initiatives. Moreover, comparisons of schools and school systems need to take account of variations in per pupil funding if they are to provide an appropriate measure of schooling efficiency.

We also need to ask what it means to describe a schooling market as 'competitive'? In principle, competitive behaviour may be observed in: price changes; changes in product delivery; reallocation of resources to reduce costs; promotion of the service; the quality and variety of the service provided and exit and entry from markets. Unless they are operating in a voucher system, state, schools typically have no control over price and extremely limited opportunities to change the locations at which they make their 'product' available. Schools may compete either through the quality of their product or through their promotion. In addition, state schools in these systems are currently operated on a 'not-for-profit' basis (at present, barring one exception in England). Therefore, the incentives for schools are in the form of (i) maintaining viability; (ii) maintaining a school size that enables the delivery of a range of curriculum that satisfies professional values; (iii) increasing senior management salaries in so far as these can be changed through financial management or increasing the size of the school; and (iv) creating scope for freedom to pursue professional objectives. Each of these incentives should encourage schools to attend to seek additional enrolments through satisfying parental preferences. There may well be conflict in the case of incentive (iv). That is, if professional objectives conflict with parental preferences then school managers must choose between them (if this is financially feasible). However, if professional and parental preferences do not directly conflict, a school may seek to satisfy parental preferences in order to create the financial opportunities to pursue other professional objectives. This incentive is also a characteristic of zonal systems for allocating school places.

Consequently, quasi-markets might encourage productive efficiency through incentives for school effectiveness or through making inefficient schools unviable. If schools are sufficiently knowledgeable about their costs and the effect of their actions on enrolment then quasi-markets can provide incentives to choose those actions that increase productive efficiency. Under these circumstances, schools might be expected to adopt some form of rational planning to ensure that the policy formed by senior management is understood and implemented at every level of the school. School managers who are sure of how to achieve the optimal objectives for the school only need to ensure that this understanding is shared by their staff and to monitor the way that staff implement their plan. In its strongest form, this model assumes that school managers already know what parents want but, without open enrolment, they do not feel under pressure to prioritise parental preferences above professional values and interests. A weaker assumption is that schools could find out exactly what parents wanted if they were prepared to incur the search costs, but previously they had no incentive to do so.

Despite accepting the substance of these arguments, recent education policy in England (noted in Chapter 7) testifies to government's lack of confidence in the sufficiency of quasi-markets incentives as a spur to productive efficiency through the adoption of rational planning. The Department of Education and Employment (DfEE) and the School Inspection Service (OfSTED) have considered it necessary to provide substantial guidance and encouragement to schools to adopt the rational planning model. Moreover, schools have been required by government to adopt prescriptive new models of teaching and learning for literacy and numeracy. At the same time, concern has been expressed about 'coasting' schools that are not threatened by market pressure because they can achieve high absolute levels of examination results with only modest levels of added value. A transmission mechanism between quasi-market incentives and school productivity has been developing too slowly, if at all, as far as government is concerned. Innovation is discouraged by information externalities which encourage producers to conform to a 'market leader' rather than experiment with new methods or outputs (Adnett and Davies 2000). Levin and Riffel (1997a) suggest that schools are slow to change in response to market pressures because they have weak processes for learning from the external environment. Bagley *et al.* (1996b) suggest that schools may be unresponsive due to the values of managers, the needs of individual children and the views of parents who see personal and social values of a school as more fundamental than its academic focus.

Orthodox economics suggests other limitations on the effectiveness of market incentives. First, productive efficiency will vary positively with the number of rival producers in the market. On this basis, an isolated rural school will face no incentive to increase productive efficiency after the introduction of a quasi-market. However, schools in urban areas where parents can choose between several alternatives should come under effective market pressure. The theory of contestable markets suggests that the incentive for productive efficiency is provided by the prospect, not just the actuality, of competition. In practice, in the presence of strong government regulation of the building of new schools and the high cost per pupil of small schools, the prospect of new schools in a market is not high. It is more feasible to anticipate the emergence of a new competitor through a school introducing free or subsidised transport arrangements. Second, in markets with restricted entry and exit, productive efficiency will vary negatively with the size of the market relative to schools' capacity. Third, peer effects will be a source of dynamic problems. For simplicity, with no loss of generality (Adnett *et al.* 2002), assume a local market with two schools. Dynamic problems arise as soon as one school achieves outcomes that are sufficiently high to attract parents from the other school. These problems are caused by the interaction of peer group effects and the average ability of pupils moving from the lower achieving to the higher achieving school. We concluded in Chapter 3 that peer effects exert a significant positive effect on pupil attainment, and in Chapter 5 that the academic ability of pupils choosing an out-of-neighbourhood school was likely to be higher than the average ability of pupils in their neighbourhood school. The loss of these pupils to the local school would affect absolute attainment in two ways. First, their departure would directly lower the school's average attainment and, second, the loss of positive peer effects would reinforce this downward movement. In these circumstances, teacher effort towards raising school effectiveness in the lower achieving school cannot raise average attainment in that school to match the higher achieving school; the viability of the school then becomes dependent on the reluctance of parents to consider an out-of-neighbourhood school or the reluctance of the other school to increase its enrolment. This problem will be experienced even with value-added measures of school performance if school effects on outcomes are insufficient to overwhelm peer effects. If parents respond to absolute measures of school performance (partly in order to secure a positive peer group effect), the problem is substantially reinforced. Fifth, schools might increase their market power by differentiating themselves from rivals. This behaviour has the merit of responding to hitherto unsatisfied consumer preference, but the creation of 'niche' markets also increases schools' bargaining power relative to parents. At the extreme, a school with a sharply defined niche creates a market in which it is the only supplier. In so far as peer group attributes influence parental choice of schools, local markets can be fragmented into a hierarchy of niches associated with different levels of average absolute pupil attainment.

We now relax the orthodox assumption of well-informed producers to see if this affects the predicted effects of market forces. Quasi-market forces could lead to an increase in school productivity even if school managers are unable to predict parent behaviour or the effect of teaching and learning on schooling outcomes. Even when schools are ill-informed, a quasi-market could penalise and eventually cull those schools that unfortunately opt for the wrong actions.

An evolutionary process can ensure the survival of the fittest. Levačić and Woods (1999) present data on fourteen schools (from their sample of 323) that were closed between 1990 and 1996. The average league table score of these schools was significantly lower than that of continuing schools, suggesting that closure was related to public measures of performance. However, it is perfectly possible that these schools were achieving above average levels of value-added when measured across all outputs on a social accounting basis.

A more positive perspective on the likely effect of market forces is provided by Austrian economics of producer behaviour. We might argue that a quasi-market will provide schools with incentives to improve their knowledge of parental preferences and their understanding of how best to organise teaching and learning. Although schools will not be able to predict in advance the benefits from researching the market and their own productive processes, if they are willing to take the risks they may reap the benefits from finding and exploiting a market niche or a new approach to teaching and learning. Given the assumption of imperfect knowledge by producers, it is consistent to assume that parents are also only partially informed. In these circumstances, schools that engage in competition through promotion may be viewed as enabling the market to work more efficiently by increasing the likelihood that parents will make informed choices.

A further, important source of uncertainty is introduced by the unpredictability of the actions of other schools. Large-scale quantitative research (e.g. Gibson and Asthana 1999; Bradley *et al.* 2000) and small-scale qualitative research (e.g. Waslander and Thrupp 1995) has typically inferred that many local schooling markets contain relatively few schools. In these circumstances, the prediction that the intensity of competition depends on the number of producers no longer holds as schools' decision-making is interdependent (McWilliams and Smart 1993; Vickers 1985, 1995; Singh *et al.* 1998). The effect on enrolments of a decision by one school to engage in a substantial promotion campaign depends on whether other schools follow suit. In markets of this size, collusion becomes a viable option, although this may be more difficult in overlapping markets in large, densely populated, urban areas. Collaborative arrangements, built on mutual trust between schools, may be explicitly intended to subvert policies intended to create competition (Wallace 1998) and, from the standpoint of orthodox theory, this collusion is against the interests of parents and pupils. We noted in Chapter 7 that co-operation between schools is encouraged by some recent policy initiatives in England. This may be justified on the basis that it enables high quality resources (particularly as embodied in skilled staff) to have an impact beyond the individual school and that it speeds the spread of information about production processes. Collusion, on the other hand, refers to tacit as well as explicit agreements between schools to maintain practices, expectations and curricula that are suboptimal from the point of view of technical and allocative efficiency.

Schools which make a first move in breaking out of a tacit or formal collusion may gain advantages through (i) cost and quality gains associated with learning from their experience in providing a new service and (ii) pre-empting space in the market, making it unattractive for other schools to provide similar services which are already available (Lieberman and Montgomery 1988). The first of these advantages is unlikely to be sustained as the learning about innovations is disseminated around the education system. First-movers also incur disadvantages. Competitor schools may be able to 'free-ride' on the costs of innovation at first-mover schools, as the results of their experience are disseminated through the education system. Competitor schools will also benefit from the resolution of market uncertainty as the size of a potential new market becomes more apparent, and parents, children and employers become more knowledgeable about the new possibilities. This reasoning suggests that differences between local schooling markets will reflect differences in costs and benefits of collusion and first-moves. Competition by promotion would also be viewed as less favourable from this perspective than from an Austrian viewpoint. The level of promotion in which schools engage would be expected to reflect the behaviour of other schools rather than the need for parents to be informed. In this kind of market, where producer decision-making is interdependent, game theory becomes the standard basis for analysis.

Each of these transmission mechanisms leads schools to respond to private rather than social outcomes. Moreover, in so far as the information available to parents (e.g. through publication of examination results as discussed in Chapter 7) biases their expressed preferences, the transmission mechanism also leads schools to be more responsive to these private outcomes than other outcomes such as personal fulfilment and consumption benefits. Whether these problems are greater in open enrolment systems than zonal systems is a question for empirical evidence.

8.2.2 Evidence on the effect of competition on efficiency

In this review we draw chiefly on evidence from the quasi-market in England and Wales. Initially we concentrate on the level and nature of competition between schools and then consider the impact of this competitive behaviour on productive efficiency. During the 1990s, self-reported competition between English secondary schools increased (Foskett 1998) and co-operation decreased (Power *et al.* 1997). In 1992 a majority (61 per cent) of headteachers (Bullock and Thomas 1997) believed that significant changes in their school roll were primarily due to demography and a minority (16 per cent) described their local markets as competitive. By 1997, 86 per cent of headteachers (ICOSS 1999) regarded their relationships with other schools as fairly or highly competitive. During this period the proportion of 16 year-olds in England achieving 5 grades A*–C in public examinations rose substantially, from 35.5 per cent in 1992 to 45.8 per cent in 1999. In the words of Bradley and Taylor (2000) this is a 'remarkable' increase. Open enrolment has also been accompanied by a steady increase in pupil attainment in some parts of the United States (Rossell and Glenn 1988; Clewell and Joy 1990) and this contrasts with the mixed assessments of the effects of voucher schemes on pupil attainment (Chapter 4). Whilst these correlations lend credence to a belief that competition between schools does lead to improvements of productive efficiency, we need to be cautious about assuming that this demonstrates cause and effect (Henig 1994). To be credible these claims require supporting evidence which shows the predicted processes of competition at work. The process of competition expected by orthodox theory and the rational planning model predicts that: (a) competition will be more intense and productive efficiency gains will be higher when there are more schools competing in a local market and the size of the market is high relative to schools' capacity; (b) in markets with restricted exit and entry, competitive behaviour will be stronger if the total size of the market is low relative to the producers' capacity: and (c) that efficiency gains will be achieved through improved deployment of resources, prioritising parents' preferences over professional judgements (with regard to output mix) and through cost effectiveness in employing inputs.

Headteachers are more likely to describe schools in their local area as highly competitive if there are more schools contesting the market (Glatter *et al.* 1997; Foskett 1998; Levačić and Woods 1999). Glatter *et al.* (1997) also note that competitive pressures were least, and the hierarchy of schools less sharply defined, in markets with a small number of widely dispersed schools. However, it is not clear from this research whether these headteachers are all referring to the same type of competitive behaviour. Do they mean that schools are competing strongly through promotion, raising standards of educational outcome or the range of educational outcomes offered? An indication of an impact of competition upon educational standards is found in the ICOSS (1999) research which found that schools' self-reported emphasis on examination results was positively correlated with a highly competitive climate. Evidence of a statistical link between competition and attainment is provided by Bradley and colleagues (Bradley and Taylor 2000; Bradley *et al.* 2000). Bradley *et al.* (2000) find that examination results of other local schools have a significant but 'negligible' influence on the performance of each school. However, in a slightly later econometric study, Bradley and Taylor find that a 1 per cent increase in the examination results of other local schools led to 0.3 per cent increase in a school's own examination performance, with the impact being nearly twice as great in metropolitan areas as in non-metropolitan areas. They also find that examination results of other local schools on academic attainment at a given school increase in effect over their period of study (1992–6).

These studies also provide some evidence of an effect of examination results on enrolment. Bradley *et al.* (2000) conclude that an improvement of 10 per cent in a school's examination performance will lead to an increase of seven pupil enrolments. As they point out, this modest increase may reflect capacity constraints faced by popular schools or reluctance of headteachers to increase their roll in case this reduces the effectiveness of the school. Despite this, Bradley and Taylor (2000) also find strong evidence suggesting that schools facing excess demand during 1993–6 have increased their pupil capacity. Evidence that competitive behaviour is more pronounced in schooling markets where market size is low relative to capacity is provided by Foskett (1998) and Levačić and Woods (1999).

Our survey of parental choice (Chapter 5) also indicated the importance to parents of a safe, well-disciplined environment that will cater for their child's security and happiness. Waslander and Thrupp (1995: 14) report the introduction of 'a new discipline system to reduce parental fears of violence and unruliness' and 'the introduction of an attractive yet inexpensive uniform' at a school struggling to attract parents at the bottom of a local hierarchy in New Zealand. The same school subsequently introduced initiatives designed to raise levels of attainment including the retention of students at the junior level for an extra year before they progress to senior classes. This initiative has the fortunate effect for the school of directly increasing its roll. Waslander and Thrupp do not report the evidence for the effect of such a policy on attainment which informed the school's principal decision. Another school in their study was considering, but so far resisting, the introduction of grouping students by ability in order to attract more higher SES status parents. This resistance was partly motivated by the impact of setting by ability on the ethnic mix of classes. According to the principal: 'there is a strong commitment to that (being non-streamed) amongst the staff but whether it will stand up to the pressures I don't know ... If we are broad-banded or streamed we would end up pretty much with a school that had three or four Pakeha (white) upper stream classes.'

Given the evidence of a modest effect of quasi-market competition on pupil attainment we turn now to the processes that might affect the likelihood of this outcome. Local management of schools provides flexibility for schools to reallocate resources within their budget (Chapter 7), although the greater flexibility given to grant-maintained schools does not appear to have led to different patterns of resource allocation (Fitz *et al.* 1993) or better educational outcomes (Levačić and Hardman 1999). Reducing the cost of an existing teaching programme increases the financial scope for the school to devote resources to school promotion or towards changing the quality and composition of the schools' educational outputs. Headteachers in England and Wales have welcomed the scope for managing resources that they have acquired under self-management and believe that this allows schools to make more effective use of resources (Levačić 1995; Bullock and Thomas 1997). They are far less sure about the effect of this 'more effective use of resources' on pupils' learning. Whilst there is a weak, positive relationship between the quality of schools' resource management and educational outcomes (Levačić and Glover 1998), evidence for the direct effect of market forces on resource management is missing. One interpretation of these findings is that school managers have used their newly acquired powers to pursue objectives that are not fully shared by parents and pupils. Whilst school self-management creates the capacity to respond to the local market, open enrolment is intended to provide the incentives to prompt this response. Are these incentives sufficiently strong? Early evidence of reforms in New Zealand (Wylie 1995) suggested that schools were paying more attention to the physical attractiveness of their facilities and promoting the school's image than to improving students' learning.

Bradley and Taylor (2000) find a strong correlation between secondary school size and pupil attainment. They conclude that an increase in roll of 100 leads to an increase in exam performance of 1 per cent. They also find that schools experiencing a rise in their pupil/teacher ratio experience a fall in pupil attainment. If schools that experience a fall in roll also experience a drop in the average ability of their students the prospect that they might improve their position in the market place through increasing their effectiveness becomes increasingly remote. This problem is most likely to affect a school that is at the bottom of its local hierarchy and this is illustrated by Waslander and Thrupp (1995) through a study of a local market in New Zealand. The school at the bottom of the hierarchy they studied experienced a dramatic fall in enrolments accompanied by a small fall in the average SES status of children at the school.

The processes and outcomes observed in quasi-markets may be particular to the nature of the constructed market. A key feature of the quasi-market in England has been the prominence afforded to the publication of league tables of schools' absolute examination performance. As discussed in the previous chapter, the form in which school performance has been reported has influenced school's choice of outputs. League tables in England have drawn particular attention to the proportion of 16-year-old pupils who achieve five or more examination passes at grades A*–C. This provides an incentive for schools to concentrate efforts on those marginal pupils who are likely to be on the borderline between achieving or not achieving this benchmark standard. In so far as parental choice is influenced by schools' absolute examination results there is an incentive for 'cream-skimming' (Gewirtz *et al.* 1995). The easiest way for schools to boost their examination results is by recruiting more able pupils. Bush *et al.* (1993) suggest that 30 per cent of the grant-maintained schools they investigated were using covert selection. West and Pennell (2000) cite a number of aspects of the processing of school admissions that lead to cream skimming in the absence of any overt bias towards more able children. Complex admission procedures favour more educated parents and these may be observed in complicated admission forms, tests and pre-admission interviews. Difficulties for less educated parents are compounded when application for enrolments at different schools must be made at different times and to different authorities. West *et al.* (1998) infer that rapid improvements in the examination results achieved by some schools must have been achieved, in part, by cream-skimming. Schools may also adopt policies designed specifically to attract middle-class parents. Most notably they may change from mixed ability teaching to setting according to ability. We noted in Chapter 5 that this is an important factor in the decision-making of some parents, and Reay (1998) provides a case study illustrating the response of one school to this pressure. Schools may also devote more effort to the achievement of outcomes that they believe will attract middle-class parents. Based on a study of schools in three local markets, Woods *et al.* (1998: 31) cite 'increased attention being given to raising academic performance as measured by examination results' in order to attract middle-class parents. We observed in Chapter 5 that studies of parental choice have yet to suggest that a desire for socialisation is significant in parental choice. Schools that shift their priorities towards academic attainment are responding rationally in the market place.

Disruptive pupils are more expensive to educate and reduce school income. They are more expensive because they demand more staff time. An indication of the extent of this extra cost is given by the degree to which the cost per pupil in a school for emotionally and behaviourally disturbed pupils exceeds the cost per pupil in comprehensive schools. They reduce school income through their negative impact on the number of parents wanting to send their child to the school. Research on parental choice reviewed in Chapter 5 suggests that parents are highly sensitive to factors that affect the safety of their child. In addition, disruptive children are likely to have a negative impact on a school's examination performance through their impact on the academic progress of other children. The rational school would therefore seek to avoid enrolling disruptive pupils and would seek to exclude pupils who develop disruptive behaviours. We would therefore predict that the introduction of a quasi-market will lead to an increase in school exclusions and this is precisely what is observed (Gewirtz *et al.* 1995; Gillborn 1996). Whilst the increase in exclusions may be attributed to a range of causes, 42 per cent of LEA Directors surveyed by Gillborn blamed increased competition between schools. Grant-maintained schools had the highest rate of exclusion of existing students and were least willing to cater for students with special educational needs (Feintuck 1994; Vincent *et al.* 1995).

Markets provide an incentive to schools to communicate more strongly with parents in the hope of convincing them of the qualities of the school. It is not surprising, therefore, to find that open enrolment incites schools to increase the quantity of resources they devote to promotion. In fact, evidence from New Zealand (Waslander and Thrupp 1995) suggests that this is usually the most immediate response that schools make. After all, if they can manage their enrolment through promoting the school, they can avoid internal changes to the running of the school that might be more costly or painful to implement. There is also considerable evidence in England and Wales that schools have increased the resources they devote to promotion. Secondary school headteachers have stressed the importance of visits to primary schools, parents' evenings and securing press coverage (Bagley *et al.* 1996a; Davies *et al.* 2002). Whilst this behaviour might be interpreted as improving the levels of information in the market place, the high priority that secondary schools attach to securing the goodwill of primary schools suggests something rather different. The conclusion of Bagley *et al.* reflects the balance of current evidence on schools' promotional behaviour: 'overall much less attention is given to this (discovering parents' preferences) than to promotional activities' (1996a: 133).

Incentives for co-operation, collusion or 'first-moves' will be affected by the local circumstances and this suggests that the impact of quasi-markets on productive efficiency will be highly variable. One source of variation is the form of school governance discussed in the previous chapter. In a comparison of schools in three localities in England and Scotland, Raab *et al.* (1997) find higher levels of competitive behaviour in the English authority which they attribute partly to the different regime for devolved school management and partly to the policy of the LEA. Levačić and Woods (1999) report significant differences in the number of headteachers reporting high levels of competition in different English LEAs. Headteachers of grant-maintained schools were more likely to view their schools as operating in a highly competitive market (ICOSS 1999). Unsurprisingly, Foskett (1998) reports more intense competition if there is a lower level of traditional collegiality amongst headteachers. Bradley *et al.* (1999) present evidence that school efficiency, particularly in grant-maintained and voluntary-aided schools, has increased 'as quasi-market forces take hold'.

Differences between local markets may also be due to headteachers' perceptions of the likely response of others to decisions they take and the value they place on different outcomes. These differences may result from variation in the systemic dispersion of conceptions about schooling markets and the role of headteachers (reviewed by Whitty *et al.* 1998). Grace (1995) identifies differences between headteachers' response to the introduction of local school markets and the rhetoric that has accompanied their introduction. These responses vary from positive endorsement to active resistance and may be expected to inform their attitude towards collusion and first moves. Headteachers' perceptions will also reflect their learning and adaptation in response to the history of their local schooling market. Rivalry is more likely where there are financial incentives that encourage growth; product differentiation is low; total market size is declining; schools have excess capacity and face high exit barriers. It may also be forced by the actions of competitors or prompted by personal rivalry.

We conclude that theories which assume that schools and parents face uncertainty as well as incomplete knowledge provide a more comprehensive explanation of current evidence. Whilst there is evidence of an overall slight increase in pupil attainment as a result of competition between schools, this has been accompanied by an increase in the difference in school level attainment causing a widening gap in the access of pupils to positive peer effects. In this respect, there is a similarity between the impact of open enrolment and the voucher schemes discussed in Chapter 4. In addition, the effect of quasi-markets on competitive behaviour varies according to local circumstances: governance, headteachers' perceptions and experience and market size relative to school capacity. These factors combine to create tendencies towards first moves or collusion that set the tone for the type of competitive behaviour that will be observed in a local market.

8.3 Stratification

8.3.1 Theoretical perspectives on stratification in schooling markets

Stratification occurs when pupils become less evenly distributed across schools according to class, ability, ethnicity or religion. Discussions of quasi-market effects in England, New Zealand and the United States have given different emphases to these elements of stratification which we note in the following summary. However, we first briefly recap the arguments discussed in Chapters 3 and 5 regarding the reasons to expect stratification to be increased by open enrolment. Given open enrolment and self-managing status, schools face an incentive to enrol pupils who will be less costly to teach and more likely to positively influence future enrolment. More able students are cheaper to teach because they are more skilled in contributing to their own learning and easier to teach in larger groups. Enrolment of more able pupils will also make it easier for the school to attract further parents in the future. Parents who are interested in absolute levels of attainment at a school (either because they judge school effec- tiveness by league tables or because they anticipate positive peer group effects) will be attracted by the presence of more able pupils at a school. Therefore, schools approaching or at capacity have an incentive to employ overt or covert selection policies to bias their intake.

The incentives for parents are less clear-cut as the impact of an open enrol- ment system replacing a zonal system depends on the distribution of housing types. Figure 8.1 illustrates the situation in a stylised way.

In Case 1 (Figure 8.1) a zonal system leads to very strong stratification of schooling by household income, which in the UK would be reflected in pupils' eligibility for free school meals. This stratification would be only slightly

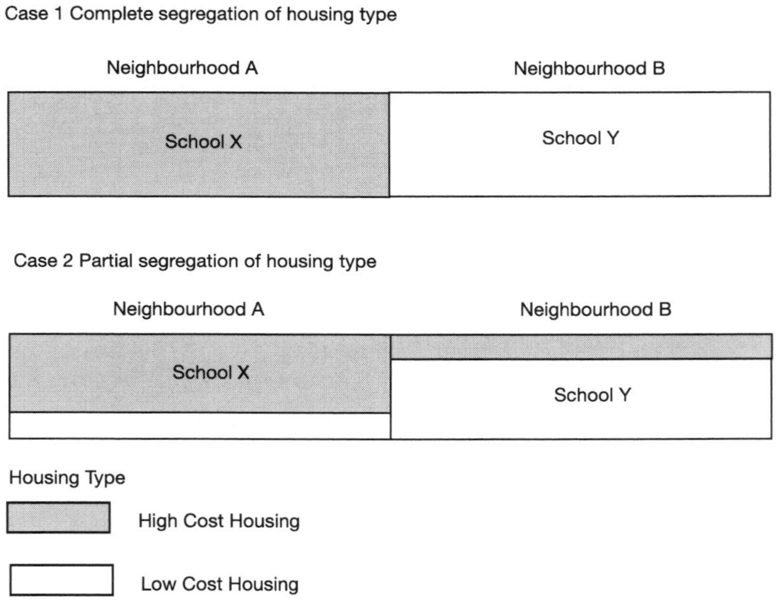

Case 1 Complete segregation of housing type

Case 2 Partial segregation of housing type

Housing Type

High Cost Housing

Low Cost Housing

Figure 8.1   The replacement of a zonal system by an open enrolment system: alternative cases

mitigated by the willingness and ability of a small number of lower income households to devote a very large proportion of their income to housing costs. As we discussed in Chapter 3, house prices partially reflect parents' willingness to pay a premium for schooling quality. Given the associations between household income, SES status and pupil attainment (also discussed in Chapter 3), we would expect the examination results of School X to clearly exceed the examination results of School Y regardless of the relative value-added by each school. On the introduction of open enrolment, parents in Neighbourhood B who judge school quality by the absolute level of examination results have an incentive to choose School X. This assumes that the housing cost differential between the two areas is sufficiently high to dwarf the additional transport and other costs that parents in the catchment area of School Y would incur in getting their children to School X. Applications to School X would therefore increase. Stratification as measured by income would decrease if School X responds to this increase in applications by accepting pupils from Neighbourhood B. It could do this if current enrolment is below capacity or it chooses to admit pupils from lower income families in preference to pupils from higher income families. As noted earlier, School X has an incentive to do this if it is able to recruit more able pupils from Neighbourhood B rather than less able pupils from Neighbourhood A. As noted in Chapter 4 this freedom is afforded to some public schools in England.

In Case 2, where housing is partially segregated, we would also expect the absolute level of examination results in School X to be higher than those in School Y, but differences in value-added might offset much of this differential. Nevertheless, parents seeking a school with a higher absolute level of examination results will choose School X. However, in contrast to Case 1 we have two classes of parent in Neighbourhood B and they may not behave in the same way. Evidence reviewed in Chapter 5 suggests that higher SES-status parents (who are more likely to live in higher-cost housing) will be significantly more likely to choose an out-of-neighbourhood school in the period immediately after the introduction of open enrolment and that this difference between parental choice by SES status will continue more modestly thereafter. To clarify the impact of this we define:

SES_A as the ratio of higher SES status parents to lower SES status parents in Neighbourhood A

SES_{AX} as the ratio of higher SES status parents to lower SES status parents from Neighbourhood A who apply for a school place for their child in School X

SES_{BX} as the ratio of higher SES status parents to lower SES status parents in Neighbourhood B who apply for a school place for their child in School X

SES_X as the ratio of higher SES status parents to lower SES status parents in School X

SES_Y as the ratio of higher SES status parents to lower SES status parents in School Y

Our analysis suggests that SES_{BX} will be greater than SES_B but it may still be lower than SES_A and SES_{AX}. The replacement of a zonal system by an open enrolment system will lead to lower (higher) stratification in applications to schools if the weighted average of SES_{AX} and SES_{BX} is less (more) than SES_A. As with Case 1 the full impact of open enrolment on stratification depends on schools' enrolment capacity and their procedures for determining intake when applications exceed capacity.

There are, therefore, several reasons why we would expect the effect of open enrolment on stratification to vary according to local factors. Open enrolment is more likely to reduce stratification where there is strong segregation of housing type according to school catchment area and popular schools are able to increase enrolments. The effect on stratification of enrolment policies of over-subscribed schools will depend on the segregation of housing type. An over-subscribed school in a neighbourhood of all high-cost housing may reduce stratification through a policy of selection by ability. An over-subscribed school in a neighbourhood of mixed housing may increase stratification by such a policy. Therefore we cannot predict the overall effect of open enrolment on stratification on the basis of theoretical analysis. We now turn to some empirical evidence.

8.3.2 Evidence of stratification in schooling markets

The ideal evidence to assess the impact of quasi-markets on stratification would include school and pupil level achievement and family background data for each local schooling market. Unfortunately, it is difficult to identify the scope of local schooling markets, not least because they frequently overlap. Attempts by researchers to circumvent this problem provide one, but not the only, source of disagreement over their conclusions. The great majority of the evidence we refer to below is taken from studies of the schooling quasi-market in England and Wales where the question of stratification has received considerable attention, and the system-wide implementation of open enrolment has facilitated quantitative as well as well as qualitative assessments upon stratification.

Stratification may occur through an unequal distribution of pupils according to ethnic background, pupils' ability, parental income, parental occupation or parental education. Whilst these characteristics are typically strongly correlated it is possible for there to be an increase in segregation according to one measure but not others. Stratification with respect to pupil ability can be observed through the distribution of pupil achievement attainment across schools. As discussed in Chapter 7, in England and Wales the most prominently reported data refer to pupils' attainment at the end of compulsory schooling when they are aged 16. These results are reported in two forms: the proportion of pupils who have achieved at least five passes at grades A*–C, and an average point score for the results of all pupils. The first of these measures is more strongly entrenched in media reporting of examination results, with the second measure only introduced in 1997 some years after the first. Given the prominence given by the media to the proportion of pupils achieving five or more passes at grades A*–C, we refer to these as 'league table results'. Between 1993 and 1997 the average point score increased from 33.1 to 35.9, with the top 10 per cent of pupils (by examination performance) experiencing an increase of 4.4 and the bottom 10 per cent of the cohort from 0.8 to 0.7 (West and Pennell 2000). Other studies have attempted to identify changes within local schooling markets. These studies have employed the notion of a local market hierarchy whereby schools are ranked in terms of league table positions. Gibson and Asthana (2000) present results of an analysis based on grouping schools into local hierarchies of this kind. They find that the annual rate of improvement in the percentage of pupils gaining 5 or more passes at grades A*–C was 1.65 for the schools at the top of their local hierarchy and 0.3 for schools at the bottom. Levačić and Woods (1999) analyse the difference between the league table score of the highest and lowest ranking schools in each local market. By this measure, the performance of high achieving schools improved relative to low achieving schools in a clear majority of the 71 local markets they investigated. The Chief Inspector of Schools in England noted a widening gap between the performance of pupils in the highest and lowest ranking schools (HMCI 1998; OfSTED 1999b). The more impressive increase in attainment achieved by the top 10 per cent of schools might be due to greater improvements in the effectiveness of these schools or a redistribution of pupils due to increasing stratification.

Case studies of the effect of quasi-markets on parental choice have led a number of researchers to conclude that social stratification has increased. Prominent amongst this research has been the work of Ball and colleagues who conclude:

> Across schools, we appear to be seeing an intensification of status hierarchies, provisional differentiation and segregation within the state system. Working class children, and particularly children with SEN, are likely to be increasingly 'ghettoized' in under-resourced and understaffed low status schools.
>
> (Gewirtz *et al.* 1985: 188)

Similar conclusions have been reached by researchers in New Zealand (Wylie 1994; Thrupp 1995), Belgium (Vandenberghe 1998) and Tanzania, where Samoff (1991: 389) reports that 'privatisation has also tended to reinforce stratification'. Noden *et al.* (1998: 234) find that once selective schools are discounted, there is no significant difference between the average examination results of first-choice schools of middle-class and working-class parents. However, they also find that there is a significant difference between the classes in the examination performance scores of destination schools. They believe that implicit bias in the recruitment procedure is partly to blame. 'Two schools that use pre-admission interviews rejected working class applicants whilst accepting middle class applicants who lived further away.' Van Cuyck-Remijssen and Dronkers (1990) note that the relative performance of public and Catholic schools in Holland varies according to which type of school is in the minority in an urban area. The minority school type outperforms other schools, and they attribute this to the greater likelihood that parents who have chosen the minority school have done so out of greater commitment to their child's education.

Waslander and Thrupp (1995) present data from local schooling markets in New Zealand using three categories of location: the local or neighbourhood school, the adjacent school and the distant school. They examine the degree of stratification by ethnic group and socio-economic status before and after the introduction of open enrolment. They find high levels of stratification in all instances and note that these figures indicate a relatively high level of stratification under the zoning system. They find that the ethnic stratification under zoning was slightly higher at the residential than the school level indicating that some Maori and Pacific Island parents were sending their children to out-of-neighbourhood schools. In contrast, they found that socio-economic segregation operated more strongly at school level than at residential level, suggesting that the socio-economic status of parents who sent their children to out-of-neighbourhood schools under the zoning system were not representative of the residential neighbourhood. Through a series of tables presenting data on dissimilarity by ethnic background and socio-economic status, they show how measured segregation by social class has tended to decline during the period of open enrolment, whilst segregation of Maori children has tended to increase. Despite an initial drop in the degree of segregation of Maori children, 'a year later many Maori students began to enrol at a school which was now increasingly marketing itself as a bicultural school in the area' (*ibid.*: 10).

The most substantial body of research evidence relating to stratification in England and Wales concerns parental income as reflected in the proportion of pupils eligible for free school meals (%FSM). Nationally, the %FSM figure rose gently in the period after the introduction of the quasi-market (Bradley and Taylor 2000). In a substantial series of papers Gorard and Fitz (e.g. 1997, 1998, 2000a, 2000b) claim to provide definitive evidence that stratification has reduced during the period since the introduction of open enrolment with the result that 'popular schools are increasing their proportion of children from academically disadvantaged families' (Gorard 1998: 254). More specifically, they present data suggesting an initial small increase followed by a significant decrease in stratification at national, regional and LEA level. As we noted in Chapter 5, an initial increase in stratification is consistent with a belief that the introduction of open enrolment allows higher income parents to further exploit existing cultural capital built up through the experience of their social networks in Tiebout choice. The social networks of lower income parents may take a little longer to adapt to the opportunities presented by open enrolment. This is the explanation favoured by Gorard and Fitz. They also use the level of appeals by parents seeking to secure their desired choice of school as a proxy for the intensity of local competition between schools. Based on the correlation between this variable and the distribution of pupils eligible for free school meals, they conclude that quasi-market forces are not responsible for the decrease in stratification they observe. However, the number of appeals is a somewhat distant proxy for the level of competition and we might reasonably expect it to be related to a wide number of variables such as: LEA policy on school expansion, social composition of the area, and initial levels of enrolment relative to capacity. As we shall see below, other researchers (Levačić and Woods 1999), using a more direct measure of competition, have come to different conclusions.

Bradley and Taylor (2000) use data from on parents' SES from the Youth Cohort Studies (YCS) as well as %FSM data to investigate changes in school segregation in England during the 1990s. Like Gorard and Fitz they investigate the distribution of %FSM within Local Education Authority Areas. However, they come to different conclusions. They base their conclusions on multiple regressions where the change in a school's %FSM is made dependent on, inter alia, the change in the %FSM of other schools in the area, the school's examination results and the examination results of other schools in the area. In comparing the 1992 and 1998 cohorts, they found that schools with the poorest exam performance experienced a 5.8 per cent increase in the proportion of pupils whose fathers are in the lowest skills group compared with a 2 per cent decrease for schools with a very good exam performance. Schools with very poor exam results experienced a 4 per cent decrease in the proportion of pupils whose fathers were in the highest skill category compared with a 3 per cent increase for schools with very high exam results. They also present an analysis of the changing distribution of %FSM across schools (Table 8.1) and note that such changes have been relatively small. Nevertheless they conclude that 'eligibility for free school meals and parental occupation therefore point in the same direction: differences in the social segregation of schools have widened during the 1990s' (*ibid.*: 16). In testing for the effect of local market conditions on the distribution across schools of children eligible for FSM they found a significant negative relationship between school examination results and the change in the proportion of pupils enrolled at the school eligible for FSM and a significant positive relationship between the examination results of other local schools and the school's % FSM. They also find some evidence that social segregation has responded more vigorously to quasi-markets in metropolitan areas than non-metropolitan areas, and that expanding schools are likely to reduce the proportion of their FSM students on their roll.

Gibson and Asthana (1998b, 2000) attempt to analyse stratification within local schooling markets (in contrast to the national, regional and LEA level focus of Gorard and Fitz). They identify local schooling markets by identifying a 'five-school market group' for each school by using postcodes to identify the four other schools whose 'catchment' areas most overlap with the target school. This procedure is criticised by Gorard and Fitz (2000a) and Gorard (2000) on

Table 8.1 Variations in %FSM according to schools' examination results

Quintile	%FSM all schools 1993*	%FSM all schools 1999*	Change in percentage %FSM*	Annual rate of percentage change**	Annual rate of change %FSM in local market group (1995–98)†
5 (Highest–best results)	5.5	5.7	0.2	0.519	−0.56
4	9.8	10.1	0.3	0.437	−0.40
3	14.4	15.6	1.2	1.190	−0.33
2	21.9	23.7	1.8	1.174	−0.14
1 (Lowest–worst results)	33.6	36.1	2.5	1.063	−0.11

Source: * Data presented by Bradley and Taylor (2000); ** Calculated from data in Bradley and Taylor (2000); † Data presented by Gibson and Asthana (2000)

the basis of the latter's analysis of school catchment areas in Wales which showed that 'although Welsh-language schools exist in the same post code locations as their more common English-language counterparts, it does not mean that their intakes are similar in terms of family background' (Gorard and Fitz 2000a: 412). Whilst this particular issue may be specific to schools in Wales, it illustrates the kind of difficulty that confronts attempts to group schools into local market areas without qualitative local information about local characteristics and dynamics. In addition, Gibson and Asthana's sample of schools experienced a fall in %FSM during a period when schools as a whole experienced a rise (Table 8.1). Nevertheless, they reach a similar conclusion to Bradley and Taylor in that grouping schools on a hierarchical basis by absolute examination results suggests that stratification between schools did increase between English schools during the period after the introduction of open enrolment and not only during the first year of this system. Moreover, this finding is implied by calculating the annual rate of percentage change and by a simple subtraction of the initial percentage %FSM from the final %FSM (Table 8.1). The importance of the distinction between these measures is stressed by Gorard and Fitz (2000a) and Gorard (2000).

The data presented by these researchers therefore leave us with a problem. How could it possibly be that measures of stratification using segregation indices at LEA and national level suggest a reduction in stratification whilst other measures suggest a small increase in stratification? One problem with LEA and national statistics is that this level of aggregated data may conceal results that would emerge from identified local markets. To illustrate this we refer to a study of Belgian schools carried out by Vandenberghe (1998). He analyses the relationship between the number of schools in a local schooling market and the dispersion between and within schools of students who have been required to repeat a year. He measures dispersion within schools on the basis of the distribution of students across the separate tracks of general, technical and professional routes. Using a Herfindahl index to measure the concentration ratio for schools in local markets he finds an inverse relationship between the number of schools in a local market and the inequality of distribution between them of students repeating a year. If the degree of market-induced stratification in local schooling markets is significantly influenced by local factors (such as the number of schools in the local market) then, at the very least, aggregate level data must be supplemented by local studies.

To examine this problem a little further we use data gathered in our investigation of two local schooling markets (Davies *et al.* 2002). Each of these markets served a small town and each was self-contained with a negligible number of pupils from outside the town attending public schools in the town. The validity of viewing each town as a distinct market was authenticated through interviews with staff focusing on competitive behaviour by schools and patterns of parental choice. We present a selection of data in Table 8.2. Column (2) presents the percentage of pupils completing compulsory education at 16 who gained five or more GCSE examination passes at grades A*–C. Columns (9) and (10) present calculations using the segregation index favoured by Gorard and Taylor (2000). This index is calculated by:

$$S = 0.5 * \Sigma \, (\, | \, A_i/A - R_i/R \, | \,)$$

where

S is the segregation index calculated for a group of schools

A_i is the number of pupils in school *i* eligible for free school meals

A is the total number of children in the group of schools eligible for free school meals

R_i is the number of pupils enrolled at the school

R is the total number of pupils enrolled in all the schools.

The segregation index increases for local market A from 0.16 to 0.22 whilst remaining constant in local market B. We concentrate first on the results for local market B as these are closer to the results obtained by Gorard and Fitz for all schools. However, the results for local market B are also consistent with those presented in Table 8.1, which suggest an increase in stratification. We now suggest how the results presented by Gorard and colleagues reported earlier might be more consistent with the findings of other studies than they suppose. That is, rather than one party being right and one wrong, with correctness consequent on appropriate methodology, it might be that methodological differences only account for part of the differences in conclusions.

We start by recalling that the interview and questionnaire data suggest

Table 8.2 Variation in %FSM and examination results in two local markets

Local market A

(1) School	(2) % A*–C	(3) Roll 1993	(4) Average school roll 1996–98	(5) % FSM 1994	(6) % FSM 1998	(7) % FSM 1998	(8) No. FSM 1998	(9) Index 1993	(10) Index 1998
5	65	986	1134	5	4	4	45	0.06	0.12
4	60	1086	1086	5	6	6	65	0.07	0.06
3	54	988	1126	6	7	7	79	0.03	0.04
2	49	877	842	7	10	10	84	0.00	0.04
1	32	630	617	15	20	20	123	0.16	0.18
Totals		4567	4805		319		397	0.16	0.22

Local market B

(1) School	(2) % A*–C	(3) Roll 1993	(4) Average school roll 1996–98	(5) % FSM 1993	(6) No. FSM 1993	(7) % FSM 1998	(8) No. FSM 1998	(9) Index 1993	(10) Index 1998
6	59	1139	1287	2	23	3	39	0.16	0.16
5	54	1005	1055	6	60	6	63	0.06	0.07
4	42	939	1024	9	85	10	102	0.01	0.00
3	41	1009	1059	13	131	11	116	0.07	0.02
2	37	765	689	10	77	15	103	0.01	0.06
1	24	658	619	21	138	24	149	0.15	0.15
Totals		5515	5733		513		573	0.23	0.23

that higher SES parents are more likely than lower SES parents to move their children to an out-of-neighbourhood school (we refer to this below as the 'SES bias proposition'). If we apply this proposition to the schools in Table 8.2 we can see that enrolment fell by 39 in school 1 in local market B. For simplicity we assume that this represents 39 'moving parents' (ignoring the overall increase in school enrolments and more complex movements). If the proportion of 'moving parents' whose children are eligible for free school meals were representative of parents at the school, then 21 per cent of these children (roughly 8) would be eligible for free school meals. If the SES bias proposition is correct then this proportion ought to be significantly less than 21 per cent. Table 8.3 shows the relationship between this proportion and the segregation index.

In the examples in Table 8.3, the proportion of pupils eligible for free school meals (FSM pupils) in School 2 (from which the movement will occur) is 20 per cent. If these pupils are fully represented in the pupils who opt for the out-of-neighbourhood School 1 then the segregation index falls significantly as

Table 8.3   The percentage of 'moving' children eligible for FSM and the Segregation Index

Example (1): Proportion of FSM in movement same as school 2

School	Roll 1993	Roll 1998	%FSM 1993	Actual FSM 1993	%FSM 1998	Actual FSM 1998	1993 index	1998 index
1	1000	1200	5	50	75	90	0.3	0.24
2	1000	800	20	200	20	160	0.3	0.24
Totals	2000	2000		250		250	0.3	0.24

Example (2): Proportion of FSM in movement same as school 1

School	Roll 1993	Roll 1998	%FSM 1993	Actual FSM 1993	% FSM 1998	Actual FSM 1998	1993 index	1998 index
1	1000	1200	5	50	5	90	0.3	0.36
2	1000	800	20	200	23.75	190	0.3	0.36
Totals	2000	2000		250		250	0.3	0.36

Example (3): Proportion of FSM in movement half way between schools 1 and 2

School	Roll 1993	Roll 1998	%FSM 1993	Actual FSM 1993	%FSM 1998	Actual FSM 1998	1993 index	1998 index
1	1000	1200	5	50	6.25	75	0.3	0.3
2	1000	800	20	200	21.88	175	0.3	0.3
Totals	2000	2000		250		250	0.3	0.3

shown in Example 1. Example 2 shows that if the proportion of FSM pupils in the movers is the same as found in School 1 then the segregation index will increase. If the proportion of FSM pupils amongst the movers is half-way between that found in School 1 and School 2 then the segregation index will be unchanged. These figures show how the SES bias proposition is consistent not only with a finding that the segregation index has not changed but also with small decreases in the segregation index. If we now return to Table 8.2 we have a situation that corresponds roughly to Example 3 in Table 8.3 in so far as the segregation index has not changed. Despite this, we note that the bottom two schools in the hierarchy have increased the number of FSM children on roll, despite decreases in total enrolments. That is, even in a case where the segregation index suggests that stratification is unchanged, the scope for increased attainment at the schools at the bottom of the local hierarchy is decreasing.

We now comment on the differences between local markets A and B. Our review of theory earlier in this section suggested that the effect of schooling markets on stratification will be strongly affected by local conditions. The distribution of housing types relative to schools will have a strong bearing on the impact on any change in stratification observed after the introduction of open enrolment. Schooling markets in which housing is more segregated are more likely to see a fall in the segregation index after the introduction of open enrolment. The data in Table 8.2 suggest this is unlikely to be the explanation for the difference between local markets A and B, given that initially the segregation index is lower in market A than in market B. A more likely explanation, presented in Davies *et al.* (2002), is that collaboration between schools in market B, fostered by local government, limited the effect of open enrolment on stratification. If accepted, this interpretation has important implications. It suggests that stratification would emerge more strongly in schooling markets if powers of local authorities to influence the behaviour of local schools were reduced, or professional ethics that emphasised a collective interest amongst local school managers and governors were weakened. This interpretation of data on stratification in England and Wales is consistent with results reported by Levačić and Woods (1999). Two of the three factors they find to be significantly related to an increase in social stratification in local markets are the proportion of grant-maintained schools and the perceived degree of competition. That is, the degree to which each school perceives itself as an independent entity competing with rivals affects the growth of stratification.

8. 4 Diversity and specialisation

8.4.1 Theoretical perspectives on school diversity and specialisation

Schools may be specialised in a number ways and a helpful typology of this diversity is provided by Glatter *et al.* (1997) and which we draw upon in Table 8.4.

The emergence of a particular type of diversity often reflects a socio-economic and cultural context in time and space. This is most apparent in the case of religious schooling as exemplified in countries such as the Netherlands and Northern Ireland. This context may also result in association between different types of diversity. For example, a strong association between curriculum and pupil ability in England underpins a history of more vocational schooling being associated with schools that specialise in the schooling of less able pupils. Our purpose here is not to trace the reasons why particular types of diversity have emerged, but rather to consider the arguments that might be advanced for maintaining or extending the degree of diversity within a schooling system. We now examine four broad lines of argument: (1) that differences

Table 8.4   Types of school diversity

Type	Description/comments
Structural	Concerning arrangements for governance, funding and ownership (e.g. private, grant-maintained, LEA maintained schools)
Curricular	Where schools specialise in or emphasise particular aspects of the curriculum (e.g. technology, music)
Style	Where schools emphasise a particular learning or teaching style or educational approach (such as child-centred or formal teaching) including related aspects such as approach to discipline, pupil grouping procedures).
Religious/philosophical	Where schools promote or emphasise a particular religious belief system or philosophy
Gender	Including schools that only admit either boys or girls and schools that arrange separate classes for girls or boys
Pupil ability	Where schools cater to pupils within a particular range of ability
Age range	Where schools vary according to the age range of the pupils

Source: Glatter *et al.* (1997)

between the schooling preferences are best met by a diversified schooling system; (2) that schools derive specialisation benefits from narrowing the range of schooling outcomes they aim to provide; (3) that competition between types of schooling system will encourage school improvement; and (4) that in the face of uncertainty about the most effective schooling type it is in the interests of the state to maintain different systems until it is clear which is most effective (as argued, for example by Hargreaves 1996).

The first argument for diversity between schools is based on the idea of allocative efficiency and was introduced in Chapter 1. An efficient schooling system will produce the range of outputs most desired by parents and pupils. Since there is a range of possible futures for which education can prepare the pupil, and since parents and pupils will to some degree differ in their valuations of the outcomes of schooling, we would expect them to differ in their most preferred type of schooling. Therefore, parents should have access to a range of schools that includes at least one school which provides something close to their most preferred type of education. According to Hargreaves (1996), parents who have chosen a particular type of school will be more committed to supporting its success and the progress of their children. A coda to this argument is that if parents are able to access alternative types of schooling the loss of benefit resulting from positional elements in educational outcomes will be reduced (as discussed in Chapter 3).

The second argument appeals to the benefits of specialisation on the production of schooling outcomes. A school that concentrates on the production of a small range of outcomes will be able to recruit teachers who are particularly skilled in these areas and purchase equipment and books that support a rich and specialised learning environment. Moreover, a school with a narrow set of aims is less likely to suffer from 'goal confusion' (Chubb and Moe 1990). That is, a school that has many aims will face frequent tensions between those aims. On occasions it will lose continuity by switching its focus between aims, and in some cases it will find that the achievement of one aim is at the expense of another. In Chapter 3 we noted evidence of competitive supply in the case of schooling outcomes. The specialisation of a school may also be assisted by a homogeneous student body. The more homogeneous the preferences of the pupils the easier they will be to satisfy given that they will be taught in groups. In addition, teachers will face fewer differentiation problems if all the pupils in the class have similar levels of prior understanding and aptitude for learning. Whilst the commitment of many teachers to meeting diverse needs in one class cannot be doubted, the scale of the difficulties they face is evident in current research (Savage and Desforges 1995).

We developed two further arguments in Chapter 7. The third argument may be illustrated with reference to local authority schools in England. If schools have the option of an alternative governance status (they may choose to be more or less independent of state support) there will be pressure on state bodies (Local Education Authorities (LEAs), in this instance) to provide services that are technically and allocatively efficient. The fourth argument takes no account of ongoing benefits from competition between alternative schooling systems. Rather, it focuses an idea of a 'most effective system' as if that is independent of the competitive system. Following this argument, diversity is only maintained until there is convincing evidence that one system is more effective than all others.

We introduced the argument against diversity in Chapter 1. This argument begins by contesting the assumption of significant difference between parental preferences. Brown (1992) develops an argument for a common curriculum based on the uncertainty that parents face about their child's future. Parents will not be able to judge the relative strengths of their child until quite late in their schooling and some parents may have considerable difficulty in making such judgements at any stage. This problem will be compounded if parents are not able to accurately predict future labour markets and social networks, although the stability over time of broad earnings differentials between occupations weakens this supporting argument, as discussed in Chapter 2. Nevertheless, if Brown's central assumption is accepted, there is an incentive for parents to avoid the risks posed by early specialisation. They may prefer to accept the loss of benefit implied by a more general education (compared to one ideally suited to their child's future) rather than risk a greater loss of benefit that would result from choosing a specialised education which later turns out to be inappropriate for their child.

Diversity may also be judged inappropriate even if it is suggested by preferences expressed by parents. There are three arguments to consider here. First, the state may judge that parents' interests conflict with those of the child. As discussed in Chapter 1, this judgement underpins compulsory education. Children at school are not earning money for the household. The parent might also gain satisfaction from seeing their child educated to follow 'in their footsteps', with a similar job and social network. A state which is prepared to override parental preferences with regard to school attendance may also feel justified in overriding preferences with regard to curriculum content. At the same time, the state may feel unjustified in risking a prediction of what is best for each individual child and therefore will provide a common curriculum for all. Second, the state may believe it is better equipped than most parents to make accurate predictions of future labour markets and accurate assessments of pupils' strengths. That is, it may believe that the child's interests are better served by the state's judgement than that of a well-intentioned parent. In this case, the state may allocate children to school types following its own assessment procedures (as in the case of grammar schools and secondary modern schools in some local education authorities in England). However, just as in the case of overriding parental self-interest, the state may yet feel unjustified in replacing parental choice by state choice. In this case, it will provide a common schooling until the child is judged responsible for his or her own (mis)judgements. Third, the state may judge that externalities in schooling outcomes justify enforcing a common schooling experience for all. For example, all pupils might be encouraged to be more tolerant, less prejudiced, more open to reason and less prone to violence. The most far-reaching expression of this argument is found in the belief that education consists in inducting new generations into society's cultural heritage and traditions of knowledge. This process requires a collective experience rather than one which is available for individuals to choose. The National Curriculum in England and Wales is one example of this argument put into practice. Whether it is a good example is very much open to debate. Contrasting examples are provided by Lawton (1996) and the DES (1983, 1985).

We now turn to the question of whether quasi-market forces might be expected to encourage school diversity. In simplistic terms this may seem self-evident. Open enrolment allows parents to express their preference for a particular type of schooling and thus encourages schools to specialise to secure the allegiance of sufficient parents to maintain viability. However, in relying on the assumption of fully informed producers and consumers, orthodox theory is ill-equipped to explain how such a process of change would actually happen. Fully informed consumers and producers would instantaneously move to a 'best' outcome in which schools adjusted their specialism to maximise aggregate benefits to parents. If we begin to introduce more realistic assumptions, specialisation seems less straightforward.

Suppose we begin from a position where all schools are offering the same curriculum and there are restricted opportunities for new schools to enter the market. Given that change is costly (in terms of recruiting new staff, retraining staff and buying new resources), each school has to weigh the potential benefits from specialisation against the costs of change. The potential benefits from specialisation depend on the preferences of parents and the responses of other schools. Suppose that one school makes a 'first-move' to specialise in technology with a strong emphasis on information and communications technology (ICT). If the school has correctly judged parental preferences then rival schools might respond by specialising in the same way and the advantage to the 'first-mover' is lost. From the point of view of 'specialisation', this might seem a bizarre outcome, but it follows a reasonable logic. The first-mover school reveals information to other schools through parental response to its actions (Adnett and Davies 2000). It becomes known that some parents will choose schools in response to a particular curriculum opportunity. Contrasting preferences of other parents remain less well known. There is less risk, although less potential benefit, in responding to the preferences that have become known compared with guessing at those that are still unclear.

In addition, schools only have an incentive to respond to the preferences of parents who seriously consider an out-of neighbourhood school (active choosers as identified in Chapter 5). If the curriculum preferences of these parents are not representative of all parents further problems may arise in the effect of a quasi-market on school specialisation. The extreme case occurs when active choosers have a homogeneous set of preferences. In this case, all schools have an incentive to satisfy these preferences regardless of the wishes of other parents. In these circumstances, the effect of a quasi-market would be to encourage conformity rather than diversity. There are, therefore, theoretical reasons why we might expect curriculum diversity to emerge only fitfully in response to an increase in the role of market forces in schooling.

8.4.2 Evidence of diversity and specialisation

In this section we first consider whether two types of diversity (according to pupil ability and curriculum) identified in Table 8.4 have increased following the introduction of quasi-markets. We reviewed religious diversity in Chapter 4 and diversity according to ability in relation to stratification in the previous section, so our major concern here lies with curriculum diversity. The arguments for diversity cited in Section 8.4.1 do not apply equally to different types of diversity. Schools that cater for different ranges of pupil ability may be welcomed on the basis that this allows schools to employ specialist resources and adopt a curriculum best suited to these pupils. However, gains from this type of specialisation would need to be very substantial to offset the peer group effects (noted in Chapter 3 and earlier in this chapter) which would disadvantage low-ability pupils. Curriculum specialisation in schools may be justified on the basis of increasing allocative efficiency (although given the potential for a loss of technical efficiency noted earlier in this chapter, assessment of any net efficiency gain may take some time).

As discussed in the previous section, the incentive for schools to 'cream-skim' and the greater likelihood that parents of more able children will consider out-of-neighbourhood schools create market pressures for specialisation according to ability. As noted in the previous section, the implications of this for diversity depend on the stratification created under the pre-existing (usually zonal) system. Reporting on the effect of market reforms in England, Fitz *et al.* (1993) observe that many of the schools in the first phasing of opting out of local authority control were selective, single sex and had traditional (academic) sixth forms and sought to increase their elite status. This suggests some increase in the degree of specialisation by ability subsequent to these market reforms. Such growing specialisation can influence headteachers' assessment of their market position. Waslander and Thrupp report a New Zealand school principal as saying

> there is a perception abroad in the community that we don't stretch and extend the top academic group and that they should probably go elsewhere and that's probably true because it takes an awful lot of specialised effort to bring up the bottom group. Parents of, what they think are reasonably academic kids ... see their kids as being sacrificed to less able kids who take more attention and are more likely to be disruptive and demand more of teachers' time.
>
> (Waslander and Thrupp 1995: 17)

According to Glatter *et al.* (1997) diversity according to pupil ability emerged as the prominent effect on diversity of market reforms in England. In their view this has resulted in a hierarchy of schools in each local market, with this hierarchy defined by the absolute level of examination results of each school. A particular form of diversity becomes dominant if it is more effective in attracting parents. Glatter *et al.* (1997) note that parents who expressed a preference for a school stressing academic attainment did so more strongly than parents who expressed any other kind of preference. This dominance is reinforced if other forms of diversity are associated with it. For example, if an 'academic curriculum' is associated in parents' minds with higher absolute levels of examination results then any school opting to specialise in a vocational curriculum conveys a negative message about absolute attainment (Davies and Adnett 1999). This may explain why Glatter *et al.* (1997) observe no incentives for innovation by the schools at the top of the hierarchy and no belief amongst the schools that attempts to differentiate themselves will attract parents. Similar findings emerge in our research (Davies *et al.* 2000). As Glatter and colleagues note, a convergence of schools towards an 'academic' emphasis is consistent with the belief that parents who are more likely to move their child to an out-of-neighbourhood school are also more likely to place a strong emphasis on academic outputs from schooling. As we saw in chapter 5, this belief is supported by the balance of evidence on parental choice. Recent research (Jesson 1999) comparing the value-added by selective and non-selective schools in England concludes that very able pupils succeed as well in non-selective schools as in selective, whilst less able pupils achieve less in a selective system. This finding is consistent with our general assessment of the peer effects literature and suggests that any tendency for market reforms to encourage diversity according to ability will reduce overall welfare.

With regard to curriculum diversity, research in England has tended to the conclusion that schools have not become more diverse (Woods 1992; Tomlinson 1994) and a number of researchers have suggested that schools have become more, rather than less, similar following the introduction of quasi-markets (Glatter *et al.* 1997; Gordon and Whitty 1997; Halpin *et al.* 1997). For example, the City Technology College (CTC) programme announced in 1986 was promoted as offering 'a good education with *vocational relevance*' (CTC Trust 1991). Despite this, research on the nature of these new schools (Walford 1991; Gewirtz *et al.* 1991; Whitty *et al.* 1993) concluded that CTCs were doing no more than put a new spin on the traditional academic quality yardstick. Edwards and Whitty (1997: 37) illustrate this conclusion with 'typical' comments from parents in their research: 'I think you can class the CTC just like that, as a grammar school' and 'I couldn't believe our luck when she got in, because it's just like getting a private education'. Woods (1992) reports in his study of local school markets that former secondary modern schools explained their emphasis on academic attainment in terms of an attempt to attract more pupils from the high end of the ability range.

The proposition that market forces will encourage diversity requires that schools identify what parents want and try to provide it. Evidence provided by Bagley *et al.* (1996a) and Davies *et al.* (2000, 2002) suggests that schools in England have weak procedures for discovering parental preferences. A minority of schools used questionnaires to elicit information and rather more relied on information gleaned from parents during routine interactions. However, Bagley *et al.* (1996a) do cite examples of schools changing policies on discipline, homework, examinations and extra-curricular activities as a result of information about parental preference.

The inference that open enrolment does not encourage curriculum specialisation is, however, made difficult by the impact during this period of a National Curriculum designed to ensure that all schools provide a similar basic 'entitlement' for all pupils (Whitty *et al.* 1998). Nevertheless, for many commentators (e.g. Walford 1996) the absence of emerging diversity between schools is attributable to parents' lack of interest in specialism (other than of the religious sort). This is consistent with the balance of evidence on parental choice reviewed in Chapter 5 and rejects the argument that schools will diversify in response to parental preference. However, we also noted in Chapter 5 that when commenting on their choice of school, parents are more likely to refer to school attributes that they perceive rather than missing attributes they might ideally wish for. They might only become aware of their preference for a specialised school if it became a real choice for them.

Other reasons for the lack of effect of market reforms on curriculum diversity in England may be inferred from research carried out by Švecová (2000) in the Czech Republic. She reports a rapid growth in specialised private schools in the period following the liberalisation of schooling provision in 1989. By 1996 many schools advertised specialist provision for a particular subject, amongst which 209 schools specialised in business. She also reports an increase in private kindergartens. She argues that 'the prevailing opinion certainly is that private schools are more open to the modernization of the education process (in terms of methods and content of study, in the CIT use, and, especially, in the school environment) than in state schools.' We might infer from this that the lack of change in curriculum diversity in English schools reflected stable political and economic conditions which provided little reason for radical change in the school curriculum. Alternatively, it might be argued that the incentives for not-for-profit schools were insufficient for them to justify risky innovation, a proposition discussed in Section 8.2.1.

In the face of the failure of market reforms to deliver curriculum specialisation, policy in England has turned to direct government policy incentives (as discussed in Chapter 7). Public schools have been encouraged to adopt a specialist status whereby they declare the subject of their specialism, secure supporting sponsorship and attract additional government funding to improve their specialist resources. These schools are allowed to select up to 10 per cent of their intake, but only 7 per cent of them were choosing do so in 2000 (Jesson 2001). Complementing this initiative, the restrictions imposed by the National Curriculum have been relaxed, enabling schools greater scope to determine the character of the curriculum offered to pupils. To date, assessments of the degree of curriculum specialism offered by these schools are lacking, but their performance relative to non-specialist schools is reported by Jesson (2001). He finds that specialist schools achieved a significantly higher value-added than non-specialist schools in 2000. The average GCSE points (measuring grade point scores across subjects taken by 16-year-old pupils in public examinations) was 41.3 for non-selective specialist schools and 36.3 for all other comprehensive schools.

Jesson considers a number of possible explanations for these results. We may group these into school commitment to target-setting and monitoring, readiness to consider innovative production processes and increased pupil motivation consequent upon state-of-the-art resources. The first interesting point about these explanations is that they do not include gains from specialisation. A second is the degree to which they suggest a bias in the selection of schools that have gained specialist status towards schools with high potential for school effectiveness and improvement. Such bias might be introduced through self-selection by schools applying to the scheme or by officials choosing between applicant schools. Until these possibilities can be discounted the link between specialisation and school performance in England remains uncertain.

Interest in the promotion of specialist schools is far from exclusive to England and Wales. These initiatives are long predated by the reform in 1974 of schools in Central Park East District 4 in East Harlem in New York City. Several very large failing schools were reorganised to produce a much larger number of smaller schools, each of which was encouraged to specialise according to its perceived expertise, and involve the local community in sharing the school's direction. These schools compete for enrolments from within the school district (Best 1993). By 1989 the percentage of students reading at or above the expected level for their age had risen from 16 per cent to 62 per cent. In other countries the state has intervened specifically to create diversity between schools. In Australia, the state of New South Wales designated some schools as specialised language and technology schools to secure a good geographical distribution of diversity. Schools in many parts of Sweden were encouraged to specialise in the 1990s. As in England, a key part of this encouragement was a relaxation in national prescription of the curriculum. There is encouraging data associated with the introduction of specialist school schemes in a number of countries, but the impact of 'specialism' per se remains compounded with other aspects of these initiatives.

8.5 Conclusions

Our assessment of school behaviour in this chapter goes to the heart of the aims of educational reforms that seek to improve schools through market reforms. Yet, given the variety of possible combinations of policy (as set out in Box 4.1), our conclusions here are limited in scope, referring only to the form of quasi-market introduced in England and Wales. Nevertheless, we have assumed in this book that comparisons of empirical data from different market experiments are as useful as comparisons of predictions from theoretical models of different policy combinations. We now present a number of conclusions.

First, the effects of an open-enrolment schooling quasi-market are heavily dependent on local circumstances: the distribution of housing types, the distribution of parents by socio-economic status, the number of schools, the degree of initial differentiation between the schools, the spare capacity within schools in a local market, the professional ethics and collegiality of headteachers, and the stance adopted by the Local Education Authority. This observation is important for interpretation of data and for policy formation. The number of schools in a local area and the amount of spare capacity can be changed over time, with predictable consequences for competitive behaviour. Likewise, professional cultures and the role of local government bodies may also change for reasons unconnected with schooling markets. However, assessments of the desirability of such changes should consider the subsequent impact on schools' competitive behaviour.

Second, open enrolment has increased the level of competitive behaviours by schools. In part, this has reinforced efforts to raise academic standards with a small, but significant, effect on attainment at 16. We are not aware of any attempt that has been made to measure the effects of competition on other schooling outputs such as personal fulfilment, socialisation or pupils' happiness at school. We cannot, therefore, preclude the possibility that these outputs have declined, given the incentives created for schools to concentrate on academic attainment. Schools have also engaged in competitive behaviours not closely related to raising attainment: notably the acquisition of resources that parents will find attractive and the promotion of the school through marketing. Given evidence that schools have generally undertaken very little market research to identify what parents really want, these competitive behaviours do not appear to be geared to improve technical or allocative efficiency.

Third, our theoretical analysis of stratification suggests that the effect of a move from a zonal to an open-enrolment system will vary strongly between local markets according to the distribution of housing and schools. This may be one reason for the difference between the evidence provided by Gorard (1999, 2000) suggesting a reduction in stratification and the evidence from Gibson and Asthana (2000) and Davies *et al.* (2002) suggesting an increase in stratification. Another may be the focus on local schooling markets in the latter. The conflict between Gorard's evidence and that of Bradley and Taylor (2000) (who also suggest an increase in stratification) is more problematic. We have shown that the proposition that parents who choose out-of-neighbourhoods are unrepresentative of the parents in the schools from which they move does not necessarily imply an increase in stratification and may, therefore, be consistent with Gorard's data.

Fourth, one of our observations has been that the full effect of the introduction of a quasi-market will take time to emerge. This principle is supported by evidence provided by Gorard (1999), although he reckons that the full effects of a change in a market regime will be seen much more quickly than we estimate. Evidence on parental choice presented in Chapter 5 combined with the theory of school behaviour discussed in Section 8.2 suggests a longer period of adjustment with an unstable equilibrium. From the point of view of policy, a key question is whether individual school improvements will be consistently rewarded with increased applications for enrolment. If an improved performance by a low-performing school is not rewarded, the market is failing to providing the incentives that are expected to generate positive change. Given the role of peer effects in pupil attainment, the most worrying possibility is that there will be dynamic cycles of decline for schools with low levels of absolute average pupil attainment and improvement for schools with high levels of absolute average attainment that are not reversible by the efforts of the schools themselves (Adnett *et al.* 2001). In our own research (Davies *et al.* 2002), the schools at the bottom of the two local market hierarchies (Table 8.2) managed to increase their absolute academic performance and their performance relative to the number of FSM pupils on roll. This is the good news from the point of view of overall efficiency. The bad news for these schools is that, having started with the lowest enrolment levels they experienced significant falls in enrolment. By the year 2001 the headteacher of one of these schools was openly calling for it to be closed on the grounds that the dynamic of competition in the town had made it financially unviable despite its achievement of strong added-value. Taylor *et al.* (2000) present contrasting evidence from five LEAs in England. Each of these LEAs covers a larger area than seems plausible for a local school market, but, even allowing for this, their data suggest that no schools experienced a spiral of decline in enrolments. Being closely linked to stratification, we may expect substantial local variations in this phenomenon. Further data is required before any summary conclusion can be offered.

Fifth, current evidence provides little support for the expectation that market forces will foster curriculum diversity between schools. There are a number of possible reasons for this and current evidence does not permit a robust evaluation of their relative importance. However, in closing this chapter we draw attention to two explanations that have important implications, if correct, for predictions of the future impact of markets on the curriculum. One possible explanation, from Austrian economics, is that parental demand for curriculum specialisation is latent, and will only become apparent if innovative schools perceive it and aim to serve it. Risks of innovation and information externalities can deter schools from introducing new programmes until 'first-movers' have demonstrated their success. A bandwagon effect of curriculum change will then ensue. The spread of psychology in the 16–19 curriculum in English schools may reflect this phenomenon. A second explanation is that schools may believe that parents likely to choose an out-of-neighbourhood school share particular curriculum preferences which are not fully representative of all parents. Davies *et al.* (2000) report beliefs amongst headteachers that these parents are seeking an academic curriculum. This results in incentives to all schools to provide a curriculum that suits the preferences of these but not other parents. The significance of these explanations for policy is that both suggest that open enrolment may not provide sufficient incentives for curriculum development. This provides a justification for the kind of state intervention in curriculum change that has been observed in England. However, evidence of school innovation in other types of market system around the world (e.g. Švecová 2000) shows how the relationship between schooling markets and innovation is dependent on the nature of the market and the context that market is serving.

9 Conclusions

Introduction

In this book we have sought to challenge the views of both proponents and opponents of an increased role for market forces in schooling markets. We have argued that proponents too often ignore the presence of extensive market failures in schooling markets and, given dysfunctional effects, the need to examine the interactions between individual reforms. Opponents, on the other hand, are often complacent about current schooling outcomes, neglecting the evidence of widespread government failures and the potential benefits from carefully designed and co-ordinated schooling reforms.

Schooling quasi-markets are recent phenomena and it should not be too surprising that, at the end of our analysis, we are left with more questions than answers. These reforms were not based upon imitation of a model of what was perceived to be 'successful' schooling systems, such as those of certain Pacific Rim countries. Instead, they originated from a widespread belief that the transplanting of market mechanisms could generate continual improvements in public schooling. One consequence is that there is no international body of empirical research that serves as a starting point for the development of an assessment of market-based reforms. Indeed, as Reynolds (1999) points out, the most recent reforms in England and Wales are increasingly ethnocentric, in the sense that they seek to utilise within-Britain variation in school performance, rather than learn from international best practice. This absence of long runs of performance data for market-based school systems suggests that, currently, caution should be exercised in reaching any firm conclusions as to their impact. In addition, as we noted in Chapter 5, the variations in research methods and their application cause problems in making comparisons across studies, and even within discipline boundaries. It also takes time for the reforms to be implemented and for them to be fully 'bedded in'. Indeed, much of our previous discussion explained why we would expect the short-term reactions of parents and pupils, teachers and school managers to quasi-market processes and incentives to differ from their longer-term responses. At this point of time, the difficulties in distinguishing between these short- and long-term responses further preclude firm conclusions from being made.

In drawing together our tentative conclusions we initially review the key findings of each of the previous chapters. In doing so we explore the extent to which common findings have emerged from these specialist assessments. In Section 9.3 we return to the three key policy questions which we set out at the end of our introductory chapter. These concern resource allocation, incentive mechanisms and the dangers of increased polarisation within schooling quasi-markets. Finally, in Section 9.4, we provide an economic interpretation of present attempts to simultaneously promote both competition and co-operation in local schooling markets.

9.2 A review of our arguments

In Chapter 1 we introduced the economic analysis of schooling markets. We examined the fundamental nature of the market mechanism and defined key terms, such as 'efficiency', which facilitated our later analysis. In developing this framework we pointed out some of the weaknesses of the orthodox economic analysis of markets and its limited applicability to schooling issues. The latter analysis still remains dominated by human capital theory which, as conventionally framed, concentrates upon the labour market consequences of educational decision-making and ignores the diversity, particularly the consumption elements, of schooling outputs. A key part of this chapter was our identification of the sources of both market and government failure in schooling markets. Rejecting all or nothing extremes, we argued that our concern should be to examine the determinants of the appropriate form and extent of market forces in state schooling systems.

Apart from providing our basic analysis and terminology, Chapter 1 identified the special characteristics of education which create problems for the design and implementation of market-based reforms. First, we noted the multiple goals of public education, which to some extent are substitutes in a school's production process. Most of these goals are not precisely measurable, and identifying accurately a school's own contribution to educational value-added is problematic, if not impossible. Second, schooling markets involve multiple principals with diverse preferences regarding the weights that should be attached to these goals of state schooling. Assessing allocative efficiency, therefore, requires some prior agreement amongst these principals as to the desired combination of schooling outcomes. Third, the agents (teachers and heads) that these principals seek to direct are in part motivated by professional and public service considerations. Market based incentives may therefore produce dysfunctional effects to the extent to which 'professionalism' and 'collegiate ethos' mechanisms are displaced. Fourth, from the viewpoint of many principals (parents and pupils, teachers and local government), schooling markets are local markets in which a small number of schools 'compete' for a largely fixed number of pupils. Moreover, those markets have a history that has generated an established hierarchy amongst local schools largely based upon the average absolute levels of academic attainment of their pupils.

In the succeeding chapters we detailed how these distinct characteristics of education, both individually and collectively, have caused problems for attempts to make schooling decisions more sensitive to market forces. For example, in Chapters 3 and 5 we showed that many of the disputes about the desirability of increased school choice are in reality disputes about the weights that should be attached to different schooling outputs. Reforms which increase parental power in schooling markets reduce those of other principals and lead to changes in the mix of educational outputs which local schools seek to produce. This has led to tensions between alternative government policy objectives. Governments have often been enthusiastic in making schools more receptive to parents' wishes. However, they have been generally unwilling to relinquish control over the determination of the composition of outcomes which schools are required to achieve.

In Chapter 2 we examined the economic and social context that both induced market-based reforms and frames the environment within which those reforms operate. We noted how new fashions in macroeconomic policy making, in particular a preoccupation with maintaining credibility for sustainable fiscal policy, had altered the budgetary process within which government expenditure on schooling was determined. Our brief review of recent expenditure trends in developed countries suggested a slow convergence, albeit with large national differences remaining. We also noted how overall spending per pupil was tending to increase, reflecting consumption (high income elasticity of demand), investment (high rates of return) and relative price influences. Our review of the econometric evidence indicated that schooling remains a socially and privately attractive investment. We also noted that attempts were continuing to substantiate its effect upon relative national growth rates. How to interpret the source of these private and social returns is also the subject of current debate, and we outlined alternative screening and status-conflict theories.

A major part of our analysis in Chapter 2 concerned the implications of the new/knowledge-based/globalised economy for the desired combinations of schooling outcomes. A key issue was how technological and organisational changes in the nature of work and social interactions were impacting on the level and distribution of schooling premiums. We questioned whether the adoption of simple national schooling targets was an appropriate response to the disparate requirements of the 'new economy'. We then linked this concern to the associated problems of growing labour market inequality and social exclusion in developed economies. Concentrating upon the need to raise the relative earnings of the least educated, we outlined Heckman's argument for a fundamental switching of public expenditure towards the youngest age groups and in favour of developing their communication skills, social adaptability and motivation.

Our economic analysis of individual parental, pupil and school behaviour was developed in Chapter 3. Here, we linked a review of theory with summaries of recent research evidence, concentrating especially on educational choice and optimal school and class size. In drawing together this analysis, we stressed the role of information and incentives in promoting allocative and technical efficiency in schooling markets. We noted that governments, in providing information and designing incentive mechanisms for schools and teachers, were likely to distort parental choices. It follows that the evaluation of education reforms should focus on their impact on choice processes as well as on schooling outcomes. We also introduced the possibility of positional demands for schooling. The extent to which schooling choice reflects individual decision-making rather than social processes now became a major issue. Only if the former dominates, can we assume that orthodox economic analysis' presumption in favour of market choice necessarily applies.

In Chapter 3 we also provided evidence indicating that home background and peer effects outweighed school effects in determining a child's academic attainment. Resource levels appear to have some effect on schooling outputs, but their effects are likely to be outweighed by levels and changes in school size. We further noted that average costs of schooling appear to be more strongly related to school size than the average attainment level of their pupils. Taken together these findings suggest that open enrolment triggers both demand and supply responses that result in an increase in the sorting of pupils by home background. In addition, schools with unfavourable peer effects will tend to lose market share. This will cause them to experience rising unit costs and falling cost effectiveness, as measured by the cost of a particular level of value-added. The interaction between these two processes could promote cumulative decline, an outcome that would be difficult to reverse.

The first three chapters provided the base for our analysis of market-based reforms of state schooling systems. In Chapter 4 we sorted those reforms into five categories: – school funding; open enrolment; teacher training and pay; local school management, and information and monitoring. The analysis of these policies was to form the content of the next group of chapters, with the remainder of Chapter 4 containing our initial analysis of the nature of the reforms to school funding and enrolment. We noted the growth of private sources of funding for schooling and the different approaches taken to involving business expertise in schooling markets. We explained how the emergence of another principal could change the preferred level and mix of schooling outputs. The evidence reviewed suggested that sponsored schools achieve higher private outcomes, though whether this reflects a school or sample selection effect remains unclear. Sponsors did not appear to have managed to instil a distinct curriculum on their schools, and in England CTCs had not managed to secure a significant market share. Difficulties in attracting financial contributions from the business sector were also apparent in attempts to adopt a partnership model, though here we concluded that it remains too early to assess its impact on schooling outcomes.

In Chapter 4 we also outlined and compared the variety of open-enrolment reforms, the consequences of which were analysed in Chapter 5. In that chapter we investigated both how parents and pupils had utilised their greater choice, and whether quasi-markets have altered the basis on which those choices are made. We concluded that both consumption and investment considerations affect parental choice, with some suggestion that middle-class parents were placing more emphasis upon investment outcomes. The relative ranking of peer group and school effectiveness considerations were difficult to identify, though interview data strongly suggested that parents stressed the importance of their preferred peer group. The quality of a school's resources was a significant, though rarely dominant, consideration in exercising choice. Overall, though parents appear to take a variety of factors into account, often they ultimately appear to employ simple heuristics in finally making their choice. The resulting differences in the implicit weights attached to location, peer group, school effectiveness and curriculum in exercising school choice contributed to the polarisation of intake on the basis of social class, ethnic background and religion.

In Chapter 6 we turned to examine how quasi-market reforms had impacted upon the licensing, training and remuneration of teachers. In the absence of a national pay system for teachers, increased competition between schools should lead to a greater dispersion of teacher's pay for given levels of effort. In practice, national pay systems and the high degree of unionisation of teachers have limited such effects. Of greater concern have been persistent recruitment and retention problems and a perceived lack of incentives to reward high-quality classroom teachers; though, in the case of the former two problems, there had been a marked reluctance to adopt one common market solution: raising relative pay. Governments have also been concerned that teacher unions and the profession's prevailing collegiate ethos may have distorted the pattern of schooling outcomes from that desired by governments. Indeed, we suggested that market-based reforms of state schooling, through strengthening rival stakeholders' power and imposing managerial values, could themselves be viewed as a vehicle for changing professional norms and ethics. We analysed specific policies aimed at strengthening performance-related pay and concluded that, whilst measured outcomes may be stimulated by such schemes, dysfunctional effects were likely, causing uncertainty about their overall impact on the level and quality of schooling outcomes.

Chapter 7 addressed the remaining two categories of quasi-market reforms: local management of schools and increased performance monitoring. If the increasing of market pressures on schools is to induce greater allocative and technical efficiency, schools need to be empowered to respond to market signals. The increased devolution of financial decision-making to individual schools has been one aspect of that empowerment. At the same time, the increase in parental choice and use of targeted incentives necessitated the increased monitoring of school performance. Our review of the evidence concerning the impact of local management of schools pointed to its popularity with headteachers and resulting improvements in x-efficiency. These improvements were contrary to the expectations of Hanushek and orthodox economics, perhaps reflecting their adoption jointly with enhanced monitoring. Our analysis of the consequences of increased performance monitoring suggested that it had encouraged a concentration on a narrow range of schooling outcomes.

These have been largely associated with the academic attainment levels of those of average and above average ability. To tackle the perceived dysfunctional effects of increased school choice and performance monitoring, a diverse array of supplementary policies had been introduced. Often the effect of these had been to reduce the extent of direct inter-school competition (e.g. specialist schools initiatives), or actively encourage cross-school co-operation (e.g. Beacon schools).

Finally, in Chapter 8, we examined the behaviour of schools in the quasi-market and brought together our findings on the overall impact on schooling of the reforms. We concentrated on the consequences of schooling markets for productive efficiency, the distribution of educational benefits across individuals and the diversity of provision within the schooling system. We concluded that there was evidence of a slight increase in the overall level of pupil attainment as a result of increasing competition between schools. This conclusion is consistent with our earlier analysis of the anticipated effects of both greater direct competition and competition by comparison. However, this increase in the overall level seemed to be accompanied by a widening of the gap between the levels attained by pupils in the highest and lowest ranked schools. We also noted the diversity of behaviour in local schooling markets and concluded that local factors, such as headteachers' behaviour and local market conditions, were normally the source of this diversity.

Our arguments developed in Chapters 3 and 5 suggested that the introduction of open enrolment and local school management would lead to pupils becoming less evenly distributed across schools by class, ethnicity and religion. Schools now had greater incentives to enrol students who were cheaper to teach and were more likely to influence positively future enrolment levels . Our review of the evidence in Chapter 8 provided some, but not overwhelming, support for this prediction. The widening of the gap between pupil attainment levels in the highest and lowest ranking schools has been attributed to greater stratification by ability. We also found that the bulk of evidence also suggested greater polarisation by class and ethnicity.

In the earlier chapters the analysis developed produced conflicting predictions concerning the impact of schooling markets on school diversity. The basic economic analysis of markets suggested that open enrolment would encourage segmentation of the market, reflecting the diversity of parent and pupil preferences. However, imperfect information, risk and uncertainty, sunk costs and the dominant position of active choosers may all favour conformity of school provision rather than diversity. Our review, in Chapter 8, of the evidence suggested that each of these factors might have contributed to the failure of schooling markets to generate significant increases in diversity.

9.3 Three key policy questions

At the end of Chapter 1 we set ourselves three questions. We now draw together our arguments of the previous chapters to develop answers.

9.3.1 Should resources be reallocated away from 'unsuccessful' schools?

We have identified a process that can lead to a cycle of decline in schools losing market share in local schooling markets. This process can be instigated by factors independent of the actual performance of a school. Cream-skimming and/or the exercise of parental preferences reallocate positive peer group effects away from lower-ranked schools. A process that may be further encouraged by the publication of school performance tables based upon unadjusted measures of pupil attainment. Resulting falls in average pupil attainment levels can lead to a continuing loss of the most able remaining pupils. If enrolments fall, then budgetary constraints are tightened while average teaching costs per pupil rise. Schools in this predicament lack the resources necessary to fund curricula innovations and promote themselves in the local market place. A cycle of decline results. We stressed that, given the processes at work in contemporary quasi-markets, a school can face this outcome regardless of their absolute or relative success in promoting educational value-added. Indeed, for any school even 'doing the right thing' may not be sufficient for it to maintain market share against less effective schools who have an intake of higher average ability.

The prevailing logic of schooling markets, which we have outlined above, is that success should be rewarded and failure punished. Given open enrolment, success in schooling markets has come to be proxied by market share. In markets with excess capacity, the closure of those schools losing market share has sometimes occurred, though the costs to those parents, pupils and staff displaced may not necessarily be less than the resulting benefits. Normally, closure has been a final resort and in practice various special measures often provide additional financial support for remedial investment. We have now provided a rationale for this reluctance to accept the judgement of the market, though its survival may seem more surprising given that currently schools, on average, are often significantly below 'optimal' size.

A similar problem concerns the allocation of financial incentives for co-operation between rival providers. The creation of Beacon schools consolidates local hierarchies both in terms of funding and prestige. The logic of LMS and Fair Funding would suggest that allowing the 'less successful' schools to buy in expertise from rival providers would create greater value for money. It also prevents the higher-ranked schools from exercising their market power to effectively 'top-slice' the additional resources meant to assist less-advantaged schools.

9.3.2 Does the increased use of incentives have to jeopardise co-operation?

Market-based reforms have largely strengthened incentives for individual schools and teachers to improve their *relative* performance in local schooling markets. However, the multiple outputs of schooling prevent the creation of an accurate, unidimensional and widely accepted measure of school or teacher performance. Hence, as Dixit (2000) argues, a design of powerful incentive schemes based upon a limited measure of performance is likely to fail. As we noted in Chapter 6, the increased use of incentives based upon individual school or teacher performance is likely to reduce beneficial co-operation. Co-operation with other schools and teachers will be largely limited to situations where there are direct mutual benefits to each party from such actions. The logical consequence of such selectivity is that beneficial co-operation both between and within schools largely disappears within a local market. The quality and extent of information flows deteriorate, inertia and duplication increase and the overall quality of the schooling process and educational decision-making are negatively affected over time.

As we noted in Chapter 7, local management of schools while producing greater freedom and flexibility for schools leads to greater isolation. In the UK, the reduced role of LEAs has also led to a reduction in their access to external expertise. Levačić (1995) found some evidence that one response in certain local schooling markets is for greater co-operation amongst schools. Orthodox economic analysis usually viewed competition and co-operation as incompatible, since the latter was viewed as a mechanism for collusion aimed at subverting consumer welfare. As Brandenburger and Nalebuff (1997) explain, in practice the optimal strategy for a business usually involves a mix of competition and co-operation. A practice they termed 'co-opetition'. Such co-operation may merely involve the exchange of information, avoiding socially wasteful replication of research, but it can extend up to joint production where start-up costs are high or the pooling of specialist expertise particularly beneficial.

Given the pressures of competition, then co-operation within networks of secondary schools or networks of primary schools is less likely to persist over time than between primary and secondary schools. Our findings above are consistent with this assessment and Levačić (1995) finds evidence that secondary schools often subsidise the costs of networking with their feeder primary schools. However, co-operation between secondary and primary schools can be seen as the former attempting to secure market share and suppressing potentially beneficial competition from rival providers. The potential benefits of sharing information, specialist services, in-service training and curriculum development and exploiting economies of scope (such as avoiding duplication of minority subject provisions) together suggest that the benefits from co-operation are likely to be greater within the primary and secondary sectors than across them. However, even beneficial collusion between rival providers is unstable given the potential benefits to any individual school from breaking the agreement. The research outlined in Chapter 8 suggests that co-operation is more likely when a public service ethos dominates the local schooling market, and in which the needs of all the children in the local community drive school behaviour.

As we noted in Chapter 6, a similar process can occur within schools when individual performance-related pay is introduced. Remunerating teachers in this way encourages them to make decisions about the reallocation of their time and effort. They are encouraged both to neglect those aspects of their duties that are not monitored and to no longer internalise the consequences of their behaviour for fellow teachers and overall school performance. Hence, the benefits gained from increased motivation need to be compared to the costs resulting from reduced co-operation. More positively, incentive mechanisms need to be designed which reduce these dysfunctional responses. Rewards need to target absolute performance rather than relative, and collective performance rather than individual.

9.3.3 Is increased polarisation inevitable?

In the UK, we have noted how the increase in parental choice and the ability of schools to improve unadjusted examination by recruiting fewer socially disadvantaged pupils has distorted competition in local schooling markets. The underlying issue basically concerns the ownership of the externalities produced by one pupil on the educational outcomes of their co-pupils. Should the peer group effect be owned by the pupil who generates them or by society as a whole and internalised by governments within their schooling policies? Orthodox theory argues that the allocation of property rights is irrelevant since markets adjust their behaviour in response to any allocation. We have, in effect, questioned this conclusion. Open enrolment in practice privatised peer group effects, the consequence has been a redistribution of these effects across schools. The resulting polarisation has widened the distribution of schooling outcomes to the likely detriment of aggregate social welfare and overall economic performance.

Different policies have been introduced to try to address the issue of increased polarisation. In some local school markets in New Zealand, over-subscribed schools, in order to promote social mix, are required to select intake via ballot instead of academic merit or proximity (Lauder *et al.* 1999). In Finland, some local authorities have paid the bus fares of those opting for specialist academic provision in schools outside of the neighbourhood (Ahonen 2000). In the Netherlands, rather than trying to fight social segregation directly, policy focuses on providing a high quality education for all by weighting funding towards schools with high proportions of pupils from disadvantaged backgrounds (Ritzen *et al.* 1997). As we have seen, social inclusion considerations have also led to a similar skewing of funding in the UK. In addition, the British government has introduced Beacon schools and 'superhead' initiatives as a way of imitating desegregation without requiring the same degree of short-run costs to be borne by the parents of those in highly ranked schools. Value-added league tables which provide information relevant to all parents, regardless of the ability of their children, are a further mechanism to try to encourage a diversity in the frames of reference employed in schooling choices and a less-polarised outcome.

9.4 Generating beneficial co-opetition in local schooling markets

As quasi-market policies have developed in Western countries, there has been a gradual realisation of the need to reinforce the school choice and the delegation of financial decision-making reforms with additional targeted interventions. These interventions have effectively sought to change the relative prices faced by decision-makers to promote the behaviour desired by government. Examples of such policies are incentive pay and training grants in the case of teachers, and student grants in the case of post-compulsory schooling. Ironically, though governments have been enthusiastic supporters of the absence of a link between resources and school performance, their actual behaviour presupposes just such a link at the margins of policy, as is indicated by the financial inducements given to schools to become specialist providers. A consequence of this process has been that, in their totality, policies lack coherence and consistency, with individual decision-takers often facing conflicting policy-induced incentives. Effective policy co-ordination requires that the dysfunctional effects of reforms be minimised at the time that policy is designed and implemented, rather than these effects later providing a rationale for further interventions. The need is for co-ordinated and mutually consistent policy. For example, the provision of simple signals of school performance to parents and pupils that do not distort decision-making in a way inconsistent with raising overall levels of educational attainment in a local market.

A further irony concerns changing attitudes to the role of for-profit businesses in the state schooling sector. Initial reforms presupposed that establishing an effective quasi-market enabled increased technical and allocative efficiency to be generated, whilst retaining the social and equity advantages of public provision and funding. Currently, as we discussed in Chapter 4, rather than trying to refine quasi-market structures to achieve these gains, governments are experimenting with alternative plans for extending private sector involvement. Previously contractually based private sector involvement was rejected on the basis of an inability to specify fully contractual obligations in schooling markets (Broadbent and Laughlin 1997). The narrowing of educational objectives which quasi-market reforms have promoted has perversely simplified the specification of schooling contracts, effectively removing the previous rationale for the retention of public sector provision. A final irony may be that, in increasing the role of the private sector in schooling markets, the government has at last enabled the emergence of a powerful multi-party pressure group to champion increased public expenditure on state schooling.

We have emphasised the potential benefits from increased inter-school co-operation within schooling markets. We have also been concerned that quasi-markets have, in aggregate, reduced such behaviour. Earlier, we noted that research indicates that the range of variation of performance within schools often exceeds that between schools, suggesting also the need for greater beneficial co-operation within schools. Over-reliance on competition and rewarding the performance of individual teachers reduces the incentives to co-operate. Since *relative* performance determines the extent of market success, co-operation now occurs only when both parties believe that their relative performance will improve. Previous co-operation, where both parties gained but unequally, will now no longer take place. Consider the case where teachers in a local schooling market freely exchange teaching materials, encouraging the rapid dissemination of best practice. Increased inter- and intra-school competition encourage the retention of one's 'best practice' materials to gain competitive advantage. Indeed, in this case it has the extra advantage of imposing additional costs on competitors, since they have to incur costs in developing their own materials. Thus markets, to the extent that they displace behaviour based upon professional ethics and collegiate ethos, can destroy even mutually beneficial co-operation. Hence the need for governments to introduce financial incentives aimed at restoring or creating co-operation. How to target such incentives to blend efficiently competition and co-operation – co-opetition – is the current key challenge for policy makers.

References

Acemoglu, D. (1996) 'A microfoundation for social increasing returns in human capital accumulation', *Quarterly Journal of Economics* 111, 3: 779–804.
—— (1999) 'Changes in unemployment and wage inequality: an alternative theory and some evidence', *American Economic Review* 89, 5: 1259–78.
Ackerman, F. (1997) 'Consumed in theory: alternative perspectives on the economics of consumption', *Journal of Economic Issues* 31, 3: 651–64.
Adnett, N. (1997) 'Recent education reforms: some neglected macroeconomics and misapplied microeconomics', *Review of Policy Issues* 3, 3: 59–78.
—— (2001) 'Modernising the European social model: developing the guidelines, *Journal of Common Market Studies* 39, 2: 353–64.
—— (forthcoming) 'Reforming teachers' pay: incentive payments, collegiate ethos and UK policy', *Cambridge Journal of Economics*.
Adnett, N. and Davies, P. (1999) 'Schooling quasi-markets: reconciling economic and sociological analyses', *British Journal of Educational Studies* 47, 3: 221–34.
—— (2000) 'Competition and curriculum diversity in local schooling markets: theory and evidence', *Journal of Education Policy* 15, 2: 157–67.
Adnett, N., Bougheas, S. and Davies, P. (2002) 'Market-based reforms of public schooling: some unpleasant dynamics', *Economics of Education Review* (forthcoming).
Adnett, N., Davies, P. and Pugh, G. (2000) *School Benchmarking Project: Scotland, report for the DfEE* (mimeo), Centre for Economics and Business Education, Staffordshire University Business School.
Aghion, P. and Howitt, P. (1998) *Endogenous Growth Theory*, Cambridge MA: MIT Press.
Ahonen, S. (2000) 'What happens to the Common School in the market?', *Journal of Curriculum Studies*, 32, 4: 483–93.
Alderman, H., Orazem, P. and Paterno, E.M. (1996) *School Quality, School Cost and the Public/Private School Choices of Low-Income Households in Pakistan*, Working Paper on the Impact of Education Reforms No. 2, World Bank.
Ancil, R. and Hakes, D. (1991) 'Antecedents and implications of Hirsch's positional goods', *History of Political Economy* 23, 2: 263–78.
Anderson, D. (1988) 'Values, religion, social class and the choice of private school in Australia', *International Journal of Educational Research* 12, 4: 351–73.
Anderson, L. (2001) 'A "Third Way" towards self-governing schools? New Labour and opting-out', *British Journal of Educational Studies* 49, 1: 56–70.
Andrews, M., Bradley, S. and Stott, D. (2001) 'The school-to-work transition, skill preferences and matching', *University of Lancaster Management School Discussion Paper* No. EC1/01.
Angrist, J. and Lavy, V. (1999) 'Using Maimondies' rule to estimate the effect of class size on scholastic achievement', *Quarterly Journal of Economics* 114, 2: 533–575.

Argys, L., Rees, D. and Brewer, D. (1996) 'Detracking America's schools: equity at zero cost?', *Journal of Policy Analysis and Management* 15, 4: 623–45.

Armstrong, D. (1997) 'School performance and staying on: a microanalysis for Northern Ireland', *The Manchester School* 67, 2: 203–30.

Arnott, R. and Rowse, J. (1987) 'Peer group effects and educational attainment', *Journal of Public Economics* 32: 287–305.

Ashenfelter, O., Harmon, C. and Oosterbeek, H. (1999) 'A review of estimates of the schooling-earnings relationship with tests for publication bias', *Labour Economics* 6, 4: 453–79.

Audit Commission (1996) *Trading Places: The supply and allocation of school places*, London: HMSO.

—— (1999) *Local Authority Performance Indicators 1997/8: Education Services*, Abingdon UK, Audit Commission.

Autor, D. (2001) 'Wiring the labor market', *Journal of Economic Perspectives* 15, 1: 25–40.

Bagley, C., Woods, P. and Glatter, R. (1996a) 'Scanning the market: school strategies for discovering parental preferences', *Educational Management and Administration* 24, 2: 125–38.

Bagley, C., Woods, P. and Glatter, R. (1996b) 'Barriers to school responsiveness in the education quasi-market', *School Organisation* 16, 1: 45–58.

Ball, S. (1993) 'Education markets, choice and social class: the market as a class strategy in the UK and the USA', *British Journal of Sociology of Education* 14, 1: 3–19.

—— (1999) 'Labour, learning and the economy: a 'policy sociology' perspective', *Cambridge Journal of Education* 29, 2: 195–206.

Ball, S., Bowe, R. and Gewirtz, S. (1996) 'School choice, social class and distinction: the realization of social advantage in education', *Journal of Education Policy* 11, 1: 89–112.

Ball, S., Bowe, R. and Gewirtz, S. (1997) 'Circuits of schooling: a sociological exploration of parental choice in social class contexts' in A.H. Halsey, H. Lauder, P. Brown and A. Wells (eds) *Education: Culture, Economy and Society*, Oxford: Oxford University Press.

Ballou, D. and Podgursky, M. (1997a) *Teacher Pay and Teacher Quality*, Kalamazoo: W.E. Upjohn Institute for Employment Research.

—— (1997b) 'Reforming teacher training and recruitment', *Government Union Review* 17, 4: 1–38.

—— (2000) 'Reforming teacher preparation and licensing: what is the evidence?', *Teachers College Record* 102, 1: 5–27.

—— (2001) 'Let the market decide', *Education Matters* 1, 1: 1–8.

Ballou, D. and Soler, S. (1998) 'Addressing the looming teacher crunch, Policy Briefing http://www.dlcppi.org/texts/social/tcrunch.htm.

Banks, M., Bates, I., Bynner, J., Breakwell, G., Elmer, N., Jamieson, L. and Roberts, K. (1992) *Careers and Identities*, Milton Keynes: Open University Press.

Barnes, D. (1976) *From Communication to Curriculum*, Harmondsworth: Penguin.

Barro, R. and Sala-I-Martin, X. (1995) *Economic Growth*, Cambridge MA: Harvard University Press.

Barrow, M. (1996) 'The reform of school funding: some case study lessons', *Environment and Planning* 14: 351–66.

Baudrillard, J. (1998) *The consumer society- myths and structures*, London: Sage.

Baumol, W. (1967) 'Macroeconomics of unbalanced growth: the anatomy of urban crisis', *American Economic Review* 162: 415–26.

Becker, G.S. (1967) 'Investment in human capital: a theoretical analysis', *Journal of Political Economy* 70, (supplement to October Issue) 5, 2: 59–549.

—— (1975) *Human capital: a theoretical and empirical analysis* 2nd edn., New York: National Bureau of Economic Research.

—— (1996) *Accounting for Tastes*, Cambridge MA: Harvard University Press.

Behrman, J. and Stacey, N. (1997) *The Social Benefits of Education*, Ann Arbor, Mich.: Michigan University Press.

Belfield, C. (2000) *Economic Principles for Education: Theory and evidence*, Cheltenham: Edward Elgar.

Bell, M. (1994) *Childerley: nature and morality in a country village*, Chicago, Il: University of Chicago Press.

Benn, C. and Chitty, C. (1996) *Thirty Years On: Is comprehensive education alive and well or struggling to survive?*, London: David Fulton.

Bennett, R., Glennerster, H. and Nevison, D. (1997) 'Investing in skill: to stay on or not to stay on?', *Oxford Review of Economic Policy* 8, 2: 130–45.

Bernheim, B. and Whinston, M. (1998) 'Incomplete contracts and strategic ambiguity', *American Economic Review* 88, 4: 902–32.

Best, J. (1992) 'Perspectives on deregulation of schooling in America', *British Journal of Educational Studies* 41, 2: 122–33.

Betts, J. and Shkolnik, J. (2000) 'The effects of ability grouping on student achievement and resource allocation in secondary schools', *Economics of Education Review* 19: 1–15.

Biggs, M. and Dutta, J. (1999) 'The distributional effects of education expenditures, *National Institute Economic Review* July: 68–77.

Bikhchandani, S., Hirshleifer, D. and Welch, I. (1998) 'Learning from the behavior of others: conformity, fads, and informational cascades', *Journal of Economic Perspectives* 12, 3: 151–70.

Billiet, J. (1977) *Secularisering en Verzuiling in het Onderwijs*, Leuven: Universitaire Pers.

Bils, M. and Klenow, P. (2000) 'Does schooling cause growth?', *American Economic Review* 90, 5: 1160–83.

Bishop, J. (1996) 'Signalling, incentives, and school organization in France, the Netherlands, Britain and the United States', in E. Hanushek and D. Jorgenson (eds) *Improving America's Schools: The Role of Incentives*, Washington DC: National Academy Press.

—— (1997) 'The effects of national standards and curriculum-based exams on achievement', *American Economic Review* 87, 2: 260–4.

—— (1998) 'Are national exit examinations important for educational efficiency?', *Cornell University, Centre for Advanced Human Resource Studies, Working Paper*.

Black, S. (1999) 'Do better schools matter? Parental valuation of elementary education', *Quarterly Journal of Economics* May: 577–99.

Blatchford, P. and Mortimore, P. (1994) 'Issue of class size for young children in schools: what can we learn from research?', *Oxford Review of Education* 20: 411–28.

Blau, F. and Kahn, L. (2000a) 'Gender and youth employment outcomes: the United States and West Germany, 1984–1991', in D. Blanchflower and R. Freeman (eds) *Youth Employment and Joblessness in Advanced Countries*, Chicago: University of Chicago Press.

—— (2000b) 'Gender differences in pay', *Journal of Economic Perspectives* 14, 4: 75–100.

—— (2001) 'Do cognitive tests explain higher US wage inequality?', *National Bureau of Economic Research Working Paper*, No. W8210.

Blundell, R., Dearden, L., Goodman, A. and Reed, H. (1997) *Higher Education, Employment and Earnings in Britain*, London: Institute for Fiscal Studies.

Blundell, R., Dearden, L., Meghir, C. and Sianes, B. (1999) 'Human capital investment: the returns from education and training to the individual, the firm and the economy', *Fiscal Studies* 20, 1: 1–23.

Blyth, E. and Milner, J. (1996) 'Unsaleable goods and the education market', in C. Pole and R. Chawla-Duggan (eds) *Reshaping Education in the 1990s: perspectives on secondary schooling*, London: Falmer Press.

Bogart, W. and Cromwell, B. (2000) 'How much is a neighbourhood school worth?', *Journal of Urban Economics* 47, 2: 280–305.

Bondi, L. (1991) 'Attainment in primary schools: an analysis of variations between schools', *British Educational Research Journal* 17, 3: 203–17.

Borghans, L. and de Grip, A. (eds) (2000) *The Overeducated Worker? The economics of skill utilization*, Cheltenham: Edward Elgar.

Bowe, R., Ball, S. and Gewirtz, S. (1994a) '"Parental choice", consumption and social theory: the operation of micro-markets in education', *British Journal of Educational Studies* 42, 1: 38–52.

Bowe, R., Gewirtz, S. and Ball, S.J. (1994b) 'Captured by the discourse? Issues and concerns in researching "parental choice"', *British Journal of Sociology of Education* 15: 63–78.

Bourdieu, P. (1990) *The Logic of Practice*, Cambridge: Polity Press.

Bourdieu, P. and Passeron, J-C. (1977) *Reproduction in Education, Society and Culture*, London: Sage.

Boyer, E.L. (1993) 'Foreword', in E. Rassell and R. Rothstein (eds) *School Choice Examining the Evidence*, Washington, DC: Economic Policy Institute.

Bradley, H. (1996) 'Parental choice of schools in an area containing grant-maintained schools', *School Organisation* 16, 1: 59–69.

Bradley, J., Johnes, G., and Millington, J. (1999) 'School choice, competition and the efficiency of secondary schools in England', *University of Lancaster Management School Discussion Paper* EC/3.

Bradley, S. and Taylor, J. (2000) 'The effect of the quasi-market on the efficiency-equity trade-off in the secondary school sector', *Lancaster University Management School Discussion Paper* EC9/00.

Bradley, S. Crouchley, R., Millington, J. and Taylor, J. (2000) 'Testing for quasi-market forces in secondary education', *Oxford Bulletin of Economics and Statistics* 62, 3: 357–90.

Brandenburger, A. and Nalebuff, B. (1997) *Co-opetition*, London: Harper Collins Business.

Broadbent, J. and Laughlin, R. (1997) 'Contracts and competition? A reflection on the nature and effects of recent legislation on the modes of control in schools', *Cambridge Journal of Economics* 21: 277–90.

Brown, B. (1992) 'Why governments run schools', *Economics of Education Review* 11, 4: 287–300.

Brown, B. and Saks, D. (1975) 'The production and distribution of cognitive skills within schools', *Journal of Political Economy* 83: 571–93.

Brueckner, J. and Lee, K. (1989) 'Club theory with a peer-group effect', *Regional Science and Urban Economics* 19: 399–420.

Brunello, G. and Comi, S. (2000) *Education and Earnings Growth: Evidence from 11 European Countries*, mimeo.

Brutsaert, H. (1998) 'Home and school influences on academic performance: state and catholic elementary schools in Belgium compared', *Educational Review* 50, 1: 37–43.

Burgess, S. and Metcalfe, P. (1999) 'The use of incentive schemes in the public and private sectors: evidence from British establishments', *University of Bristol, CMPO Working Paper*, No. 00/15.

Bullock, A. and Thomas, H. (1997) *Schools at the Centre*, London: Routledge.

Bush, T., Coleman, M. and Glover, D. (1993) *Managing Autonomous Schools*, London: Paul Chapman Publishing.

Caille, J.P. (1993) *Le choix d'un collège public situé en dehors du secteur de domiciliation*, Note d'information, DEP, 93–19.

Card, D. and Krueger, A. (1992) 'Does school quality matter? Returns to education and the characteristics of public schools in the US', *Journal of Political Economy* 100: 1–40.

—— (1996) 'School resources and school outcomes: an overview of the literature and new evidence from North and South California', *Journal of Economic Perspectives*, 10, Fall: 31–50.

Carl, J. (1994) 'Parental choice as national policy in England and the United States', *Comparative Education Review* 38, 3: 294–322.

Carnoy, M. (1998) 'National voucher plans in Chile and Sweden: did privatisation reforms make for better education?', *Comparative Education Review* 42, 3: 309–37.

Carroll, J.B. (1963) 'A model of school learning', *Teachers College Record*, 64: 723–33.

Challis, L. Day, P., Klein, R. and Scrivens, E. (1994) 'Managing quasi-markets: institutions of regulation', in W. Bartlett, C. Propper, D. Wilson and J. Le Grand (eds) *Quasi-Markets in the Welfare State: The Emerging Findings*, Bristol: SAUS Publications.

Cheng. Y. (1995) *Staying on in full-time education after 16: do schools make a difference?*, England and Wales Youth Cohort Study for the Department for Education and Employment, London: Department for Education and Employment.

Chubb, J. and Moe, T. (1988) 'Politics, markets and the organization of schools', *American Political Science Review* 82, 4: 1065–87.

—— (1990) *Politics, Markets and America's Schools*, Washington DC: Brookings Institution.

City Technology College Trust (1991) *A Good Education with Vocational Relevance*, London: CTC Trust.

Clark, B.R. (1984) 'The school and the university: what went wrong in America', paper presented at the Rockefeller Institute of Government Policy Forum, Albany, NY.

Clewell, B. and Joy, M. (1990) *Choice in Montclair, New Jersey*, Princeton: ETS.

Coldron, J. and Boulton, P. (1991) '"Happiness" as a criterion of parents' choice of school', *Journal of Education Policy* 6, 2:169–78.

Coleman, J.S., Hoffer, T. and Kilgore, S. (1982) *High School Achievement: Public, Catholic and Private Schools Compared*, New York: Basic Books.

Collins, A. and Snell, M. (1998) 'Parental Preferences and Choice of Secondary School', University of Portsmouth, Department of Economics Discussion Paper, No. 110.

Coltham, J. (1972) 'Educational accountability: an English experiment and its outcome', *School Review* 81: 15–34.

Conduit, E., Brookes, R., Bramley, G. and Fletcher, C.L. (1996) 'The value of school locations', *British Educational Research Journal*, 22, 2: 199–206.

Congleton, R. (1989) 'Efficient status seeking: externalities and the evolution of status games', *Journal of Economic Behaviour and Organization* 11: 175–90.

Conlisk, J. (1996) 'Why bounded rationality?', *Journal of Economic Literature* 34, June: 669–700.

Cowper, J. and Samuels, M. (1997) 'Performance benchmarking in the public sector: the UK experience', in *Benchmarking, Evaluation and Strategic Management in the Public Sector*, Paris: OECD.

Croxford, L. (1994) 'Equal opportunities in the secondary school curriculum in Scotland, 1977–91', *British Educational Research Journal* 20, 4: 371–91.

Corneo, G. and Jeanne, O. (1997) 'Conspicuous consumption, snobbism and conformism', *Journal of Public Economics*, 66: 55–71.

Costrell, R. (1994) 'A simple model of educational standards', *American Economic Review* 84, 4: 956–71.

Cookson, P. (1992) 'The ideology of consumership and the coming deregulation of the public school system', *Journal of Education Policy* 7, 3: 303–11.

Crafts, N. (1996) 'Post-Neoclassical endogenous growth theory: what are its main policy implications?', *Oxford Review of Economic Policy* 12, 2: 30–47.

Creemers, B. (1994) *The Effective Classroom*, London: Cassell.

Cullingford, C. and Daniels, S. (1999) 'Effects of OFSTED inspections on school performance', in C. Cullingford (ed.) *An Inspector Calls*, London: Kogan Page.

Cutler, T. and Waine, B. (1999) 'Rewarding better teachers? performance related pay in schools', *Educational Management and Administration* 27, 1: 55–70.

Cutler, T. and Waine, B. (2000) 'Mutual benefits or managerial control? The role of appraisal in performance related pay for teachers', *British Journal of Educational Studies* 48, 2: 170–82.

Daly, M., Büchel, F. and Duncan, G. (2000) 'Premiums and penalties for surplus and deficit education: evidence from the United States and Germany', *Economics of Education Review* 19: 169–78.

Darling-Hammond, L. (2000) 'Reforming teacher preparation and licensing: debating the evidence', *Teachers College Record* 102, 1: 1–25.

Davies, P. and Adnett, N. (1999) 'Quasi-market reforms and vocational schooling in England: an economic analysis', *Journal of Education and Work* 12, 2: 141–56.

Davies, P., Adnett, N. and Mangan, J.(2002) 'Diversity and dynamics of competition: analysis and evidence from two local schooling markets', *Oxford Review of Education* (forthcoming).

Davies, P., Adnett, N. and Turnbull, A. (2000) 'Market forces and diversity in local schooling markets: evidence from the 14–19 curriculum', paper presented at the British Educational Research Association Annual Conference, Cardiff University, 7–10 September 2000.

de Bartolome, C. (1990) 'Equilibrium and inefficiency in a community model with peer group effects', *Journal of Political Economy* 98, 1: 110–33.

Dearden, L. (1998) 'Ability, families, education and earnings in Britain', Institute for Fiscal Studies Working Paper No. 98/14.

Dearden, L., Machin, S. and Reed, H. (1997) 'Intergenerational mobility in Britain', *Economic Journal* 107: 47–66.

Dee, T.S. (1998) 'Competition and the quality of public schools', *Economics of Education Review* 17, 4: 419–27.

—— (2000) 'The capitalization of education finance reforms', *Journal of Law and Economics* 43, 1: 185–214.

Department of Education and Science (DES) (1983) *Curriculum 11–16: Towards a statement of entitlement (Curricular Re-appraisal in Action)*, London: HMSO.

—— (1985) *Better Schools*, London: HMSO.

Dex, S., Joshi, H., Macran, S. and McCulluch, A. (1998) 'Women's employment transitions around child bearing', *Oxford Bulletin of Economics and Statistics* 60, 1: 79–97.

DfEE (Department for Education and Employment) (1998) *Teachers: Facing the Challenge of Change*, London: HMSO.

—— (2000) *A Model of Teacher Effectiveness*, Report by Hay McBer to the Department for Education and Employment, London: DfEE.

—— (2001a) *Schools: Building on Success*, Cm. 5050, London: HMSO.

—— (2001b) *Press Notice*, 6 March 2001.

—— (2001c) *DfEE Public Private Partnerships website*, notice posted 19th January 2001, DfEE

—— (2001d) *Investing in Excellence: Business Opportunities in Education and Employment*, DfEE Web Site, DfEE.

—— (2001e) *City Academies: A Prospectus for Sponsors and Other Partners*, London, DfEE.

—— (2001f) *Education Action Zones Web Site*, http://www.standards.dfee.gov.uk /eaz/London, DfEE.

Department for Education and Skills (DFES) (2001) *Code of Practice on School Admissions* (London: Stationery Office).

Department of Trade and Industry (1998) *Our Competitive Future: Building the Knowledge-Driven Economy*, Cm. 4176, London: Stationery Office.

Dijkstra, A. and Peschar, A. (1996) 'Religious determinants of academic attainment in the Netherlands', *Comparative Education Review* 40, 1: 47–65.

Dixit, A. (2000) *Incentives and Organizations in the Public Sector: An Interpretative Review*, revised version of paper presented at National Academy of Sciences Conference on Devising Incentives to Promote Human Capital, Irvine, CA., 17–18 December 1999.

Dolton. P. and van der Klaauw, W. (1999) 'The turnover of teachers: a competing risks explanation', *Review of Economics and Statistics* 81, 3: 543–55.

Dolton, P., Makepeace, G., Hutton, S. and Audas, R. (1999) *Making the Grade: Education, the Labour Market and Young People*, York: Joseph Rowntree Foundation.

Dougherty, C. (2000) 'Numeracy, literacy and earnings: evidence from the National Longitudinal Survey of Youth', *London School of Economics and Political Science, Centre for Economic Performance*, Discussion Paper 478.

Dutta, J., Sefton, J. and Weale, M. (1999) 'Education and public policy', *Fiscal Studies* 20, 4: 351–86.

Easen, P. (2000) 'Education action zones: partnership is no panacea for progress', *Westminster Studies in Education* 23: 55–69.

Easterlin, R. (1995) 'Will raising the incomes of all increase the happiness of all?', *Journal of Economic Behavior and Organization* 26: 35–47.

Echols, F. and Willms, J. (1993) *Scottish Parents and Reasons for School Choice*, Vancouver: Department of Social and Educational Studies, University of British Columbia.

—— (1995) 'Reasons for school choice in Scotland', *Journal of Education Policy* 10, 2: 143–56.

Echols, F., McPherson, A. and Willms, J. (1990) 'Parental choice in Scotland', *Journal of Educational Policy* 5, 3: 207–22.

Edwards, T. and Whitty, G. (1994) 'Education: opportunity, equality and efficiency, in A. Glyn and D. Miliband (eds) *Paying for Inequality: The Economic Costs of Social Injustice*, London: Institute for Public Policy Research.

—— (1997) 'Marketing quality', in R. Glatter, P. Woods and C. Bagley (eds) *Choice and Diversity in Schooling: Perspectives and Prospects*, London: Routledge.

Edwards, T., Whitty, G. and Power, S. (1999) 'Moving back from comprehensive education?', in J. Demaine (ed.) *Education Policy and Contemporary Politics*, Basingstoke: Macmillan.

Edwards, T., Taylor Fitz-Gibbon, C., Hardman, F., Haywood, R. and Meacher, N. (1997) *Separate But Equal? A-levels and GNVQs*, London: Routledge.

Elam, S., Rose, L. and Gallup, A. (1996) 'The 28th annual Phi Delta Kappa/Gallup Poll of the public's attitudes towards public schools', *Phi Delta Kappa* 78: 41–64.

Epple, D. and Romano, R. (1998) 'Competition between private and public schools, vouchers and peer-group effects', *American Economic Review* 88, 1: 33–62.

Ermisch, J. and Francesconi, M. (2000) 'The effect of parent's employment on children's educational attainment', Discussion Paper No. 215, Bonn: IZA.

Eshel, I., Samuelson, L. and Shaked, A. (1998) 'Altruists, egotists, and hooligans in a local interaction model', *American Economic Review*, 88, 1: 157–79.

Espinola, V. (1995) *Seminario Regional sobre Descentralizacion Educativa: Organizacion y Manejo de las Escuelas a Nivel Local: El Caso de Chile*, paper presented at IDB, World Bank, Dominican Republic's Ministry of Education Conference, Santo Domingo, March 1995.

European Commission, Directorate-General for Education and Culture (2000) *European Report on Quality of School Education: Sixteen Quality Indicators*, Brussels: European Commission.

Evans, W. and Schwab, R. (1995) 'Finishing high school and starting college: do Catholic schools make a difference?', *Quarterly Journal of Economics* 110: 947–74.

Evans, W., Oates, W. and Schwab, R. (1992) 'Measuring peer group effects: a study of teenage behavior', *Journal of Political Economy* 100, 5: 966–91.

Fehr, E. and Gätcher, S. (2000) 'Fairness and retaliation: the economics of reciprocity', *Journal of Economic Perspectives* 14, 3: 159–181.

Feinstein, L. and Symons, J. (1999) 'Attainment at secondary school', *Oxford Economic Papers* 51: 300–21.

Feintuck, M. (1994) *Accountability and Choice in Schooling*, Milton Keynes: Open University Press.

Fels, R. (1995) 'Making US schools competitive', in W. Becker and W. Baumol (eds) *Assessing Educational Practices: The Contribution of Economics*, Cambridge, Mass/New York: MIT Press/Russell Sage Foundation.

Fevre, R., Rees, G. and Gorard, S. (1999) 'Some sociological alternatives to human capital theory and their implications for research on post-compulsory education and training', *Journal of Education and Work* 12, 2: 117–40.

Fielding, A. (1995) 'Institutional disparities in the cost effectiveness of GCE A-level Provision: A Multi-level Approach', *Education Economics* 3, 2: 159–72.

—— (1998) 'Perspectives on performance indicators: GCE Advanced level and differences between institution types in cost effectiveness', *School Effectiveness and School Improvement* 9, 2: 218–31.

Figlio, D.N. and Stone, J.A. (1997) 'School choice and student performance: are private schools really better?', Discussion Paper No. 1141-97, University of Wisconsin-Madison: Institute for Research on Poverty.

Finkelstein, N. and Grubb, W. (2000) 'Making sense of education and training markets: lessons from England', *American Educational Research Journal* 37, 3: 601–32.

Finn, C., Manno, B. and Vanourek, G. (2000) *Charter Schools in Action: Renewing Public Education*, Princeton, NJ: Princeton University Press.

Fiske, E. and Ladd, H. (2000) *When Schools Compete: A Cautionary Tale*, Washington D.: Brookings Institution.

Fitz, J., Halpin, D. and Power, S. (1993) *Grant Maintained Schools: Education in the Marketplace*, London: Kogan Page.

Fitz-Gibbon, C. (1996) *Monitoring Education: Indicators, quality and effectiveness*, London: Cassell.

—— (1999) 'Long-term consequences of curriculum choices with particular reference to mathematics and science', *School Effectiveness and School Improvement*, 10, 2: 217–32.

Fitz-Gibbon, C. and Stephenson-Foster, N. (1999) 'Is OFSTED helpful?', in C. Cullingford (ed.) *An Inspector Calls*, London: Kogan Page.

Flecknoe, M. (2001) 'Target setting: will it help to raise achievement?', *Educational Management and Administration* 29, 2: 217–28.

Flores, F. and Gray, J. (2000) *Entrepreneurship and the wired life: Work in the wake of careers*, London, Demos.

Fortune, J. and O'Neil, J. (1994) 'Production function analyses and the study of educational funding equity: a methodological critique', *Journal of Educational Finance*, 20: 21–46.

Foskett, N. (1998) 'Schools and marketization: cultural challenges and responses', *Educational Management and Administration* 26, 2: 197–210.

Foskett, N. and Hesketh, A. (1997) 'Constructing choice in contiguous and parallel markets: institutional and school leavers' responses to the new post-16 marketplace', *Oxford Review of Education* 23, 3: 299–319.

Fowler, W. and Walberg, H. (1991) 'School size, characteristics and outcomes', *Educational Evaluation and Policy Analysis* 13: 189–202.

Fox, I. (1985) *Private schools and public issues: The Parents' View*, Basingstoke: Macmillan.

Francesconi, F., Orszag, J., Phelps, E. and Zoega, G. (2000) 'Education and the natural rate of unemployment', *Oxford Economic Papers* 52: 204–23.

Francis, G., Hinton, M., Holloway, J. and Mayle, D. (1999) *Effective Benchmarking: A Guide To Good Practice*, London: Chartered Institute for Management Accountants.

Francois, P. (2000) '"Public service motivation" as an argument for government provision', *Journal of Public Economics* 78: 275–99.

Frank, R. (1985) *Choosing the Right Pond: Human Behavior and the Quest for Status*, Oxford: Oxford University Press.

—— (1997) 'The frame of reference as a public good', *Economic Journal* 107:1832–47.

Freeman, R. (2000) 'The divergence in employment in the EU and the US', in B. Marin, D. Meulders and D. Snower (eds) *Innovative Employment Initiatives*, Aldershot: Ashgate.

Frey, B. (1993) 'Does monitoring increase work effort? The rivalry with trust and loyalty', *Economic Inquiry* 31: 663–70.

Friedman, M. (1955) 'The role of government in education', in R. Solo (ed.) *Economics and the Public Interest*, New Brunswick: Rutgers University Press.

Gambetta, D. (1987) *Were They Pushed Or Did They Jump? Individual Decision Mechanisms in Education*, Cambridge: Cambridge University Press.

Garces, E., Thomas, D. and Currie, J. (2000) 'Longer term effects of Head Start', *National Bureau of Economic Research Working Paper* No. W8054.

Gewirtz, S. (1998) 'Can all schools be successful? An exploration of the determinants of school "success"', *Oxford Review of Education* 24, 4: 439–57.

Gewirtz, S., Ball, S. and Bowe, R. (1995) *Markets, Choice and Equity in Education* Buckingham: Open University Press.

—— (1994) 'Parents, privilege and the education market-place', *Research Papers in Education*, 9,1:3–29.

Gewirtz, S., Walford, G. and Miller, H. (1991) 'Parents individualistic and collectivist strategies', *International Studies in Sociology of Education* 1, 1: 173–92.

Gibbons, R. (1998) 'Incentives in organisations', *Journal of Economic Perspectives* 12, 4:115–32.

Gibson, A. and Asthana, S. (1998a) 'School performance, school effectiveness and the 1997 White Paper', *Oxford Review of Education* 24, 2: 195–210.

—— (1998b) 'Schools, pupils and exam results: contextualising school "performance"', *British Educational Research Journal* 24, 3: 269–82.

—— (1999) 'Local markets and the polarization of schools in England and Wales', mimeo, Exeter University, UK: Department of Geography.

—— (2000) 'What's in a number? Commentary on Gorard and Fitz's "Investigating the determinants of segregation between schools"', *Research Papers in Education* 15, 2: 133–53.

Gillborn, D. (1996) *Exclusions From School*, Viewpoint Number 5, London: University of London, Institute of Education.

Glass, G. and Smith, M. (1979) 'Meta-analysis of research on the relationship of class size and achievement', *Educational Evaluation and Policy Analysis* 1: 2–16.

Glatter, R., Woods, P. and Bagley, C. (1997) 'Diversity, differentiation and hierarchy', in R. Glatter, P. Woods and C. Bagley (eds) *Choice and Diversity in Schooling: Perspectives and Prospects*, London: Routledge.

Glenn, C. (1989) *Four Variations on the Education of Immigrant Pupils*, Boston: Commonwealth of Massachusetts Department of Education.

Glennerster, H. (1991) 'Quasi-markets for education?', *Economic Journal* 101: 1268–76.

Glover, D. (1992) 'An investigation of the criteria used by parents and community in judgement of school quality', *Educational Research* 34, 1: 35–44.

Goldhaber, D.D. and Brewer, D. (1997) 'Why don't schools and teachers seem to matter?', *Journal of Human Resources* 32, 3: 505–23.

Goldstein, H. (1995) *Multilevel Statistical Models*, 2nd edn, London: Hodder & Stoughton.

Goldstein, H. and Blatchford, P. (1998) 'Class size and educational achievement: a review of methodology with particular reference to study design', *British Educational Research Journal* 24, 3: 255–67.

Goldstein, H. and Spiegelhalter, D. (1996) 'League tables and their limitations: statistical issues in comparisons of institutional performance', *Journal of Royal Statistical Society A* 159, 3: 385–443.

Goldstein, H. and Thomas, S. (1996) 'Using examination results as indicators of school and college performance', *Journal of Royal Statistical Society A* 159, 1: 149–63.

Goldstein, H., Rasbash, J., Yang, M., Woodhouse, G., Pan, H., Nuttall, D. and Thomas, S. (1993) 'A multilevel analysis of school examination results (1)', *Oxford Review of Education* 19, 4: 425–33.

Gorard, S. (1997a) *School Choice in an established market*, Aldershot: Ashgate.

—— (1997b) 'Who pays the piper? Intergenerational aspects of school choice', *School Leadership and Management* 17, 2: 245–56.

—— (1998) 'Social movement in underdeveloped markets: an apparent contradiction', *Educational Review* 50, 3: 249–58.

—— (1999) ' "Well, that about wraps it up for school choice research": a state of the art review', *School Leadership and Management* 19, 1: 25–47.

—— (2000) 'Here we go again: a reply to "What's in a number" ', *Research Papers in Education* 15, 2: 155–62.

Gorard, S. and Fitz, J. (1998) 'The more things change ... The missing impact of marketisation?', *British Journal of Sociology of Education*, 19, 3: 365–76.

—— (2000a) 'Investigating the determinants of segregation between schools', *Research Papers in Education* 15, 2: 115–32.

—— (2000b) 'Markets and stratification: a view from England and Wales', *Educational Policy* 14, 3: 405–28.

Gorard, S. and Taylor, C. (2000) *A comparison of segregation indices used for assessing the socio-economic composition of schools*, Cardiff University School of Social Sciences, Working Paper 37.

Gordon, L. and Whitty, G. (1997) 'Giving the "hidden hand" a helping hand? The rhetoric and reality of neoliberal education reform in England and New Zealand', *Comparative Education* 33, 3: 453–67.

Grace, G. (1995) *School leadership: beyond education management. An essay in policy scholarship*, London: Falmer.

Gradstein, M. (2000) 'An economic rationale for public education: the value of commitment', *Journal of Monetary Economics* 45: 463–74.

Gradstein, M. and Justman, M. (2000) 'Human capital, social capital and public schooling', *European Economic Review* 44: 879–90.

Greeley, A. and Rossi, P. (1966) *The Education of Catholic Americans*, Chicago: Aldine.

Green, F., McIntosh, S. and Vignoles, A. (1999) ' "Overeducation" and skills: clarifying the concepts', London School of Economics and Political Science, Centre for Economic Performance, Discussion Paper No. 435.

Greenaway, D. and Nelson, D. (2000) 'The assessment: globalization and labour market adjustment', *Oxford Review of Economic Policy* 16, 3: 1–11.

Greenaway, D., Uppward, R. and Wright, P. (2000) 'Sectoral transformation and labour market flows', *Oxford Review of Economic Policy* 16, 3: 57–75.

Greenwood, D. (1997) 'New developments in the intergenerational impacts of education', *International Journal of Educational Research* 27: 503–11.

Gregg, P. and Machin, S. (2000) 'Child development and success or failure in the youth labor market', in D. Blanchflower and R. Freeman (eds) *Youth Employment and Joblessness in Advanced Countries*, Chicago: University of Chicago Press.

Grubb, N. (1999) 'Improvement or control? A US view of English inspection', in C. Cullingford (ed.) *An Inspector Calls*, London: Kogan Page.

Gundlach, E., Wossman, L. and Gmelin, J. (2001) 'The decline of schooling productivity in OECD countries', *Economic Journal* 111: C135–47.

Haller, E.J. (1992) 'High school size and student indiscipline: another aspect of the school consolidation issue?', *Educational Evaluation and Policy Analysis* 14, 2: 145–56.

Halpin, D., Power, S. and Fitz, J. (1997) 'Opting into the past? Grant maintained schools and the reinvention of tradition', in R. Glatter, P. Woods and C. Bagley (eds) *Choice and Diversity in Schooling: Perspectives and Prospects*, London: Routledge.

Hammond, T. and Dennison, W. (1995) 'School choice in less populated areas', *Educational Management and Administration* 23, 2: 104–13.

Handy, F. (1995) 'Reputations as collateral: an economic analysis of the role of trustees of nonprofits', *Nonprofit and Voluntary Sector Quarterly* 24, 4: 293–305.

Handy, F. and Katz, E. (1998) 'The wage differential between nonprofit institutions and corporations: getting more by paying less?', *Journal of Comparative Economics* 26: 241–61.

Hannaway, J. (1992) 'Higher order skills, job design, and incentives: an analysis and proposal', *American Educational Research Journal* 29, 1: 3–21.

Hansmann, H. (1987) 'Economic theories of nonprofit organization', in W.W. Powell (ed.) *The Nonprofit Sector*, New Haven: Yale University Press.

Hanushek, E. (1986) 'The economics of schooling: production and efficiency in public schools', *Journal of Economic Literature* 24, 3: 1141–77.

—— (1989) 'The impact of differential expenditure on school performance', *Educational Researcher* 18: 45–51.

—— (1992) 'The trade-off between child quantity and quality, *Journal of Political Economy* 100: 84–117.

—— (1994) *Making Schools Work: Improving Performance and Controlling Costs*, Washington DC: Brookings Institution.

—— (1996a) 'Measuring investment in education', *Journal of Economic Perspectives*, 10: 9–30.

—— (1996b) 'School resources and student performance', in G. Burtless (ed.) *Does Money Matter? The Effect of School Resources on Student Achievement and Adult Success*, Washington, DC: Brookings Institution.

—— (1996c) 'Outcomes, costs, and incentives in schools', in E. Hanushek and D. Jorgenson (eds) *Improving America's Schools: The Role of Incentives*, Washington DC: National Academy Press.

—— (1997a) 'Outcomes, incentives, and beliefs: reflections on analysis of the economics of schools', *Educational Evaluation and Policy Analysis* 19, 4: 301–8.

—— (1997b) 'Effects of school resources on economic performance', *Education Evaluation and Policy Analysis* 19, 2: 141–64.

Hanushek, E. and Kimko, D. (2000) 'Schooling, labour-force quality and the growth of nations', *American Economic Review*, 90, 5: 1184–1208.

Hanushek, E., Kain, J., and Rivkin, S. (1998) 'Teachers, schools and academic achievement', National Bureau of Economics Research, Working Paper No. 6691,

Hanushek, E., Rivkin, S. and Taylor, L. (1996) 'The identification of school resource effects', *Education Economics* 4, 2: 105–25.

Hargreaves, A. and Dawe, R. (1990) 'Paths of professional development: contrived collegiality, collaborative culture and the case of peer coaching', *Teaching and Teacher Education* 6: 227–41.

Hargreaves, D. (1996) 'Diversity and choice in school education: a modified libertarian approach', *Oxford Review of Education* 22, 2: 131–41.

Harkness, S. (1996) 'The gender earnings gap: evidence from the UK, *Fiscal Studies* 17, 2: 1–36.

Harmon, C. and Walker, I. (2000) 'The returns to the quantity and quality of education: evidence for men in England and Wales', *Economica* 67: 19–35.

Haskel, J. and Slaughter, M. (2001) 'Trade, technology and UK wage inequality', *Economic Journal* 111, 468: 163–87.

Hatcher, R. (1998) 'Class differentiation in education: rational choices?', *British Journal of Sociology of Education* 19, 1: 5–24.

Haveman, R. and Wolfe, B. (1995) 'The determinants of children's attainments: a review of methods and findings', *Journal of Economic Literature* 33: 1829–78.

Heckman J. (2000) 'Policies to foster human capital', *Research in Economics* 54: 3–56.

Hedges, L., Laine, R. and Greenwald, R. (1994) 'Does money matter? A meta-analysis of studies of the effects of school inputs on student outcomes', *Educational Researcher* 23, 3: 5–14.

Hemsley-Brown, J. (1999) 'College choice, perceptions and priorities', *Educational Management and Administration* 27, 1: 85–98.

Henderson, V., Mieszkowski, P. and Sauvageau, Y. (1978) *Peer Group Effects and Educational Production Functions*, Ottawa, Canada: Economic Council of Canada.

Henig, J.R. (1994) *Rethinking School Choice: Limits of the Market Metaphor*, Princeton: Princeton University Press.

Hermalin, B. (1998) 'Toward an economic theory of leadership: leading by example', *American Economic Review* 88, 5: 1188–1206.

Hess, G.A. (1992) 'Chicago and Britain: experiments in empowering parents', *Journal of Education Policy* 7, 2: 155–71.

Heyneman, S. (2000) 'Educational qualifications: the economic and trade issues, *Assessment in Education* 7, 3: 417–38.

Hill, P.T., Foster, G.E. and Gendler, T. (1990) *High Schools with Character* (RAND R-3944-RC), Santa Monica CA: Rand Corporation.

Hirsch, F. (1976) *Social Limits to Growth*, London: Routledge.

HMCI (1998) *Secondary Education 1993–1997: A Review of Secondary Schools in England* London: OfSTED.

Hodkinson, P., Sparkes, A. and Hodkinson, H. (1996) *Triumph and Tears: Young People, Markets and the Transition from School to Work*, London: David Fulton.

Hoenack, S.A. (1997) 'An application of a structural model of school demand and supply to evaluate alternative designs of voucher education systems', *Economics of Education Review* 16, 1: 1–14.

Hoffer, T.B. (1992) 'Middle school ability grouping and student achievement in science and mathematics', *Educational Evaluation and Policy Analysis* 14: 205–27.

Hofman, R., Hofman, W. and Guldemond, H. (1999) 'Social and cognitive outcomes: a comparison of contexts of learning', *School Effectiveness and School Improvement* 10, 3: 352–66.

Holmstrom, B. and Milgrom, P. (1991) 'Multitask principal agent analyses: incentive contracts, asset ownership, and job design', *Journal of Law, Economics and Organization* 7, sp: 24–52.

House, E. (1996) 'A framework for appraising educational reforms', *Educational Researcher* 25, 7: 6–14.

Howieson, C. and Croxford, L. (1996) *Using the YCS to Analyse the Outcomes of Careers Education and Guidance*, Department for Education and Employment Research Studies 40, London: Stationery Office.

Hoxby, C. (1996a) 'How teachers' unions affect education production', *Quarterly Journal of Economics* 111, 3: 671–718.

—— (1996b) 'Are efficiency and equity in school finance substitutes or complements?', *Journal of Economic Perspectives* 10, 4: 51–72.

—— (1998a) 'What do America's "traditional" forms of school choice teach us about school choice reforms?', *Federal Reserve Bank of New York Economic Policy Review* 4, 1: 47–60.

—— (1998b) 'The effects of class size and composition on student achievement: new evidence from natural population variation', National Bureau of Economic Research Working Paper No. 6869.

—— (2000) 'Does competition among public schools benefit students and taxpayers?', *American Economic Review* 90, 5: 1209–38.

—— (2001) 'Changing the profession', *Education Matters* 1, 1: 1–11.

ICOSS (1999) *Responses to Competitive Pressures on Secondary Schools: Headteachers' Perceptions*, The Impact of Competition on Secondary Schools, ESRC/Open University Research Programme, 7 January 1999.

Ilon, L. (1992) 'School choice in a privatized market: equity implications in Zimbabwe', *Journal of Education Finance*, : 303–17.

Jackson, N. and Lund, H. (2000) 'Introduction to benchmarking', in N. Jackson and H. Lund (eds) *Benchmarking for Higher Education*, Buckingham: Society for Research into Higher Education/Open University Press.

James, E. (1991) 'Public policies towards private education: an international comparison', *International Journal of Educational Research* 15, 5: 355–76.

Jesson, D. (1999) *Do grammar schools get better results?*, paper presented to CASE Seminar, Westminster Central Hall, London, November 1999.

—— (2001) *Educational outcomes and value added analysis of specialist schools for the year 2000*, London, Technology Colleges Trust.

Jimenez, E., Lockheed, M., Luna, E. and Paqueo, V. (1991) 'School effects and costs for private and public schools in the Dominican Republic', *International Journal of Educational Research*, 15, 5: 393–410.

Jimenez, E. and Sawada, Y. (1999) 'Do community-managed schools work? An evaluation of El Salvador's EDUCO Program', *World Bank Economic Review*, 13, 3: 415–41.

Johnson, D. and Johnson, R. (1994) *Learning Together and Alone: Cooperative, Competitive, and Individualistic Learning*, 4th edn, Needham Heights, MA: Allyn & Bacon.

Johnson, G. and Scholes, K. (1999) *Exploring Corporate Strategy*, 5th edn, Harlow: Financial Times/ Prentice-Hall.

Jonathan, R. (1990) 'State education service or prisoner's dilemma: the "hidden hand" as source of education policy', *Educational Philosophy and Theory* 22, 1: 16–24.

Jones, K. and Hatcher, R. (1994) 'Educational progress and economic change: notes on some recent proposals', *British Journal of Educational Studies* 42, 3: 245–60.

Joshi, H., and Paci, P. (1998) *Unequal Pay for Women and Men*, Cambridge, MA.: MIT Press.

Kanellopoulos, C. and Psacharopoulos, G. (1997) 'Private education expenditure in a "free education" country: the case of Greece', *International Journal of Educational Development* 17, 1: 73–81.

Karsten, S. (2000) 'Neoliberal education reform in the Netherlands', *Comparative Education* 35, 3: 303–18.

Katz, L. and Autor, D. (1999) 'Changes in the wage structure and earnings inequality', in O. Ashenfelter and D. Card (eds) *Handbook of Labor Economics*, Volume 3A, Amsterdam: Elsevier.

Keays, W., Maychell, K., Evans, C., Brooks, R., Lee, B. and Pathak, S. (1998) *Staying On: A Study of Young People's Decisions About Sixth Forms, Sixth-Form Colleges and Colleges of Further Education*, Slough: NFER.

Keep, E. and Mayhew, K (1999) 'The assessment: knowledge, skills and competitiveness', *Oxford Review of Economic Policy* 15, 1: 1–15.

Kerkhoff, A. (1986) 'Effects of ability grouping in British secondary schools', *American Sociological Review* 51: 842–58.

Kersh, N. (1998) 'Aspects of the privatisation of education in Latvia', in P. Bersford-Hill (ed.) *Education and Privatisation in Eastern Europe and the Baltic Republics*, Wallingford: Triangle Books.

King, E. and Bellew, R. (1993) 'Educating women: lessons from experience', in E.King and Hill (eds)*Women's Education in Developing Countries: Barriers, Benefits and Policies*, Baltimore MD: John Hopkins University Press.

King, E., Rawlings, L., Gutierrez, M., Pardo, C. and Torres, C. (1997) 'Colombia's targeted education voucher program: features, coverage and participation', Impact Evaluation of Education Reforms Working Papers 3, Development Economics Research Group, World Bank.

King, R.A. and MacPhail-Wilcox, B. (1994) 'Unravelling the production function: the continuing quest for resources that make a difference', *Journal of Education Finance* 20: 47–65.

Kleiner, M. (2000) 'Occupational Licensing', *Journal of Economic Perspectives* 14, 4: 89–202.

Kleinman, M., West, A. and Sparkes, J. (1998) *Investing in employability: theories of business and government in the transition to work*, London: London School of Economics (commissioned by BT).

Klemperer, P. (1987) 'Markets with consumer switching costs', *Quarterly Journal of Economics* 102, 2: 375–94.

Kogan, M. and Maden. M. (1999) *The Ofsted System of School Inspection: An Independent Evaluation*, London: Centre for the Evaluation of Public Policy and Practice, Brunel University and Helix Consulting Group.

Koretz, D. (1996) 'Using student assessments for educational accountability', in E. Hanushek and D. Jorgenson (eds) *Improving America's Schools: The Role of Incentives*, Washington DC, National Academy Press.

Kozol, J. (1991) *Savage Inequalities: Children in America's Schools*, New York, Crown Publishers.

Kreitzberg, P. and Priimagi, S. (1998) 'Educational transition in Estonia 1987–1996', in P. Bersford-Hill (ed.) *Education and Privatisation in Eastern Europe and the Baltic Republics*, Wallingford: Triangle Books.

Kremer, M. (1995) 'Research on schooling: what we know and what we don't. A comment on Hanushek', *World Bank Research Observer* 10, August: 247–54.

Krueger, A.(1999) 'Experimental estimates of education production functions', *Quarterly Journal of Economics* 114, 2: 497–532.

Kuh, D., Head, J. and Wadsworth, M. (1997) 'The influence of education and family background on women's earnings in midlife: evidence from a British national birth cohort study', *British Journal of Sociology of Education* 18, 3: 385–405.

Kumar, R.C. (1983) 'Economies of scale in school operation: evidence from Canada', *Applied Economics* 15: 323–40.

Lakdawalla, D. (2001) 'The declining quality of teachers', National Bureau of Economic Research, Working Paper No. W8263.

Lamdin, D. (1995) 'Testing for the effect of school size on student achievement within a school district', *Education Economics* 3, 1: 33–42.

Lamdin, D. and Mintrom, M. (1997) 'School choice in theory and practice: taking stock and looking ahead', *Education Economics* 5, 3: 211–44.

Lassibille, G., Tan, J-P. and Sumra, S. (2000) 'Expansion of private education: lessons from recent experience in Tanzania', *Comparative Education Review* 44, 1: 1–28.

Lauder, H., Hughes, D., Dupuis, A. and McGlinn, J. (1992) *To Be Somebody: Class, Gender and the Rationality of Educational Decision-making*, Wellington: New Zealand Ministry of Education.

Lauder, H. and Hughes D., and Watson, S., Waslander, S., Thrupp, M., Strathdee, R., Simiyu, I, Dupuis, A., McGlinn, J. and Hamlin, J. (1999) *Trading in Futures: Why Markets in Education Don't Work*, Buckingham: Open University Press.

Lawton, D. (1996) 'The changing context: the National Curriculum', in S. Hodkinson and M. Jephcote (eds) *Teaching Economics and Business*, London: Heinemann.

Lawton, S. (1992) 'Why restructure? An international survey of the roots of reform', *Journal of Education Policy* 7, 2: 139–54.

Lazear, E. (1999) 'Personnel economics: past lessons and future directions', *Journal of Labor Economics* 17, 2: 199–36.

—— (2000) 'Economic imperialism', *Quarterly Journal of Economics* 115, February: 99–146

Lee, J-W and Barro, R. (1997) 'Schooling quality in a cross section of countries', National Bureau of Economic Research, Working Paper No. 6198.

Leibenstein, H. (1950) 'Bandwagon, snob and Veblen effects in the theory of consumers' demand', *Quarterly Journal of Economics* 64: 198–207.

Leigh, J. (1986) 'Accounting for tastes: correlates of risk and time preferences *Journal of Post-Keynesian Economics* 9, 11: 17–31.

—— (1998) 'The social benefits of education: a review article', *Economics of Education Review* 17, 3: 363–368.

Leland, H. (1979) 'Quacks, lemons and licensing: a theory of minimum quality standards', *Journal of Political Economy* 87: 1328–46.

Levačić, R. (1995) *Local Management of Schools: Analysis and Practice*, Milton Keynes: Open University Press.

—— (1999) 'Local management of schools in England: results after six years', *Journal of Education Policy* 13, 3: 331–50.

Levačić, R. and Glover, D. (1998) 'Relationship between efficient resource management and school effectiveness: evidence from OFSTED secondary school inspections', *School Effectiveness and School Improvement* 9, 1: 95–122.

Levačić, R. and Hardman, J. (1999) 'The performance of grant-maintained schools in England: an experiment in autonomy', *Journal of Educational Policy* 14, 2: 185–212.

Levačić, R. and Ross, K. (1998) *Principles for Designing Needs-Based School Funding Formulae*, Paris: International Institute for Educational Planning.

Levačić, R. and Woods, P. (1999) 'Polarisation and inequalities between secondary schools in England: effects on school practice and performance', paper presented at British Educational Research Association Annual Conference, University of Sussex, September 1999.

Levin, B. and Riffel, J. (1997a) 'School system responses to external change: implications for parental choice in schools, in R. Glatter, P. Woods and C. Bagley (eds) *Choice and Diversity in Schooling: Perspectives and Prospects*, London: Routledge.

—— (1997b) 'Schools' understanding of changing communities', *Journal of Education Policy* 12, 1–2: 45–51.

Levin, H. (1991) 'The economics of educational choice', *Economics of Education Review* 10, 2: 137–58.

—— (1994) 'Economics of school reform for at-risk students', in E. Hanushek and D. Jorgenson (eds) *Improving America's Schools: The role of Incentives*, Washington DC: National Academy Press.

—— (1997) 'Raising school productivity: an x-efficiency approach', *Economics of Education Review* 16, 3: 303–11.

Levin, H. and Kelley, C. (1994) 'Can education do it alone?', *Economics of Education Review* 13: 97–108.

Levy, D. (1987) 'A comparison of private and public educational organizations, in W. Powell (ed.) *The Nonprofit Sector A Research Handbook*, New Haven: Yale University Press.

Lieberman, M. and Montgomery, D. (1988) 'First-mover advantages', *Strategic Management Journal* 9: 41–58.

Liebowitz, S. and Margolis, S. (1994) 'Network externality: an uncommon tragedy', *Journal of Economic Perspectives* 8, 2: 133–50.

Lindbeck, A. and Snower, D. (2000) 'Multitask learning and the reorganisation of work: from Tayloristic to holistic organization', *Journal of Labor Economics* 18, 3: 353–76.

Loeb, S. and Page, M. (2000) 'Examining the link between teacher wages and student outcomes: the importance of alternative labor market opportunities and non-pecuniary variation', *Review of Economics and Statistics* 82, 3: 393–408.

Lord, R. (1984) *Value for Money in Education*, London: Public Money.

Louis, K. and van Velzen, B. (1991) 'A look at choice in the Netherlands', *Educational Leadership* 48, 4: 66–72.

Luyten, H. (1994) 'School size effects on achievement in secondary education: evidence from the Netherlands, Sweden and the USA', *School Effectiveness and School Improvement* 5: 75–99.

Machin, S. (1998) 'Recent shifts in wage inequality and the wage returns to education in Britain', *National Institute Economic Review* 166: 87–96.

Macran, S., Joshi, H. and Dex, S. (1996) 'Employment after childbearing: a survival analysis', *Work, Employment and Society* 10, 2: 273–96.

Mancebón, M-J. and Bandrés, E. (1999) 'Efficiency evaluation in secondary schools: the key role of model specification and of ex post analysis of results', *Education Economics* 7, 2: 131–52.

McGeorge, C. (1995) 'Private and integrated schools in New Zealand: subsidising the illusion of choice', *Journal of Education Policy* 10, 3: 259–70.

McMahon, W. (1998) 'Conceptual framework for the analysis of the social benefits of lifelong learning', *Education Economics* 6, 3: 309–46.

McPartland, J. and McDill, E. (1982) 'Control and differentiation in the structure of American education', *Sociology of Education* 55: 77–88.

MacPhail-Wilcox, B. and King, R.A. (1986) 'Production functions re-visited in the context of educational reform', *Journal of Education Finance* 12: 191–222.

McWilliams, A. and Smart, D. (1993) 'Efficiency v. structure–conduct–performance: implications for strategy research and practice', *Journal of Management* 19: 63–78.

Maguire, M., Ball, S. and Macrae, S. (1999) 'Promotion, persuasion and class taste: marketing (in) the UK post-compulsory sector', *British Journal of Sociology of Education* 20, 3: 291–308.

Maital, S. and Maital, S. (1977) 'Time preference, delay of gratification and the intergenerational transmission of economic inequality', in O. Ashenfelter and W. Oates (eds) *Essays in Labor Market Analysis*, New York: Wiley/Israel University Press.

Mangan, J., Adnett, N. and Davies, P. (2001) 'Movers and stayers: determinants of post-16 educational choice', *Research in Post-Compulsory Education* 6, 1: 31–50.

Manski, C. (2000) 'Economic analysis of social interactions', *Journal of Economic Perspectives* 14, 3: 115–36.

Marlow, M. (2000) 'Spending, school structure, and public education quality: evidence from California', *Economics of Education Review* 19: 89–106.

Marsden, D. (2000) 'Teachers before the "Threshold"', Discussion Paper 454, London: Centre for Economic Performance.

Marsden, D. and French, S. (1998) *What a Performance: Performance Related Pay in the Public Services*, London: Centre for Economic Performance.

Martin, J. (1998) 'Education and economic performance in the OECD countries: an elusive relationship', *Journal of the Statistical and Social Inquiry Society of Ireland* XXVII, V: 99–128.

Mason, R. (1998) *The Economics of Conspicuous Consumption: Theory and Thought since 1700*, Cheltenham: Edward Elgar.

Matthews, R. (1991) 'The economics of professional ethics: should the professions be more like business?', *Economic Journal* 101: 737–50.

Menéndez Weidman, L. (2001) 'Policy trends and structural divergence in educational governance: the case of the French national ministry and US Department of Education', *Oxford Review of Education* 27, 1: 75–84.

Merkies, A. (2000) 'Economies of scale and school consolidation in Dutch primary school industry', in Blank J. (ed.) *Public Provision and Performance. Contributions from Efficiency and Productivity Measurement*, Amsterdam: Elsevier.

Merrifield, J. (1999) 'Monopsony power in the market for teachers: why teachers should support market-based education reform', *Journal of Labor Research* 20, 3: 377–91.

Meyer, R.(1997) 'Value-added indicators of school performance: a primer', *Economics of Education Review* 16, 3: 283–301.

Michelson, S. (1972) 'Equal school resource allocation', *Journal of Human Resources* 7: 283–306.

Micklewright, J. (1988) 'Schooling choice, educational maintenance allowances and panel attrition', Department of Economics, Queen Mary College, Working Paper No. 185.

—— (1989) 'Choice at sixteen', *Economica* 56: 25–39.

Milgrom, P. and Roberts, J. (1992) *Economics Organization and Management*, Englewood Cliffs, NJ: Prentice Hall.

Mok, K-H. (1997) 'Retreat of the state: marketization of education in the Pearl River Delta', *Comparative Education Review* 41, 3: 260–76.

Mok, K-H. and Wat, K-Y. (1998) 'Merging the public and private boundary: education and the market place in China', *International Journal of Educational Development* 18, 3: 255–67.

Monk, D. (1994) 'Subject area preparation of secondary mathematics and student achievement, *Economics of Education Review* 13, 2: 125–45.

Morris, A. (1997) 'Same mission, same methods, same results? Academic and religious outcomes from different models of Catholic schooling', *British Journal of Educational Studies* 45, 4: 378–91.

—— (1998) 'By their fruits you will know them: distinctive features of Catholic education', *Research Papers in Education* 13, 1: 87–112.

Mortimore, P., Sammons, P., Stoll, L., Lewis, D. and Ecob, R. (1988) *School Matters: The Junior Years* Somerset: Open Books.

Mortimore, P. (1993) 'School effectiveness and the management of effective learning and teaching', *School Effectiveness and School Improvement* 4, 4: 290–310.

Munich, D. and Filer, R. (2000) 'Responses of private and public schools to voucher funding: the Czech and Hungarian experience', University of Michigan, William Davidson Institute, Working Paper No. 360.

Murnane, R. (1986) 'Comparisons of private and public schools: what can we learn?', in D. Levy (ed.) *Private Education: Studies in Choice and Public Policy*, New York: Oxford University Press.

—— (1991) *Who will teach? Policies that matter*, Cambridge, MA: Harvard University Press.

—— (1996) 'Staffing the nation's schools with skilled teachers', in E. Hanushek and D. Jorgenson (eds) *Improving America's Schools: The Role of Incentives*, Washington DC, National Academy Press.

Murnane, R. and Cohen, D., (1986) 'Merit pay and the evaluation problem: why most merit pay plans fail and a few survive', *Harvard Educational Review* 56, 1: 1–17.

Murnane, R. and Phillips, B. (1981) 'What do effective teachers of inner city children have in common?', *Social Science Research* 10: 83–100.

Murphy, J. (1997) 'Restructuring through school-based management: insights for improving tomorrow's schools', in T. Townsend (ed.) *Restructuring and Quality: Issues for tomorrows schools*, London: Routledge.

Murray, M and Wallace, S. (1997) 'The implications of expanded school choice', *Public Finance Review* 25, 2: 459–73.

Neal, D. (1997) 'The effect of Catholic secondary schooling on educational attainment', *Journal of Labor Economics* 15: 98–123.

Nickell, S. (1998) 'The collapse in demand for the unskilled: what can be done?', in R. Freeman and P. Gottschalk (eds) *Generating Jobs: How to Increase Demand for Less-Skilled Workers*, New York: Russell/Sage Foundation.

Noden, P., West, A., David, M. and Edge, A. (1998) 'Choices and destinations at transfer to secondary schools in London', *Journal of Education Policy* 13, 2: 221–36.

Odden, A. (2001) 'Rewarding expertise', *Education Matters* 1, 1: 1–11.

Office for Standards in Education (OfSTED) (1998a) *Guidance on the Inspection of Secondary Schools*, London: OfSTED.

—— (1998b) *Inspection of Calderdale Local Education Authority*, London: HMSO.

—— (1999a) *Inspection of Walsall Local Education Authority*, London: HMSO.

—— (1999b) *The Annual Report of Her Majesty's Chief Inspector of Schools*, London: Stationery Office.

—— (2001) *Education Action Zones: Commentary on the first six zone inspections*, London: Stationery Office.

Office for National Statistics (1998) *Social Focus on Men and Women*, London: HMSO.

Organisation for Economic Co-operation and Development (OECD) (1994) *School: a matter of choice* (Paris: OECD).

—— (1997) 'Benchmarking, evaluation and strategic management in the public sector', OECD Working Papers, Vol. V, Paris: OECD.

—— (1998) *Education at a Glance*, 1998 edn, Paris: OECD.

—— (2000) *Education at a Glance*, 2000 edn, Paris: OECD.

—— (2001) *Education Policy Analysis*, Paris: OECD.

Peltzman, S. (1993) 'The political economy of the decline of American public education', *Journal of Law and Economics* 36, 2: 331–70.

Persson, T. and Tabellini, G. (1994) 'Is inequality harmful for growth?', *American Economic Review* 84: 600–21.

Petch, A. (1986) 'Parents' reasons for choosing secondary schools, in A. Stillman (ed.) *The Balancing Act of 1980: Parents and Education*, Windsor: Nelson NFER.

Peters, T. and Waterman, R. (1982) *In Search of Excellence*, New York: Harper & Row.

Pollitt, C. and Bouckaert, G. (2000) *Public Management Reform: A comparative analysis*, Oxford: Oxford University Press.

Poole, M. and Jenkins, G. (1998) 'Human resource management and the theory of rewards: evidence from a national survey', *British Journal of Industrial Relations* 36, 2: 227–47.

Power, S., Halpin, D. and Whitty, G. (1997) 'Managing the state and the market: "new" education management in five countries', *British Journal of Educational Studies* 45, 4: 342–62.

Prais, S. (2001) '"Grammar schools" achievements and the DfEE's measures of value-added: an attempt at clarification', *Oxford Review of Education* 27, 1: 69–73.

Pratten, C., Robertson, D. and Tatch, J. (1997) 'A Study of the Factors Affecting Participation in Post-Compulsory, Full-Time Education and Government Supported Training By 16–18 Year Olds in England and Wales', University of Cambridge, Department of Applied Economics, DAE Working Papers, No. 9711.

Prendergast, C. (1999) 'The provision of incentives in firms', *Journal of Economic Literature* 37:7–63.

Price, S. (2000) 'Prudence and pragmatism and the fiscal stance', *Economic Outlook* January: 12–18.

Pritchett, L. and Filmer, D. (1999) 'What education production functions really show: a positive theory of education expenditure', *Economics of Education Review*, 18: 223–39.

Psacharopoulos, G. (1987) 'Public versus private schools in developing countries: evidence from Colombia and Tanzania', *International Journal of Educational Development* 7, 1: 59–67.

Raab, C.D., Munn, P., McAvoy, L., Bailey, L., Arnott, M. and Adler, M. (1997) 'Devolving the management of schools in Britain', *Educational Administration Quarterly* 33, 2: 140–57.

Rabin, M. (1998) 'Psychology and economics', *Journal of Economic Literature* 36, March: 11–46.

Rangazas, P. (1997) 'Competition and private school vouchers', *Education Economics* 5, 3: 245–63.

Ranson, S. (1993) 'Markets or democracy for education', *British Journal of Educational Studies* 41, 4: 333–52.

Raggatt, P. and Williams, S. (1999) *Government, Markets and Vocational Qualifications: An Anatomy of Policy*, London: Falmer.

Rapp, G. (2000) 'Agency and choice in education: does school choice enhance the work effort of teachers?', *Education Economics* 8, 1: 37–63.

Reay, D. (1996) 'Contextualising choice: social power and parental involvement', *British Educational Research Journal* 22, 5: 581–96.

—— (1998) 'Setting the agenda: the growing impact of market forces on pupil grouping in British secondary schooling', *Journal of Curriculum Studies* 30, 5: 545–58.

Reay, D. and Ball, S. (1997) ' "Spoilt for choice": the working classes and educational markets', *Oxford Review of Education* 23, 1: 89–116.

Reay, D. and Lucey, H. (2000) 'Children, school choice and social differences', *Educational Studies* 26, 1: 83–100.

Reezigt, G.J., Guldemond, H. and Creemers, B.P.M. (1999) 'Empirical validity for a comprehensive model on educational effectiveness', *School Effectiveness and School Improvement* 10, 2: 193–216.

Reich, R. (1991) *The Work of Nations: Preparing Ourselves for the 21st Century Capitalism*, New York: Vantage Books.

Reynolds, D. (1999) 'School effectiveness, school improvement and contemporary educational policies', in J. Demaine (ed.) *Education Policy and Contemporary Politics*, Basingstoke: Macmillan.

Reynolds, D. and Farrell, S. (1996) *Worlds Apart? A Review of International Studies of Educational Achievement Involving England*, London: HMSO.

Reynolds, D., Sammons, P., Stoll, L., Barber, M. and Hillman, J. (1996) 'School effectiveness and school improvement in the United Kingdom', *School Effectiveness and School Improvement* 7, 2: 133–58.

Richardson, R. (1999) *Performance Related Pay in Schools: An Assessment of the Green Papers*, London: National Union of Teachers.

Riley, K. and Rowles, D. (1997) 'Inspection and school improvement in England and Wales: national contexts and local realities', in T. Townsend (ed.) *Restructuring and Quality: Issues for Tomorrow's Schools*, London: Routledge.

Riley, K., Watling, R., Rowles, D. and Hopkins, D. (1998) *Education Action Zones: Some Lessons Learned From the First Wave of Applications*, London: Education Network.

Ritzen, J., Van Dommelin, J. and de Viljder, F. (1997) 'School finance and school choice in the Netherlands', *Economics of Education Review* 16, 3: 329–35.

Robertson, D. and Symons, J. (1996) 'Do peer groups matter? Peer groups versus school effects in academic attainment', London: Centre for Economic Performance, London School of Economics, Discussion Paper No. 311.

Robertson, C., Cowell, B. and Olson, J. (1998) 'A case study of integration and destreaming: teachers and students in an Ontario secondary school respond', *Journal of Curriculum Studies* 30, 6: 691–717.

Robertson, S. (1996) 'Teacher's work, restructuring and postFordism: constructing the new "professionalism" ', in I. Goodson, and A. Hargreaves (eds) *Teachers' Professional Lives*, London: Falmer.

Robinson, P. and Manacorda, M. (1997) 'Qualifications and the labour market in Britain 1984–94: Skill-based change in the demand for labour or credentialism?', London School of Economics and Political Science, Centre for Economic Performance, Discussion Paper No. 330.

Rosenthal, L. (2001) 'The value of secondary school quality', paper presented at Royal Economic Society Annual Conference, April 2001.

Rossoll, C.H. and Glenn, C.L. (1988) 'The Cambridge controlled choice plan', *Urban Review* 20, 2: 75–94.

Rounds Parry, T. (1996) 'Will the pursuit of higher quality sacrifice ethical opportunity in education? An analysis of the voucher scheme in Santiago', *Social Science Quarterly* 77: 821–41.

Rubery, J., Humphries, J., Fagan, C. Grimshaw, D. and Smith, M. (2000) *Equal Opportunities as a Productive Factor*, Manchester School of Management, European Work and Employment Research Centre.

Rubinson, R. and Browne, I. (1994) 'Education and the economy', in N. Smelser and R. Swedberg (eds) *The Handbook of Economic Sociology*, Princeton, NJ: Princeton University Press.

Salganik, L. and Karweit, N. (1982) 'Voluntarism and governance in education', *Sociology of Education* 55: 152–61.

Sammons, P., Hillman, J. and Mortimore, P. (1995) *Key Characteristics of Effective Schools: A Review of School Effectiveness Research*, London: OfSTED.

Samoff, J. (1991) 'Local initiatives and national policies: the politics of private schooling in Tanzania', *International Journal of Educational Research* 15, 5: 377–92.

Sander, W. (1993) 'Expenditure and student achievement in Illinois', *Journal of Public Economics* 52: 403–16.

—— (1995) 'Schooling and smoking', *Economics of Education Review*, 14, 3: 1–23.

—— (1997) 'Catholic high schools and rural academic achievement', *American Journal of Agricultural Economics* 79: 1–12.

Savage, J. and Desforges, C. (1995) 'The role of informal assessment in teachers' practical action', *Educational Studies*, 21, 3: 433–46.

Schagen, I. (1999) 'A methodology for judging departmental performance within schools', *Educational Research* 41, 1: 3–10.

Schiefelbein, E. (1991) 'Restructuring education through economic competition: the case of Chile', *Journal of Education Administration* 29, 4: 17–29.

Schmid, G., Schütz, H. and Speckesser, S. (1999) 'Broadening the scope of benchmarking: radar charts and employment systems', *Labour* 13, 4: 879–99.

Select Committee on Education and Employment (1999) *Minutes of Evidence Taken Before the Education and Employment Committee (Education Sub-Committee)*, HC355–1, Session 1998–99, London: HMSO.

Shann, M. (1999) 'Academics and a culture of caring: the relationship between school achievement and prosocial and antisocial behaviors in four urban middle schools', *School Effectiveness and School Improvement* 10, 4: 390–413.

Shapiro, C. (1986) 'Investment, moral hazard and occupational licensing', *Review of Economic Studies* LIII: 843–62.

Shleifer, A. (1998) 'State versus private ownership', *Journal of Economic Perspectives* 12, 4: 133–50.

Shokrail, N. and Youseff, S. (1998) *School Choice Programs: What's happening in the States*, Washington DC: Heritage Foundation.

Singh, S., Utton, M. and Waterson, M. (1998) 'Strategic behaviour of incumbant firms in the UK', *International Journal of Industrial Organisation* 16: 229–51.

Sloane, P., Battu, H. and Seaman, P. (1999) 'Overeducation, undereducation and the British labour market', *Applied Economics* 31, 11: 1437–54.

Smedley, D. (1995) 'Marketing secondary schools to parents: some lessons from the research on parental choice', *Education Management and Administration* 23, 2: 96–103.

Smet, M. and Nonneman, W. (1998) 'Economies of scale and scope in Flemish schools', *Applied Economics*, 30: 1251–8.

Smith, P. (1993) 'Outcome-related performance indicators and organizational control in the public sector', *British Journal of Management* 4, 3: 135–52.

—— (1995) 'Performance indicators and control in the public sector, in A. Bery, J. Broadbent and D. Otley (eds) *Management Control: Theories, issues and practices*, London: Macmillan.

Snower, D. (1996) 'The low-skill, bad-job trap', in A. Booth and D. Snower (eds) *Acquiring Skills: Market Failures, Their Symptoms and Policy Responses*, Cambridge: Cambridge University Press.

Solnick, S. and Hemenway, D. (1998) 'Is more always better? A survey on positional concerns', *Journal of Economic Behavior and Organization* 37: 373–83.

Somanathan, R. (1998) 'School heterogeneity, human capital accumulation and standards', *Journal of Public Finance* 67: 369–97.

Sommerland, H. and Sanderson, P. (1997) 'The legal labour market and the training needs of women returners in the UK', *Journal of Vocational Education and Training* 49, 1: 45–64.

Sørensen, A. (1994) 'Firms, wages and incentives', in N. Smelser and R. Swedberg (eds) *The Handbook of Economic Sociology*, Princeton NJ: Princeton University Press.

Spear, M., Gould, K. and Lee, B. (2000) *Who would be a teacher? A review of factors motivating and demotivating prospective and practising teachers*, Slough: National Foundation for Educational Research.

Spender, J.-C. (2001) 'Business policy and strategy as a professional field', in H.W. Volberda and T. Elfring (eds) *Rethinking Strategy*, London: Sage.

Starrett, D. (1981) 'Land value capitalization in local public finance', *Journal of Political Economy* 89, 2: 306–27.

Stevans, L.K. and Sessions, D.N. (2000) 'Private/public school choice and student performance revisited', *Education Economics*, 8, 2: 169–84.

Storey, A. (2000) 'A leap of faith? Performance pay for teachers', *Journal of Education Policy* 15, 5: 509–23.

Summers, A. and Johnson, A. (1996) 'The effects of school-based management plans, in E. Hanushek and D. Jorgenson (eds) *Improving America's Schools: The Role of Incentives*, Washington DC: National Academy Press.

Summers, A. and Wolfe, B. (1977) 'Do schools make a difference?', *American Economic Review* 67: 639–52.

Švecová, J. (2000) 'Privatization of education in the Czech Republic', *International Journal of Educational Development* 20: 127–33.

Swaffield, J. (2000) 'Gender, motivation, experience and wages', London School of Economics and Political Science, Centre for Economic Performance, Discussion Paper, No. 457.

Talbert, J. and McLaughlin, M. (1996) 'Teacher professionalism in local school contexts', in I. Goodson and A. Hargreaves (eds) *Teachers' Professional Lives*, London: Falmer.

Taylor, J. and Bradley, S. (2000) 'Resource allocation and economies of size in secondary schools, *Bulletin of Economic Research* 52: 123–50.

Taylor, C., Gorard, S. and Fitz, J. (2000) 'Size matters: does school choice lead to spirals of decline?', Measuring Markets Working Paper 34, Cardiff: Cardiff University School of Social Science.

Teelken, C. (1998) *Market Mechanisms in Education: A Comparative Study of School Choice in the Netherlands, England and Scotland*, PhD Thesis.

Thomas, A. and Dennison, B. (1991) 'Parent or pupil choice: who really decides in urban schools?', *Educational Management and Administration* 19, 4: 243–51.

Thomas, G. and McClelland, R. (1997) 'Parents in the market-place: some responses to information, diversity and power', *Educational Research* 39, 2: 243–51.

Thomas, W. (2000) 'The role of the peer group in the staying-on decision at sixteen', Faculty of Economics and Social Science, University of the West of England, Bristol, Working Paper No. 32.

Thrupp, M. (1998) 'Exploring the politics of blame', *Comparative Education* 34, 2: 195–210.

Tiebout, C.M. (1956) 'A pure theory of local public expenditures', *Journal of Political Economy* 64, 5: 416–28.

Times Educational Supplement (TES) (2001a) *Parents would pay for small classes*, 13.4.2001, p. 13.

—— (2001b) *Budget cuts give Labour some explaining to do*, 25.4.2001, p. 6.

Tooley, J. (1995) 'Markets or democracy for education? A reply to Stewart Ranson', *British Journal of Educational Studies* 43, 1: 21–34.

—— (1997) 'On school choice and social class: a response to Ball, Bowe and Gewirtz', *British Journal of Sociology of Education* 18, 2: 217–30.

Tomlinson, S. (1994) *What is Really Going on in School?*, Parliamentary Brief on Education, December 1994: 103–100.

Topel, R. (1999) 'Labour markets and economic growth', in O. Ashenfelter and D. Card (eds) *Handbook of Labor Economics*, Volume 3C, Amsterdam: Elsevier.

Tronti, L. (1998) 'Benchmarking labour market performance and policies', *Labour* 12, 3: 489–513.

Tyack, D. (1990) '"Restructuring" in historical perspective: tinkering toward Utopia', *Diagnostique* 25, 2–3: 127–33.

Van Cuyck-Remijssen, A. and Dronkers, J. (1990) 'Catholic and Protestant schools, a better choice in the Netherlands?', *School Effectiveness and School Improvement* 1, 3: 211–20.

Van de Grift, W. and Houtveen, A. (1999) 'Educational leadership and pupil achievement in primary education', *School Effectiveness and School Improvement* 10, 4: 373–89.

Van Zenten, A. (1996) 'Market trends in the French school system: overt policy, hidden strategies, actual changes', *Oxford Studies in Comparative Education* 6, 1: 63–8.

Vandenberghe, V. (1998) 'Educational quasi-markets: the Belgian experience', in W. Bartlett, J.Roberts and J. Le Grand (eds) *A Revolution in Social Policy: Lessons from the Development of Quasi-market Reforms in the 1990s*, Bristol: Policy Press.

—— (1999a) 'Combining market and bureaucratic control in education: an answer to market and bureaucratic failure? *Comparative Education* 35, 3: 271–82.

——(1999b) 'Economics of education: the need to go beyond human capital theory and production function analysis', *Educational Studies* 25, 2: 129–43.

Vedder, R. and Hall, J. (2000) 'Private school competition and public school teacher salaries', *Journal of Labor Research* 21, 1: 161–8.

Vickers, J. (1985) 'Strategic Competition among the few: some recent developments in the economics of industry', *Oxford Review of Economic Policy*, 1: 39–62.

Vickers, J. (1995) 'Concepts of competition', *Oxford Economic Papers* 47: 1–23.

Vignoles, A., Levačić, R., Walker, J., Machin, S. and Reynolds, D. (2000) *The Relationship Between Resource Allocation and Pupil Attainment: A review*, Department for Education and Employment Research Report RR228, Norwich: HMSO.

Vila, L. (2000) 'The non-monetary benefits of education', *European Journal of Education* 35, 1: 21–32.

Vincent C., Evans, L., Lunt, I. and Young, P. (1995) 'Policy and practice: the changing nature of special educational provision in schools', *British Journal of Special Education* 22, 1: 4–11.

Walberg, H.J. (1984) 'Improving the quality of America's schools', *Education Leadership* 41: 19–27.

Waldfogel. J. (1998) 'The family gap for young women in the US and Britain: can maternity leave make a difference?', *Journal of Labor Economics* 16, 3: 505–45.

Walford, G. (1991) 'Choice of school at the first city technology college', *Educational Studies* 17, 1: 65–75.

—— (1996) 'Diversity and choice on school education: an alternative view', *Oxford Review of Education* 22, 2: 143–54.

—— (2000) 'A policy adventure: sponsored grant-maintained schools', *Educational Studies* 26, 2: 247–62.

—— (2001) 'Does the market ensure quality?', *Westminster Studies in Education* 24, 1: 23–33.

Wallace, M. (1998) 'A counter-policy to subvert education reform? Collaboration among schools and colleges in a competitive climate', *British Educational Research Journal* 24: 195–215.

Waslander, S. and Thrupp, M. (1995) 'Choice, competition and segregation: an empirical analysis', *Journal of Education Policy* 10, 1: 1–26.

Weiss, A. (1995) 'Human capital vs. signalling explanations of wages', *Journal of Economic Perspectives* 9, 4: 133–54.

Wells, A.S. (1993) 'The sociology of school choice: why some win and others lose in the educational marketplace', in E. Rasell and R. Rothstein (eds) *School Choice: Examining the Evidence*, Arlington: Economic Policy Institute.

West, A. (1992) 'Factors affecting choice of school for middle class parents: implications for marketing', *Educational Management and Administration* 20, 4: 212–21.

West, A. and Varlaam, A. (1991) 'Choosing a secondary school: parents of junior school children', *Educational Research* 33, 1: 22–30.

West, A. and Pennell, H. (2000) 'Publishing school examination results in England: incentives and consequences', *Educational Studies* 26, 4: 423–36.

West, A., Pennell, H. and Noden, P. (1998b) 'School admissions: increasing equity, accountability and transparency', *British Journal of Educational Studies* 46, 2: 188–200.

West, A., David, M., Hailes, J. and Ribbens, J. (1995) 'Parents and the process of choosing secondary schools: implications for schools', *Educational Management and Administration* 23, 1: 28–38.

West, A., Noden, P., Edge, A. and David, M. (1998a) 'Parental involvement in education and out of school', *British Educational Research Journal* 24, 4: 461–84.

West, A., Noden, P., Edge, A., David, M. and Davies, J. (1998b) 'Choice and expectations at primary and secondary stages in the state and private sectors', *Educational Studies* 24, 1: 45–60.

West E. (1997) 'Education vouchers in principle and practice: a survey', *World Bank Research Observer* 12, 1: 83–103.

Whitfield, K. and Wilson, R.A. (1991) 'Staying on in full-time education: the Educational participation rate of 16 year olds', *Economica* 58: 391–404.

Whitty, G., Edwards, T. and Gewirtz, S. (1993) *Specialisation and Choice in Urban Education: The City Technology Colleges*, London: Routledge.

Whitty, G., Power, S. and Halpin, D. (1998) *Devolution and Choice in Education: The School, the State and the Market*, Buckingham: Open University Press.

Williams, M., Addison, L., Hancher, K., Hutner, A., Kutner, M., Sherman, J. and Tron, E. (1983)*Private Elementary and Secondary Education*, Final Report to Congress of the Congressionally Mandated Study of School Finance, vol. 2, July.

Williams, T. and Carpenter, P. (1991) 'Private schooling and public achievement in Australia', *International Journal of Educational Research* 15, 5: 411–31.

Williamson, O. (1985) *The Economic Institutions of Capitalism: Firms, Markets, Relational Contracting*, New York: Free Press.

Willis, P. (1977) *Learning to Labour: How Working Class Kids get Working Class Jobs*, Farnborough: Saxon House.

Willms, J. (1986) 'Social class segregation and its relationship to pupils' examination results in Scotland', *American Sociological Review* 51: 224–41.

Willms, J. and Echols, F. (1992) 'Alert and inert clients: the Scottish experience of parental choice of schools', *Economics of Education Review* 11, 4: 339–50.

Winkley, D. (1999) 'An examination of OFSTED', in C. Cullingford (ed.) *An Inspector Calls*, London: Kogan Page.

Witherspoon, S. (1995) 'Careers advice and the careers service: the experiences of young people', Employment Department Research Series, Youth Cohort Report No. 33, Sheffield: Employment Department.

Witte, J. (1992) 'Private school versus public school achievement: are there findings that should affect the educational choice debate?', *Economics of Education Review* 11: 371–94.

—— (1996a) 'School choice and student performance', in H. Ladd (ed.) *Holding Schools Accountable: Performance-Based Reform in Education*, Washington, DC: Brookings.

—— (1996b) 'Who benefits from the Milwaukee choice program?', in B. Fuller and R. Elmore (eds) *Who Chooses? Who Loses? Culture, Institutions and the Unequal Effects of School Choice*, New York: Teachers' College Press.

Witte, J., Thorn, C., Pritchard, K. and Claiburn, M. (1994) *Fourth Year Report: Milwaukee Parental Choice Program*, Madison: Department of Public Instruction.

Wolfe, B. and Zuvekas, S. (1997) 'Nonmarket outcomes of schooling', *International Journal of Educational Research* 27, 6: 491–502.

Wood, A. (1998) 'Globalisation and the rise in economic inequalities', *Economic Journal* 108, 450: 1463–82.

Woods, P. (1992) 'Empowerment through choice? Towards an understanding of parental choice and school responsiveness', *Educational Management and Administration* 20, 4: 204–11.

—— (1996) 'Choice, class and effectiveness', *School Effectiveness and School Improvement* 7, 4: 324–41.

Woods, P., Bagley, C. and Glatter, R. (1998) *School Choice and Competition: Markets in the Public Interest*, London: Routledge.

Wylie, C. (1994) *Self Managing Schools in New Zealand: The Fifth Year*, Wellington: New Zealand Council for Educational Research.

—— (1995) 'Contrary currents: the application of the public sector reform framework in education', *New Zealand Journal of Educational Studies* 20, 2: 149–64.

Zanzig, B. (1997) 'Measuring the impact of competition in local government education markets on the cognitive achievement of students', *Economics of Education Review* 16, 4: 431–41.

Index

Printed and bound by CPI Group (UK) Ltd, Croydon, CR0 4YY

11/05/2025

01866596-0001